DNS in Action

A detailed and practical guide to DNS
implementation, configuration, and administration

Libor Dostálek

Alena Kabelová

BIRMINGHAM - MUMBAI

DNS in Action

A detailed and practical guide to DNS implementation, configuration, and administration

First published: March 2006

Production Reference: 1240206

Published by Packt Publishing Ltd.
32 Lincoln Road
Olton
Birmingham, B27 6PA, UK.

ISBN 1-904811-78-7

www.packtpub.com

Cover Design by www.visionwt.com

This is an authorized and updated translation from the Czech language.

Copyright © Computer Press 2003 *Velký průvodce protokoly TCP/IP a systémem DNS*. ISBN: 80-722-6675-6. All rights reserved.

Credits

Authors
Libor Dostálek
Alena Kabelová

Technical Editors
Darshan Parekh
Abhishek Shirodkar

Editorial Manager
Dipali Chittar

Development Editor
Louay Fatoohi

Indexer
Abhishek Shirodkar

Proofreader
Chris Smith

Production Coordinator
Manjiri Nadkarni

Cover Designer
Helen Wood

About the Authors

Libor Dostálek was born in 1957 in Prague, Europe. He graduated in mathematics at the Charles University in Prague. For the last 20 years he has been involved in ICT architecture and security. His experiences as the IT architect and the hostmaster of one of the first European Internet Service Providers have been used while writing this publication.

Later he became an IT architect of one of the first home banking applications fully based on the PKI architecture, and also an IT architect of one of the first GSM banking applications (mobile banking). As a head consultant, he designed the architecture of several European public certification service providers (certification authorities) and also many e-commerce and e-banking applications.

The public knows him either as an author of many publications about TCP/IP and security or as a teacher. He has taught at various schools as well as held various commercial courses. At present, he lectures on Cryptology at the Charles University in Prague.

He is currently an employee of the Siemens.

Alena Kabelová was born in 1964 in Budweis, Europe. She graduated in ICT at the Economical University in Prague. She worked together with Libor Dostálek as a hostmaster. She is mostly involved in software development and teaching. At present, she works as a senior project manager at the PVT and focuses mainly on electronic banking.

Her experiences as the hostmaster of an important European ISP are applied in this publication.

Table of Contents

Preface

Recently, while driving to my work, I listened to radio as usual. Because of the establishment of the new EU (European Union) domain, there was an interview with a representative of one of the Internet Service Providers. For some time the interview went on, boringly similar to other common radio interviews, but suddenly the presswoman started to improvise and she asked, "*But isn't the DNS too vulnerable? Is it prepared for terrorist attacks?*" The ISP representative enthusiastically answered, "*The whole Internet arose more than 30 years ago, initiated by the American Department of Defense. From the very beginning, the Internet architecture took into account that it should be able to keep the communication functional even if a part of the infrastructure of the USA were destroyed, i.e., it must be able to do without a destroyed area.*"

He went on enthusiastically, "*We have 13 root name servers in total. Theoretically, only one is enough to provide the complete DNS function.*" At this point, we must stop for a moment our radio interview to remind you that a role and principle of usage of root name servers are described in the first chapter of this book. Now, let's go back to our interview again. The presswoman, not satisfied with the answer, asked, "*All these root name servers are in the USA, aren't they? What will happen if someone or something cuts off the international connectivity, and I am not be able to reach any root name server?*" The specialist, caught by the presswoman's questions, replied, "*This would be a catastrophe. In such a case, the whole Internet would be out of order.*"

That time I did not immediately came upon the solution that an area cut off this way is by nature similar to an Intranet. In such a case, it would be enough to create national (or continental) recovery plan and put into work a fake national (or continental) name server, exactly according to the description in Chapter 9, describing closed company networks. The result would be that the Internet would be limited only to our national (or continental) network; however, it would be at least partially functional.

In fact at that time, the specialist's answer made me angry. "So what?", I thought, "Only DNS would be out of order; i.e., names could not be translated to IP addresses. If we do not use names but use IP addresses instead, we could still communicate. The whole network infrastructure would be intact in that case!"

But working according to my way would be lengthy, and I thought about it over and over. After some time I realized that the present Internet is not the same as it was in the early 1990s. At that time the handful of academics involved with the Internet would have remembered those few IP addresses. But in the present scenario, the number of IP addresses is in the millions, and the number of people using the Internet is much higher still. Most of them are not IT experts and know nothing about IP addresses and DNS. For such people, the Internet is either functional or not—similar to, for example, an automatic washing machine. From this point of view, the Internet without functional DNS would be really out of order (in fact it would still be functional, but only IT experts would be able to use it).

The goal of this publiction is to illustrate to readers the principles on which the DNS is based. This publication is generously filled with examples. Some are from a UNIX environment, some from Microsoft. The concrete examples mostly illustrate some described problem. The publication is not a text book of a DNS implementation for a concrete operating system, but it always tries to find out the base of the problem. The reader is led to create similar examples according to his or her concrete needs by him- or herself.

The goal of this book is to give the reader a deep understanding of DNS, independent of any concrete DNS implementation. After studying this book, the reader should be able to study DNS standards directly from the countless Requests for Comments (RFC). Links to particular RFCs are listed in the text. In fact, it is quite demanding to study the unfriendly RFCs directly without any preliminary training. For a beginner, only to find out the right RFC could be a problem.

Before studying this book, the reader should know the IP principles covered in the *Understanding TCP/IP* book published by Packt Publishing (ISBN: 1-904811-71-X) because this publication is a logical follow-on from that book.

The authors wish you good luck and hope that you get a lot of useful information by reading this publication.

What This Book Covers

Chapter 1 begins to explain basic DNS principles. It introduces essential names, for example, domain and zone, explaining the difference between them. It describes the iteration principle by which the DNS translates names to IP addresses. It presents a configuration of a resolver both for UNIX and for Windows. The end of the chapter explains name server principles and describes various name server types.

Chapter 2 is fully focused on the most basic DNS procedure, the DNS query. Through this procedure, the DNS translates names to IP addresses. In the very beginning, however, this chapter describes in detail the Resource Record structure. At the end of this chapter, many practical examples of DNS exchanges are listed.

Chapter 3 deals with other DNS procedures (DNS Extensions), i.e., DNS Update, DNS Notify, incremental zone transfer, negative caching, IPv6 Extensions, IPsec, and TSIG.

Chapter 4 talks about the DNS implementation. It is derived from its historical evolution. From the historical point of view, the oldest DNS implementation that is still sometimes used is BIND version 4. This implementation is very simple so it is suitable to describe basic principles with it. Next, the new generations of BIND are discussed followed by the Windows 2000 implementation.

Chapter 5 discusses the tools for debugging DNS such as nslookup, dnswalk, and dig, how to control a name server using the rndc program, and the common errors that might occur while configuring DNS.

Chapter 6 deals with the creation of DNS domains (domain delegation) and with the procedure of domain registration.

Chapter 7 also talks about domain delegation. In contrast to Chapter 6, here the domain registration relates not to forward domains but to reverse domains.

Chapter 8 deals with international organizations, called Internet Registries, which are responsible for assigning IP addresses and domain registration.

Chapter 9 describes the DNS architecture of closed intranets.

Chapter 10 talks about the DNS architecture from the point of view of firewalls.

What You Need for This Book

This publication is created to help beginners, who are already familiar with computers, to discover DNS secrets. It will be also useful for computer administrators and, specifically, for network administrators. It will be also useful as a textbook for DNS lectures.

This book discusses the fundamentals of DNS; it is not a manual for some concrete DNS implementation. It contains examples from both Windows and UNIX environments. It explains the DNS concepts to a user, independently of the hardware and software he or she uses. We can work effectively with DNS even in a *not-so-powerful* personal computer.

Conventions

In this book, you will find a number of styles of text that distinguish between different kinds of information. Here are some examples of these styles, and an explanation of their meaning.

There are three styles for code. Code words in text are shown as follows: "We can include other contexts through the use of the `include` directive."

A block of code will be set as follows:

```
[statistics-file path_name]
    [zone-statistics yes_or_no]
    [auth-nxdomain yes_or_no]
    *[deallocate-on-exit yes_or_no]
    [dialup dialup_option]
```

When we wish to draw your attention to a particular part of a code block, the relevant lines or items will be made bold:

```
[statistics-file path_name]
    [zone-statistics yes_or_no]
    [auth-nxdomain yes_or_no]
    *[deallocate-on-exit yes_or_no]
    [dialup dialup_option]
```

Any command-line input and output is written as follows:

```
$ORIGIN        default_domain
```

New terms and **important words** are introduced in a bold-type font. Words that you see on the screen, in menus or dialog boxes for example, appear in our text like this: "clicking the Next button moves you to the next screen".

Warnings or important notes appear in a box like this.

Reader Feedback

Feedback from our readers is always welcome. Let us know what you think about this book, what you liked or may have disliked. Reader feedback is important for us to develop titles that you really get the most out of.

To send us general feedback, simply drop an email to feedback@packtpub.com, making sure to mention the book title in the subject of your message.

If there is a book that you need and would like to see us publish, please send us a note in the SUGGEST A TITLE form on www.packtpub.com or email suggest@packtpub.com.

If there is a topic that you have expertise in and you are interested in either writing or contributing to a book, see our author guide on www.packtpub.com/authors.

Customer Support

Now that you are the proud owner of a Packt book, we have a number of things to help you to get the most from your purchase.

Errata

Although we have taken every care to ensure the accuracy of our contents, mistakes do happen. If you find a mistake in one of our books—maybe a mistake in text or code—we would be grateful if you would report this to us. By doing this you can save other readers from frustration, and help to improve subsequent versions of this book. If you find any errata, report them by visiting http://www.packtpub.com/support, selecting your book, clicking on the Submit Errata link, and entering the details of your errata. Once your errata have been verified, your submission will be accepted and the errata added to the list of existing errata. The existing errata can be viewed by selecting your title from http://www.packtpub.com/support.

Questions

You can contact us at questions@packtpub.com if you are having a problem with some aspect of the book, and we will do our best to address it.

1

Domain Name System

All applications that provide communication between computers on the Internet use IP addresses to identify communicating hosts. However, IP addresses are difficult for human users to remember. That is why we use the name of a network interface instead of an IP address. For each IP address, there is a name of a network interface (computer)—or to be exact, a domain name. This domain name can be used in all commands where it is possible to use an IP address. (One exception, where only an IP address can be used, is the specification of an actual name server.) A single IP address can have several domain names affiliated with it.

The relationship between the name of a computer and an IP address is defined in the **Domain Name System (DNS)** database. The DNS database is distributed worldwide. The DNS database contains individual records that are called **Resource Records (RR)**. Individual parts of the DNS database called **zones** are placed on particular name servers. DNS is a worldwide distributed database.

If you want to use an Internet browser to browse to www.google.com with the IP address 64.233.167.147 (Figure 1.1), you enter the website name www.google.com in the browser address field.

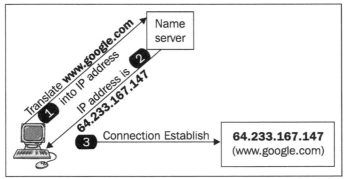

Figure 1.1: It is necessary to translate a name to an IP address before establishing a connection

Just before the connection with the www.google.com web server is made, the www.google.com DNS name is translated into an IP address and only then is the connection actually established.

It is practical to use an IP address instead of a domain name whenever we suspect that the DNS on the computer is not working correctly. Although it seems unusual, in this case, we can write something like:

```
ping 64.233.167.147
http://64.233.167.147
```

or send email to

```
dostalek@[64.233.167.147]
```

However, the reaction can be unexpected, especially for the email, HTTP, and HTTPS protocols. Mail servers do not necessarily support transport to servers listed in brackets. HTTP will return to us the primary home page, and the HTTPS protocol will complain that the server name does not match the server name in the server's certificate.

1.1 Domains and Subdomains

The entire Internet is divided into domains, i.e., name groups that logically belong together. The domains specify whether the names belong to a particular company, country, and so forth. It is possible to create subgroups within a domain that are called **subdomains**. For example, it is possible to create department subdomains for a company domain. The domain name reflects a host's membership in a group and subgroup. Each group has a name affiliated with it. The domain name of a host is composed from the individual group names. For example, the host named bob.company.com consists of a host named bob inside a subdomain called company, which is a subdomain of the domain com.

The domain name consists of strings separated by dots. The name is processed from left to right. The highest competent authority is the root domain expressed by a dot (.) on the very right (this dot is often left out). **Top Level Domains (TLD)** are defined in the root domain. We have two kind of TLD, **Generic Top Level Domain (gTLD)** and **Country Code Top Level Domain (ccTLD)**. Well known gTLDs are edu, com, net, and mil which are used mostly in the USA. According to ISO 3166, we also have two letter ccTLD for individual countries. For example, the us domain is affiliated with USA. However ccTLD are used mostly outside the USA. A detailed list of affiliated ccTLD and their details are listed in Appendix A.

The TLD domains are divided into subdomains for particular organizations, for example, coca-cola.com, mcdonalds.com, google.com. Generally, a company subdomain can be divided into lower levels of subdomains, for example, the company Company Ltd. can have its subdomain as company.com and lower levels like bill.company.com for its billing department, sec.company.com for its security department, and head.company.com for its headquarters.

The names create a tree structure as shown in the figure:

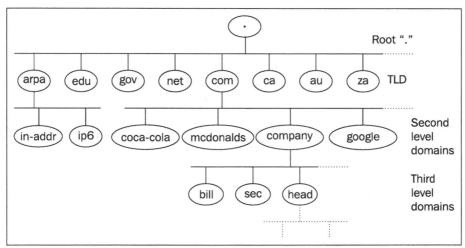

Figure 1.1a: The names in the DNS system create a tree structure

The following list contains some other registered gTLDs:

- The `.org` domain is intended to serve the noncommercial community.
- The `.aero` domain is reserved for members of the air transport industry.
- The `.biz` domain is reserved for businesses.
- The `.coop` domain is reserved for cooperative associations.
- The `.int` domain is only used for registering organizations established by international treaties between governments.
- The `.museum` domain is reserved for museums.
- The `.name` domain is reserved for individuals.
- The `.pro` domain is being established; it will be restricted to credited professionals and related entities.

1.2 Name Syntax

Names are listed in a dot notation (for example, `abc.head.company.com`). Names have the following general syntax:

```
string.string.string ........string.
```

where the first string is a computer name, followed by the name of the lowest inserted domain, then the name of a higher domain, and so on. For unambiguousness, a dot expressing the root domain is also listed at the end.

The entire name can have a maximum of 255 characters. An individual string can have a maximum of 63 characters. The string can consist of letters, numbers, and hyphens. A hyphen cannot be at the beginning or at the end of a string. There are also extensions specifying a richer repertoire of characters that can be used to create names. However, we usually avoid these additional characters because they are not supported by all applications.

Both lower and upper case letters can be used, but this is not so easy. From the point of view of saving and processing in the DNS database, lower and upper case letters are not differentiated. In other words, the name newyork.com will be saved in the same place in a DNS database as NewYork.com or NEWYORK.com. Therefore, when translating a name to an IP address, it does not matter whether the user enters upper or lower case letters. However, the name is saved in the database in upper and lower case letters; so if NewYork.com was saved in the database, then during a query, the database will return "NewYork.com.". The final dot is part of the name.

In some cases, the part of the name on the right can be omitted. We can almost always leave out the last part of the domain name in application programs. In databases describing domains the situation is more complicated:

- It is almost always possible to omit the last dot.
- It is usually possible to omit the end of the name, which is identical to the name of the domain, on computers inside the domain. For example, inside the company.com domain it is possible to just write computer.abc instead of computer.abc.company.com. (However, you cannot write a dot at the end!) The domains that the computer belongs to are directly defined by the domain and search commands in the resolver configuration file. There can be several domains of this kind defined (see Section 1.9).

1.3 Reverse Domains

We have already said that communication between hosts is based on IP addresses, not domain names. On the other hand, some applications need to find a name for an IP address—in other words, find the reverse record. This process is the translation of an IP address into a domain name, which is often called **reverse translation**.

As with domains, IP addresses also create a tree structure (see Figure 1.2). Domains created by IP addresses are often called reverse domains. The pseudodomains inaddr-arpa for IPv4 and IP6.arpa for IPv6 were created for the purpose of reverse translation. This domain name has historical origins; it is an acronym for *inverse addresses in the Arpanet*.

Under the domain in-addr.arpa, there are domains with the same name as the first number from the network IP address. For example, the in-addr.arpa domain has subdomains 0 to 255. Each of these subdomains also contains lower subdomains 0 to 255. For example, network 195.47.37.0/24 belongs to subdomain 195.in-addr.arpa. This actual subdomain belongs to domain 47.195.in-addr.arpa, and so forth. Note that the domains here are created like network IP addresses written backwards.

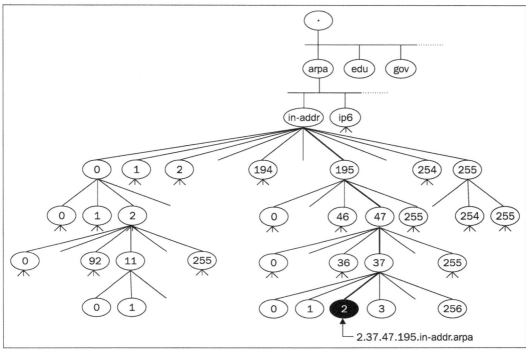

Figure 1.2: Reverse domain to IP address 195.47.37.2

This whole mechanism works if the IP addresses of classes A, B, or C are affiliated. But what should you do if you only have a subnetwork of class C affiliated? Can you even run your own name server for reverse translation? The answer is yes. Even though the IP address only has four bytes and a classic reverse domain has a maximum of three numbers (the fourth numbers are already elements of the domain—IP addresses), the reverse domains for subnets of class C are created with four numbers. For example, for subnetwork 194.149.150.16/28 we will use domain 16.150.149.194.in-addr.arpa. It is as if the IP address suddenly has five bytes! This was originally a mistake in the implementation of DNS, but later this mistake proved to be very practical so it was standardized as an RFC. We will discuss this in more detail in Chapter 7. You will learn more about reverse domains for IPv6 in Section 3.5.3.

1.4 Domain 0.0.127.in-addr.arpa

The IP address 127.0.0.1 presents an interesting complication. Network 127 is reserved for loopback, i.e., a software loop on each computer. While other IP addresses are unambiguous within the Internet, the address 127.0.0.1 occurs on every computer. Each name server is not only an authority for common domains, but also an authority (primary name server) to domain 0.0.127.in-addr.arpa. We will consider this as given and will not list it in the chart, but be careful not to forget about it. For example, even a caching-only server is a primary server for this domain. Windows 2000 pretends to be the only exception to this rule, but it would not hurt for even Windows 2000 to establish a name server for zone 0.0.127.in-addr.arpa.

1.5 Zone

We often come across the questions: What is a zone? What is the relation between a domain and a zone? Let us explain the relationship of these terms using the company.com domain.

As we have already said, a domain is a group of computers that share a common right side of their domain name. For example, a domain is a group of computers whose names end with company.com. However, the domain company.com is large. It is further divided into the subdomains bill.company. com, sec.company.com, sales.company.com, xyz.company.com, etc. We can administer the entire company.com domain on one name server, or we can create independent name servers for some subdomains. (In Figure 1.3, we have created subordinate name servers for the subdomains bill.company.com and head.company.com.) The original name server serves the domain company.com and the subdomains sec.company.com, sales.company.com, and xyz.company.com—in other words, the original name server administers the company.com zone. The zone is a part of the domain namespace that is administered by a particular name server.

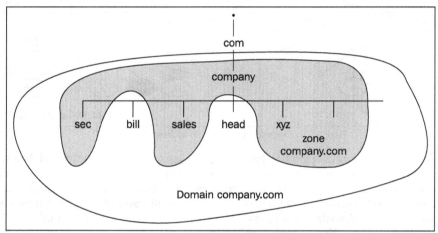

Figure 1.3: Zone company.com

A zone containing data of a lower-level domain is usually called a **subordinate zone**.

1.5.1 Special Zones

Besides classic zones, which contain data about parts of the domains or subdomains, special zones are also used for DNS implementation. Specifically, the following zones are used:

- **Zone stub**: Zone stub is actually a subordinate zone that only contains information about what name servers administer in a particular subdomain (they contain the NS records for the zone). The zone stub therefore does not contain the entire zone.

- **Zone cache/hint**: A zone hint contains a list of root name servers (non-authoritative data read into memory during the start of the name server). Only BIND version 8 and later use the name hint for this type of zone. In previous versions, a name cache zone was used. Remember that the root name servers are an authority for a root domain marked as a dot (.).

1.6 Reserved Domains and Pseudodomains

It was later decided that other domains could also be used as TLD. Some TLD were reserved in RFC 2606:

- The `test` domain for testing
- The `example` domain for creating documentation and examples
- The `invalid` domain for evoking error states
- The `localhost` domain for software loops

Domains that are not directly connected to the Internet can also exist, i.e., computers that do not even use the TCP/IP network protocol therefore do not have an IP address. These domains are sometimes called **pseudodomains**. They are meaningful especially for electronic mail. It is possible to send an email into other networks and then into the Internet with the help of a pseudodomain (like DECnet or MS Exchange).

In its internal network, a company can first use TCP/IP and then DECnet protocol. A user using TCP/IP in the internal network (for example, `Daniel@computer.company.com`) is addressed from the Internet. But how do you address a user on computers working in the DECnet protocol?

To solve this, we insert the fictive `dnet` pseudodomain into the address. The user Daniel is therefore addressed `Daniel@computer.dnet.company.com`. With the help of DNS, the entire email that was addressed into the `dnet.company.com` domain is redirected to a gateway in DECnet protocol (the gateway of the `company.com` domain), which performs the transformation from TCP/IP (for SMTP) into DECnet (for Mail-11).

1.7 Queries (Translations)

Most common queries are translation of a hostname to an IP address. It is also possible to request additional information from DNS. Queries are mediated by a resolver. The **resolver** is a DNS client that asks the name server. Because the database is distributed worldwide, the nearest name server does not need to know the final response and can ask other name servers for help. The name server, as an answer to the resolver, then returns the acquired translation or returns a negative answer. All communication consists of queries and answers.

The name server searches in its cache memory for the data for the zone it administers during its start. The primary name server reads data from the local disk; the secondary name server acquires data from the primary name server by a query zone transfer of the administered zones and also saves them into the cache memory. The data stored within the primary and secondary name servers is called **authoritative data**. Furthermore, the name server reads from its memory cache/hint the zone data, which is not part of the data from its administered zone (local disk), but nonetheless enables this data to connect with the root name servers. This data is called **nonauthoritative data**. In the terminology of BIND program version 8 and 9, we sometimes do not speak of them as primary and secondary servers, but as master servers and slave servers.

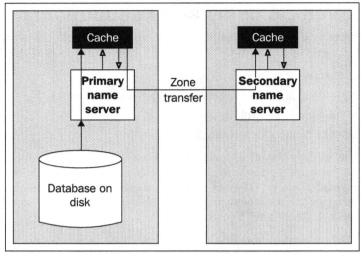

Figure 1.4: Primary name server loads data from a disk, while the secondary
server acquires data by *zone transfer* query

Name servers save into their cache memory positive (and sometimes even negative) answers to
queries that other name servers have to ask for. From the point of view of our name server, this
data acquired from other name servers is also non-authoritative, thereby saving time when
processing repeated queries.

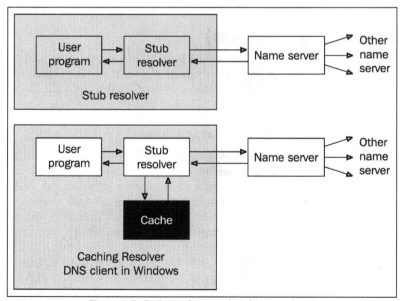

Figure 1.5: Stub resolvers and caching resolvers

Requirements for translations occur in a user program. The user program asks a component within the operating system, which is called a **resolver**, for a translation. The resolver transfers the query for translation to a name server. In smaller systems, there is usually only a stub resolver. In such cases, the resolver transfers all requirements by DNS protocol to a name server running on another computer (see Figure 1.5). A resolver without cache memory is called a *stub resolver*. It is possible to establish cache memory for a resolver even in Windows 2000, Windows XP, etc. This service in Windows is called **DNS Client**. (I think this is a little bit misleading as a stub resolver is not a *proper* DNS client!)

Some computers run only a resolver (either stub or caching); others run both a resolver and a name server. Nowadays, a wide range of combinations are possible (see Figure 1.6) but the principle remains the same:

1. The user inserts a command, then the hostname needs to be translated into an IP address (in Figure 1.6, number 1).

2. If the resolver has its own cache, it will attempt to find the result within it directly (2).

3. If the answer is not found in the resolver cache (or it is a stub), the resolver transfers the request to a name server (3).

4. The name server will look for the answer in its cache memory.

5. If the name server does not find the answer in its cache memory, it looks for help from other name servers.

6. The name server can contact more name servers by a process referred to as iteration. By iteration, the name server can access or contact a name server, which is an authority on the answer. The authoritative name server will then give a last resort answer (negatively if there is no information in DNS corresponding with the inserted name).

7. But if the process described above does not return the result fast enough, the resolver repeats its query. If there are more name servers listed in the resolver configuration, then it will send the next query to the next name server listed in the directory (i.e., another name server). The directory of name servers is processed cyclically. The cycle starts for the particular query from the name server, which is listed in the first position.

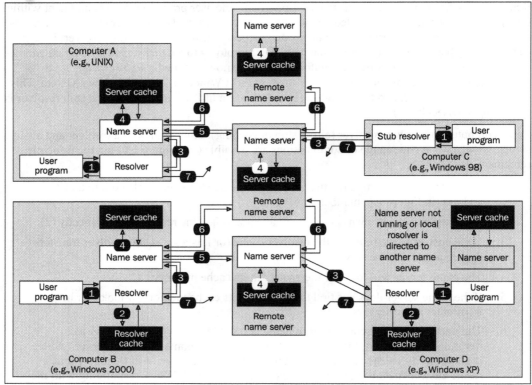

Figure 1.6: Name server and resolver

DNS uses both UDP and TCP protocols for the transport of its queries/answers. It uses port 53 for both protocols (i.e., ports 53/UDP and 53/TCP). Common queries such as the translation of a name to an IP address and vice versa are performed by UDP protocol. The length of data transported by UDP protocol is implicitly limited to 512 B (a truncation flag can be used to signal that the answer did not fit into 512 B and it is therefore necessary for the query answer to be repeated by the TCP protocol). The length of UDP packets is limited to 512 B because a fragmentation could occur for larger IP datagrams. DNS does not consider fragmentation of UDP as sensible. Queries transporting zone transfer data occur between the primary and secondary name servers and are transported by TCP protocol.

Common queries (such as the translation of a name to an IP address and vice versa) are performed with the help of datagrams in UDP protocol. The translations are required by a client (resolver) on the name server. If the name server does not know what to do, it can ask for translation (help) from other name servers. Name servers solve questions among themselves by iteration, which always starts from the root name server. More details are available in Section 1.10.

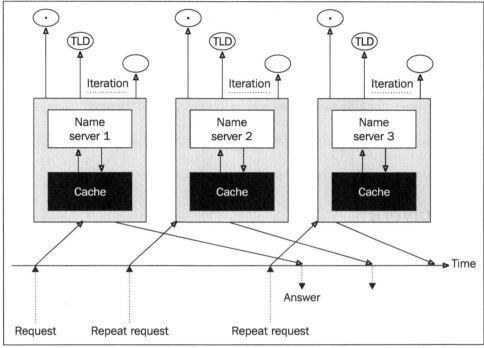

Figure 1.7: Required answer for a translation

There is a rule in the Internet that a database with data needed for translations is always saved on at least two independent computers (independent name servers). If one is unavailable, the translation can be performed by the other computer.

In general, we cannot expect that all name servers are accessible all the time. If the TCP protocol is used for a translation, attempts to establish a connection with an inaccessible name server would cause long time intervals while the TCP protocol is trying to connect. Only when this time interval is over is it possible to connect to the next name server.

The solution for this in UDP protocol is more elegant: A datagram containing a request for the translation is sent to the first server. If the answer does not come back within a short time-out interval, then a datagram with a request is sent to another name server, if the answer does not come back again, it is sent to the next one, and so on. If all possible name servers are used, it will start again from the first one, and the whole cycle repeats until the answer comes back or the set interval times out.

1.7.1 Round Robin

Round Robin is a technique that can be used to equally load several machines (Load Balancing). It is possible to use this technique for the majority of name servers (including Windows 2000/2003). This is a situation where we have more than one IP address for one name in DNS. For example, we may operate an exposed web server and because the performance of the machine is not sufficient, we buy another or two more. We start running the web server on all three of them (for example, www.company.com). The first one has an IP address 195.1.1.1, the second one 195.1.1.2, and the third one 195.1.1.3. There will be three records in DNS for www.company.com, and each of them will have a different IP address. Round Robin technique ensures that the answer to the:

1. first query (to the first user) will be that the web server return addresses 195.1.1.1, 195.1.1.2, and 195.1.1.3

2. the answer to the next query (to the second user) will be that the server return IP addresses 195.1.1.2, 195.1.1.3, and 195.1.1.1.

3. the answer to te next query (may be 3rd user) will return IP addresses 195.1.1.3, 195.1.1.1, and 195.1.1.2.

4. procedure are repeating from 1st point again and again.

1.8 Resolvers

A **resolver** is a component of the system dealing with the translation of an IP address. A resolver is a client; it is not a particular program. It is a set of library functions that are linked with application programs requiring services such as Telnet, FTP, browsers, and so on. For example, if Telnet needs to translate the name of a computer to its IP address, it calls the particular library functions.

The client (in this case, the aforementioned Telnet) calls the library functions (gethostbyname), which will formulate the query, and send it to the name server.

Time limitations must also be considered. It is possible that a resolver does not receive an answer to its first query, while the next one with the same content is answered correctly (while the server is waiting for the first query, it manages to obtain the answer for the second query from another name server, so the first query was not answered, because the response of its name server took too long). From the user's point of view, it seems that the translation was not managed on the first try, but was completed by processing it again. The use of the UDP protocol causes a similar effect. Note that it can also happen that the server did not receive the request for the translation at all, because the network is overloaded, and the UDP datagram has been lost somewhere along the way.

1.8.1 Resolver Configuration in UNIX

The configuration file for a resolver in the UNIX operating system is /etc/resolv/conf. It usually contains two types of lines (the second command can be repeated several times):

```
domain        the name of the local domain
nameserver    IP address of name server
```

If the user inserted the name without a dot at the end, the resolver will add the domain name from the domain command after the inserted name, and will try to transfer it to the name server for translation. If the translation is not performed (a negative answer has been received from the name server), the resolver will try to translate the actual name without the suffix from the domain command.

Some resolvers enable the search command. This command allows us to specify more names of local domains.

The IP address of a name server that the resolver should contact is specified by the nameserver command. It is recommended to use more nameserver commands for times when some name server is not available.

> The IP address of a name server always has to be stated in the configuration file of the resolver, not the domain name of the name server!

When configuring the resolver and name server on the same machine, the nameserver command can be directed to a local name server 127.0.0.1 (but this is not necessary).

Other parameters of the resolver (for example, the maximum number of nameserver commands) can be set in the configuration file of the operating system kernel. This file is often called /usr/include/resolv.h. Afterwards, of course, a new compilation of the kernel operating system must follow.

Generally, it is also possible to configure all computers without the use of DNS. Then all requests for address translations are performed locally with the help of the /etc/hosts file (in Windows %System_Root%/System32/Drivers/etc/hosts). It is possible to combine both methods (the most typical variant); however, we need to be careful about the content of the database /etc/hosts. Usually it is also possible to set the order in which the databases are supposed to be browsed. Usually one /etc/hosts file is browsed and afterwards the DNS.

1.8.2 Resolver Configuration in Windows

There is an interesting situation in Windows 2000 and higher. Here we still have the previously mentioned DNS Client service. It is an implementation of a caching resolver. This service is started implicitly. It is strictly recommended in the documentation not to stop this service. However, according to my tests, Windows acts like a station with a stub resolver after stopping this service.

The content of a resolver cache can even be written out by a ipconfig /displayDNS command or deleted by ipconfig /flushDNS command.

The content of a %System Root%/System32/Drivers/etc/hosts file whose content is not changed by the ipconfig /flushDNS command is also a part of the cache resolver. The cache resolver can be parameterized by the insertion or change of keys in the Windows register folder HKEY_LOCAL_MACHINE/SYSTEM/CurrentControlSet/Services/Dnscache/Parameters, for example, by a NegativeCacheTime key, where you can specify a time period within which negative answers kept in the cache resolver can be changed.

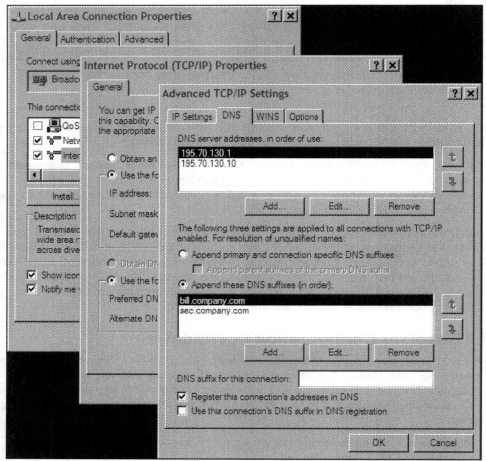

Figure 1.8: Configuration of a resolver in Windows XP

In older Windows versions, the configuration of a resolver was as simple as it was in UNIX. The difference was only in the fact that a text configuration file was not created by a text editor, but the values were inserted into a particular window. With Windows XP this particular configuration window of the resolver (Figure 1.8) contains a lot more information.

It is necessary to look at Windows XP and higher from a historical point of view. The LAN Manager System based on NetBIOS protocol was the predecessor of the Windows network. NetBIOS protocol also uses names of computers, which it needs to translate to network addresses in the network layer. When Windows uses TCP/IP as a network protocol, it needs to translate the names of computers to IP addresses and vice versa.

LAN Manager implemented its own system of names. Names with particular IP addresses were saved locally in a `%SystemRoot%/System 32/Drivers/etc/lmhosts` file. Later Windows implemented a DNS analogy, a database called WINS (Windows Internet Names Service).

18

The translation of names is an interesting problem in Windows. When a translation is not found either in an lmhosts file or on WINS server, it is then sent to a broadcast requesting whether the searched for computer is present on the LAN. Searching in DNS after the implementation of DNS into Windows has extended the entire mechanism. So programs in Windows 2000, which have LAN Manager system as a precursor search for the translation:

1. In the LAN Manager cache of a local computer (nbtstat -c command lists the cache). It is a cache of the NetBIOS protocol. Rows of the lmhosts file, having the #PRE string as a last parameter, are loaded into this cache when a computer starts. If the lmhosts file is changed, we can force reloading of these rows into a cache by the nbtstat -R command.

2. On WINS servers. By a broadcast or multicast on LAN.

3. In the lmhosts file.

4. In a resolver cache (even the content of hosts file is read into it).

5. On DNS servers.

And programs (for example, the ping command) that are Internet oriented search for the translation:

1. In the resolver cache (even the content of hosts file is read into it).

2. On DNS Servers.

3. On WINS servers.

4. By a broadcast or multicast packet of NetBIOS protocol.

5. In the lmhosts file.

So if you make a mistake in the name of the computer in the ping command, then in the record of a MS Network Monitor program or in the record of an Ethereal program (visit http://www.ethereal.com for additional information) you will also be able to see the packets of NetBIOS protocol and even the search conducted by a broadcast.

Now to the configuration of a resolver in Windows XP in Figure 1.8. First we will insert the IP addresses of name servers into the upper window (DNS server's address, in order of use). It is not necessary to insert them if we get them during the start up of the computer, for example, from a DHCP server or during the establishment of a dial-up connection with the help of PPP protocol.

Furthermore, there are two options here:

1. Select Append primary and connection specific in DNS suffixes in the DNS tab (this option is not selected in Figure 1.8); the translation is performed as follows:

   o If the required name contains a dot, then the resolver tries to translate the name without adding a suffix.

   o If the name does not contain a dot, it tries to translate the inserted name after which it has added a dot and a domain name of a Windows domain (configured on Properties in the Computer Name tab).

   o It tries to translate the inserted name after which it has added a dot and a name of a chain in a field DNS suffix for this connection.

2. Click Append these DNS suffixes (in order); the translation is performed as follows:

    o   If the required name contains a dot then the resolver tries to translate the name without adding a suffix.
    o   It tries to add particular suffixes according to a list listed in the window below the mentioned option.

So if you make a mistake in the name of the computer and hit a nonexistent name xxx, then because you have selected a second option, the resolver will first try to translate the name xxx.bill.company.com and then a name xxx.sec.company.com. In both cases, it will generate a query to the name server 195.70.130.1 for each of these translations and then if you do not receive the answer in time, it will repeat the question to the server 195.70.130.10, and the whole cycle is repeated until the time limit is exceeded.

1.9 Name Server

A name server keeps information for the translation of computer names to IP addresses (even for reverse translations). The name server takes care of a certain part from the space of names of all computers. This part is called the zone (at minimum it takes care of zone 0.0.127.in-addr.arpa).

A domain or its part creates the zone. The name server can with the help of an NS type record (in its configuration) delegate administration of a subdomain to a subordinate name server.

The name server is a program that performs the translation at the request of a resolver or another name server. In UNIX, the name server is materialized by the named program. Also the name **BIND (Berkeley Internet Name Domain)** is used for this name server.

Types of name servers differ according to the way in which they save data:

*   **Primary name server/primary master** is the main data source for the zone. It is the authoritative server for the zone. This server acquires data about its zone from databases saved on a local disk. Names of these types of servers depend on the version of BIND they use. While only the primary name server was used for version 4.x, a primary name master is used for version 8. The administrator manually creates databases for this server. The primary server must be published as an authoritative name server for the domain in the SOA resource record, while the primary master server does not need to be published. There is only one of this type of server for each zone.

*   **Master name server** is an authoritative server for the zone. The master server is always published as an authoritative server for the domain in NS records. The master sever is a source of data of a zone for the subordinate servers (slave/secondary servers). There can be several master servers. This type of server is used for Bind version 8 and later.

*   **Secondary name server/slave name server** acquires data about the zone by copying the data from the primary name server (respectively from the master server) at regular time intervals. It makes no sense to edit these databases on the secondary

name servers, although they are saved on the local server disk because they will be rewritten during further copying. This type of name server is also an authority for its zones, i.e., its data for the particular zone is considered irrevocable (authoritative). The name of this type of server depends again on the version of BIND it uses. For version 4, only the secondary name was used, the term slave server was used for a completely different type of server. In version 8 you can come across both names.

- **Caching-only name server** is neither a primary nor secondary name server (it is not an authority) for any zone. However, it uses the general characteristics of name servers, i.e., it saves data that comes through its cache. This data is called nonauthoritative. Each server is a caching server, but by the words caching, we understand that it is neither a primary nor secondary name server for any zone. (Of course, even a caching-only server is a primary name server for zone 0.0.127.in-addr.arpa, but that does not count).

- **Root name server** is an authoritative name server for the root domain (for the dot). Each root name server is a primary server, which differentiates it from other name servers.

- **Slave name server** (in BIND version 4 terminology) transmits questions for a translation to other name servers; it does not perform any iteration itself.

- **Stealth name server** is a secret server. This type of name server is not published anywhere. It is only known to the servers that have its IP address statically listed in their configuration. It is an authoritative server. It acquires the data for the zone with the help of a zone transfer. It can be the main server for the zone. Stealth servers can be used as a local backup if the local servers are unavailable.

The architecture of a master/slave system is shown in the following figure:

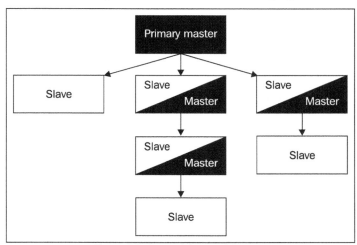

Figure 1.9: Master/slave architecture

One name server can be a master (primary) server for one zone and a slave (secondary) server for another.

From the point of view of a client, there is no difference between master (primary) and slave (secondary) name servers. Both contain data of similar importance—both are authoritative for the particular zone. The client does not even need to know which server is the master (primary server) and which one is the slave (secondary). On the other hand, a caching server is not an authority, i.e., if it is not able to perform the translation, it contacts the authoritative server for the particular zone.

So if the hostmaster change some information on the master server (i.e. adds another computer name into the database), then the databases on all slave servers are automatically corrected after a time set by a parameter in the SOA resource record (if the hostmaster only corrected the database manually on a secondary name server, the correction would disappear at the same time!). A problem occurs when the user receives the first answer from the slave server at a time when the slave server has not been updated. The answer is negative, i.e., such a computer is not in the database.

Even worse is the following case: the master server operates correctly, but there is no data for the zone on the slave server because zone transfer failed. The clients receive authoritative answers from the master server or the slave server by chance. When the client receives an answer from the master server, the answer is correct. When the client receives an answer from the slave server, the answer is negative. But the user doesn't know which server is correct and which is wrong . Then the user says, "*First I receive a response to my query and second time I do not.*"

Authoritative data comes from the database which is stored on the primary master's disk. Nonauthoritative data comes from other nameservers ("from the network"). There is only one exception. The name server needs to know the root name servers to ensure proper functioning of the name server. However, it is not an authority for them usually, still each name server has own nonauthoritative information about root servers on the disk. It is implemented by a cache command in BIND version 4 or zone cache/hint in BIND version 8 and later.

The iteration process of a translation of the name abc.company.com to an IP address is shown in the following figure below:

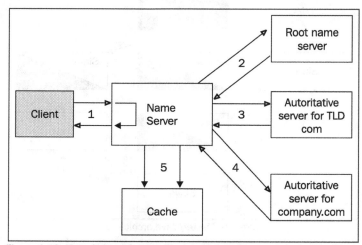

Figure 1.10: Translation of a domain name abc.company.com to IP address

The step-by-step process is as follows:

1. The resolver formulates the requirement to the name server and expects an unambiguous answer. If the name server is able to answer, it sends the answer immediately. It searches for the answer in its cache memory (5). Authoritative data from the disk databases is acquired as well as nonauthoritative data acquired during previous translations. If the server does not find the answer in its cache memory, it contacts other servers. It always begins with a root name server. If the name server does not know the answer itself, it contacts the root name server. That is why each name server must know the IP addresses of root name servers. If no root name server is available (as is, for example, the case for all closed Intranets), then after several unsuccessful attempts, the entire translation process collapses.

2. The root name server finds out that the information about the .com domain was delegated by NS resource record to the subordinate name server and it will return this subordinate name server's IP addresses (IP address of authoritative name servers for the zone .com).

3. Our name server turns to the authoritative server for the .com domain and finds out that the information about the company.com domain was delegated by NS type resource record to the subordinate name server and will return this subordinate name server's IP addresses (IP address of authoritative name servers for company.com zone).

4. Our name server then turns to the authoritative name server for the company.com domain, which will solve its query (or not). The answer from authoritative name server for relevant zone is marked as an authoritative answer. The result is transmitted to the client (1).

5. The information, which the server has gradually received, will also be saved into the cache. The answer to the next similar question is looked up in cache and returned directly from cache. But this next answer is not marked as authoritative.

The name server even saves answers into the cache memory described in the previous five points (translation of abc.company.com). It can then use the answers from the cache for the following translations to save time, but it also helps the root name servers. However, if you require the translation of a name from TLD that is not in the cache, then the root name server is really contacted. From this we can see that the root servers in the Internet will be heavily burdened and their unavailability would damage communication on the entire Internet.

The name server does not require the complete (recursive) answer. Important name servers (for example, root name servers or TLD name servers) do not even have to produce recursive answers, and hence avoid overloading themselves and restricting their availability. It is not possible to direct the resolver of your computer to them.

The nslookup program is a useful program for the administrator of the name server. If you want to perform questions on a name server with the nslookup program, then forbid iteration (recursive questions) and the addition of domain names from the configuration file of the resolver with the commands:

```
$ nslookup
  set norecurse
  set nosearch
```

1.10 Forwarder Servers

There is another type of server, called a forwarder server. The characteristics of this server are not connected with whether it is a primary or secondary server for any zone, but with the way in which the translation of DNS questions is performed.

So far we have said that the resolver transfers the request for the translation to a name server, i.e., it sends a query to a name server and waits for the final answer (the client sends a recursive query and waits for a final answer). If the name server is not able to answer itself, it performs a recursive translation via non-recursive queries. First it contacts the root name server. The root name server tells the resolver which name servers it must ask for answers to its query. Then it contacts the recommended name server. This name server sends many packets into the Internet.

If a company network is connected to the Internet by a slow line, then the name server loads the line by its translations. In such a case, it is advantageous to configure some of the name servers as forwarder servers.

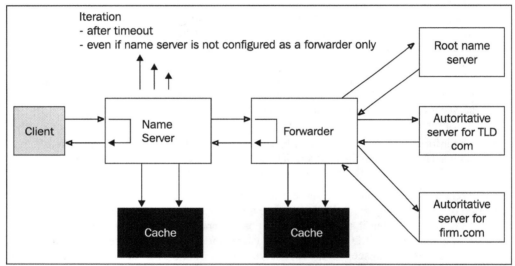

Figure 1.11: Communication of a local name server with a forwarder server

The local name server transmits the queries to the forwarder server. However, the local name server marks these queries as recursive. The forwarder server takes the request from the local name server and performs translation via non-recursive queries on the Internet by itself. It then returns only the final result to our name server.

The local name server waits for the answer from the forwarder server for the final result. If the local name server does not get the answer in the set time out limit, then it contacts the root name servers and tries to solve the case by iteration.

If the local name server is not supposed to contact the root name servers, but is supposed to only wait for the answer, then it is necessary to indicate such a server in its configuration as a *forwarder-only*. In BIND version 4.x such a server is called *slave*. Forwarder-only (slave) servers are used on intranets (behind the firewall) where contact with root name servers is not possible. The forwarder server then contacts a name server, which is part of the firewall.

The forwarder server can work as a caching-only server in both variants, and it can also be the primary or secondary name server for some zones.

It is also possible to configure forwarder servers in Windows 2003 Server as shown in the figure below:

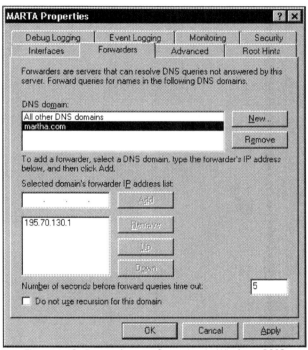

Figure 1.12: Forwarders configuration in Windows 2003

Run the DNS from the Administrative Tools. Right-click to your DNS server and choose Properties. Select the Forwarders tab. Click New and enter the name of the domain you want to resolve by forwarders. Insert the IP addresses of the forwarder servers below. You can insert into the Number of seconds before forward queries time out box a time limit during which the server waits for an answer from a forwarder server. We can establish a slave server by clicking the Do not use recursion for this domain option.

2
DNS Protocol

2.1 Resource Records

Information on domain names and their IP addresses, as well as all the other information distributed via DNS is stored in the memory of name servers as **Resource Records (RR)**.

A name server (also referred to as a DNS server) loads data into its cache in several ways. Authoritative data are read from files on a disk or obtained via a zone transfer query from another authoritative servers. Nonauthoritative data are obtained by the server from other servers as it answers of individual DNS queries. Do not forget for special kind of nonauthoritative data – information about root name servers which are loaded locally from disk file.

If a DNS client needs to obtain information from a DNS, it requests RR from the DNS according to its requirements, i.e., a client can request from a domain server an A type RR with the IP addresses of the particular domain name. A client can be a resolver or a name server that cannot resolve the query on its own.

The structure of RR is prescribed by DNS protocol. The RR structure is shown in the following figure:

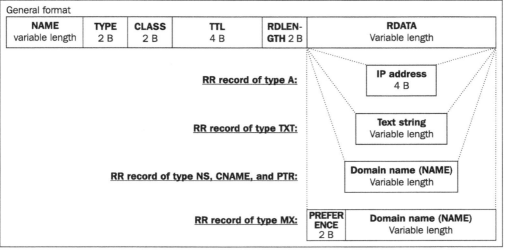

Figure 2.1: Resource Record structure

Each RR field consists of:

- **NAME**: Domain name.
- **TYPE**: Record type.
- **CLASS**: Record class.
- **TTL**: Time to live. A 32-bit number indicating the time the particular RR can be kept valid in a server cache. When this time expires, the record has to be considered invalid. The value 0 keeps nonauthoritative servers from saving the RR to their cache memory.
- **RDLENGTH**: A 16-bit number specifying the length of the RDATA field.
- **RDATA**: The data stored as a string of variable length. The format of the field depends on the RR type and class.

Note that the RR format in DNS protocol is in binary notation, i.e., it is opaque to users. This is the form in which RRs are propagated through the network via DNS protocol. On the other hand, users will want to insert their RRs into zone files in text format. As it is simple to convert binary notation to text format, individual fields are converted to text and separated by a space or a tab or a combination of these characters. Individual strings in domain names are spaced by a dot.

Type	Name	Description of the RDATA field
A	Host Address	32-bit IP address.
NS	Authoritative Name Server	The domain name of the name server, which is the authoritative name server for the particular domain.
CNAME	Canonical name for an alias	A domain name specifying a synonym to the NAME field
SOA	Start Of Authority	Each zone data file must have exactly one SOA record. This consists of 7 fields. For an explicit description, see DNS databases in Section 4.3.2.2.
PTR	Domain name pointer	Domain name. The record is used for reverse translation.
HINFO	Host information	Consists of two strings of characters. They contain descriptions of the HW and the SW used in the NAME computer respectively.
MX	Mail exchange	Consists of two fields. The first is an unsigned 16-bit containing the preference value and the second is the domain name of the exchange server.
TXT	Text string	Text string containing a description.
AAAA	IP6 address	128-bit IP address (IP version 6).
WKS	Well known service description	A description of well known server services in TCP and UDP. It consists of three parts: 32-bit address, protocol number, and service ports.
SIG	Security signature	A description record used for authentication in Secure DNS.
KEY	Security key	A public zone key used as a signature in authentication.

Type	Name	Description of the RDATA field
NXT	Next domain	Name of another domain. Authenticating a nonexistent domain name and type.
A6	A6 host address	Can contain up to three fields: prefix length, part of an IP version 6 address, and prefix name.

Table 2.1: The most common RR

2.2 DNS Protocol

The DNS protocol works with several types of operations. The most commonly used operation is a DNS QUERY. It is a query that enables the obtaining of one or more records from the DNS database. The DNS QUERY operation was for a long time the only operation possible in the DNS system. New modifications to the DNS protocol have brought new kinds of operations, as DNS NOTIFY or DNS UPDATE. These will be dealt with in the next chapter.

The DNS protocol operates on a query/answer basis. A client sends a query to a server and the server answers it. DNS protocol uses name compression in order to make DNS packets as compact as possible.

The DNS protocol is an application-layer protocol and, as such, it does not carry out packet transfer on its own. The packet transfer is delegated to a transport protocol. Unlike the overwhelming majority of other application protocols, DNS protocol uses both UDP and TCP. Each query and the answer to it are transferred by the same transport protocol.

With translation queries (asking RR), UDP is preferred. Where a DNS answer is longer than 512 B, the answer includes only a 512 B part of the information, and the truncation (TC) bit is set in the header to mark that the answer is incomplete. The complete answer can be requested by the client via TCP.

For zone transfer between a primary and a secondary name server, TCP is used. Name servers wait for queries both on the 53/UDP port and the 53/TCP port.

> Some UDP implementations do not fill in the checksum field in the UDP packet header and take advantage of this option. This feature can be useful, for example, for NFS, but it is precarious with DNS. A network failure can result in a meaningless answer, especially where SLIP has been used on the way between a server and a client. Therefore make sure before a name server installation that your system is set to fill in the checksum in the UDP packet.

2.3 DNS Query

The DNS QUERY operation consists of a query and an answer. A query contains a request for an RR (or several RRs) from the DNS database. The answer either contains the particular RR or is a denial. The RR contained in an answer can be the ultimate answer or help the client to formulate another DNS QUERY to achieve the aim, i.e., to formulate another iteration.

2.3.1 DNS Query Packet Format

DNS query uses the same packet format for both queries and answers as shown in the following figure:

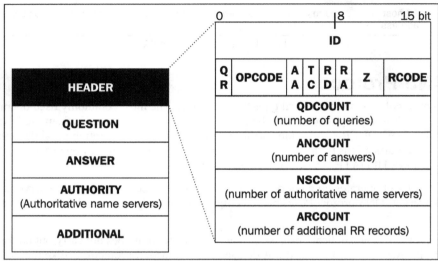

Figure 2.2: DNS Query packet format

A packet can consist of up to five sections. Each packet has to contain the HEADER section.

The term 'query' is used in two senses:

1. A DNS QUERY operation. A basic DNS protocol operation through which records (RR) are searched for in DNS databases. Several other operations will be discussed in the next chapter.

2. The DNS QUERY operation always consists of a query (sent by a client) and an answer to it sent to the client by the name server. The client is either a resolver or a name server that cannot provide the answer on its own. A resolver usually marks its query with a tag showing it is a recursive query, i.e., it asks the name server to retrieve a final answer. On the contrary, if the query is sent by a name server, it is usually marked with a tag showing it is an interactive query, i.e., the name server asks another name server to help it with the translation, but does not send a recursive query as it is able to arrive at what it needs by iteration.

2.3.2 DNS Query Packet Header

The packet header is obligatory and is contained both in the query and in the answer.

The first two bytes (16 bits) of a header contain a query identifier (**query ID**). A query ID is generated by a client and copied into the answer by a server. The ID is used to match a query with an answer. It identifies uniquely which particular query goes with which particular answer. The ID allows a client to send several queries at a time without waiting for an answer.

The next two bytes of a header contain the control bits. The significance of the control bits is shown in the following table:

Field	No. of bits	Value
QR	1	0 if the message is a query 1 if the message is an answer
Opcode	4	The query type which is the same both for the query and the answer: 0: standard query (QUERY) 1: inverse query (IQUERY) 2: status query (STATUS) 4: notify query (NOTIFY) 5: update query (UPDATE)
AA	1	0 for non-authoritative answer 1 for authoritative answer
TC	1	1: the answer was truncated to 512 bytes. If a client needs to obtain the whole answer, the query must be sent again via TCP.
RD	1	Recursion Desired - this bit may be set in a query and is copied into the response. If is set, it directs the name server to pursue the query recursively.
RA	1	Recursion Available - this be is set or cleared in a response, and denotes whether recursive query support is available in the name server.)
Z	3	Reserved for future use
Rcode	4	The result code of an answer 0: No error (Noerror) 1: Format error, The name server was unable to interpret the query (FormErr)

Table 2.2: Significance of the individual control bits in a DNS packet header

The next four 2-byte fields in a packet header hold the number of records contained in the individual sections following the header:

- **QDCOUNT** specifies the number of records a query consists of

- **ANCOUNT** specifies the number of records an answer consists of

- **NSCOUNT** specifies the number of records a section containing links to authoritative name servers consists of

- **ARCOUNT** specifies the number of records a section containing additional information consists of

The following example shows a DNS packet found in a network (for catching DNS packets I use a program called Ethereal):

```
Frame 2 (318 bytes on wire, 318 bytes captured)
Ethernet II, Src: Cisco_8e:1f:80 (00:15:63:8e:1f:80), Dst: Fujitsu_79:5d:0e
Internet Protocol, Src: 160.217.1.10 (160.217.1.10), Dst: 160.217.208.142
User Datagram Protocol, Src Port: domain (53), Dst Port: 1337 (1337)
Domain Name System (response)
Transaction ID: 0x000c
Flags: 0x8180 (Standard query response, No error)
1... .... .... .... = Response: Message is a response
.000 0... .... .... = Opcode: Standard query (0)
```

```
.... .0.. .... .... = Authoritative: Server is not an authority for domain
.... ..0. .... .... = Truncated: Message is not truncated
.... ...1 .... .... = Recursion desired: Do query recursively
.... .... 1... .... = Recursion available: Server can do recursive queries
.... .... .0.. .... = Z: reserved (0)
.... .... ..0. .... = Answer authenticated: Answer/authority portion was not
authenticated by the server
.... .... .... 0000 = Reply code: No error (0)
    Questions: 1
    Answer RRs: 3
    Authority RRs: 6
    Additional RRs: 6
    Queries
        www.google.com: type A, class IN
    Answers
        www.google.com: type CNAME, class IN, cname www.l.google.com
        www.l.google.com: type A, class IN, addr 72.14.207.99
        www.l.google.com: type A, class IN, addr 72.14.207.104
    Authoritative nameservers
        l.google.com: type NS, class IN, ns d.l.google.com
        l.google.com: type NS, class IN, ns e.l.google.com
        l.google.com: type NS, class IN, ns g.l.google.com
        l.google.com: type NS, class IN, ns a.l.google.com
        l.google.com: type NS, class IN, ns b.l.google.com
        l.google.com: type NS, class IN, ns c.l.google.com
    Additional records
        a.l.google.com: type A, class IN, addr 216.239.53.9
        b.l.google.com: type A, class IN, addr 64.233.179.9
        c.l.google.com: type A, class IN, addr 64.233.161.9
        d.l.google.com: type A, class IN, addr 64.233.183.9
        e.l.google.com: type A, class IN, addr 66.102.11.9
        g.l.google.com: type A, class IN, addr 64.233.167.9
```

2.3.3 Question Section

DNS query packets mostly contain only one section: it is a question section for one question (QDCOUNT=1). The question section consists of three fields:

- **QNAME** contains a domain name. In DNS protocol dot (.) notation is not used with domain names. Each part of a domain name (commonly stated between dots) is preceded by a byte containing the length of the string. The domain name is concluded by a zero marking its end (zero length of the string). An example of the content of this field in a query for the info.pvt.net domain name translation is as follows: $04_{16}info03_{16}pvt03_{16}net00_{16}$. The lengths of strings are in binary notation.

- **QTYPE** specifies the query type, i.e., the RR type required in the answer. The most common types of queries are shown in the following table:

Type	Value (in decimal notation)	Description
A	1	IP address version 4
NS	2	Authoritative name servers
CNAME	5	The canonical name for an alias
SOA	6	Marks the start of a zone of authority
WKS	11	A well known service description

Type	Value (in decimal notation)	Description
PTR	12	A domain name pointer
HINFO	13	Host information
MX	15	Mail exchange
TXT	16	Text strings
SIG	24	For a security signature
KEY	25	For a security key
NXT	30	Next Domain
AAAA	28	IP6 Address
CERT	37	CERT (see Chapter 3.8)
A6	38	IP address version 6
AXFR	252	Transfer of an entire zone
IXFR	251	Incremental transfer
*	255	A request for all records

Table 2.3: Query type values

- **QCLASS** stands for query class.

Numerical value (in decimal notation)	Description
1	IN: Internet
3	CH: Chaos
4	HS: Hesiod
255	*: all classes (as QCLASS only)

Table 2.4: Query Classes

An example of a DNS packet found in a network is as follows (the question section is shown in bold):

```
Frame 2 (318 bytes on wire, 318 bytes captured)
Ethernet II, Src: Cisco_8e:1f:80 (00:15:63:8e:1f:80), Dst: Fujitsu_79:5d:0e
Internet Protocol, Src: 160.217.1.10 (160.217.1.10), Dst: 160.217.208.142
User Datagram Protocol, Src Port: domain (53), Dst Port: 1337 (1337)
Domain Name System (response)
     Transaction ID: 0x000c
     Flags: 0x8180 (Standard query response, No error)
     Questions: 1
     Answer RRs: 3
     Authority RRs: 6
     Additional RRs: 6
     Queries
          www.google.com: type A, class IN
               Name: www.google.com
               Type: A (Host address)
               Class: IN (0x0001)
     Answers
     Authoritative nameservers
     Additional records
```

2.3.4 The Answer Section, Authoritative Servers, and Additional Information

Along with a header section and a repeated question section, answer packets contain another three sections: an answer section, an authoritative servers section, and an additional information section. The answer itself is included in the answer section. The authoritative name server section holds the names of the name servers in NS records. The additional information section usually holds IP addresses of authoritative name servers. Records in these sections are common resource records similar to name server cache records and use the same format as:

- **NAME**: The domain name, the same format as in the QNAME question section.
- **TYPE**: The record type, the same format as in the QTYPE question section.
- **CLASS**: The record class, the same format as in the QCLASS question section.
- **TTL**: RR expiry date, i.e., the time an answer can be kept in a server cache as valid.
- **RDLENGTH**: RDATA section length.
- **RDATA**: the right side of RR (an IP address or a domain name).

An example of a DNS packet with answer, authoritative servers, and additional information sections is as follows:

```
Frame 2 (318 bytes on wire, 318 bytes captured)
Ethernet II, Src: Cisco_8e:1f:80 (00:15:63:8e:1f:80), Dst: Fujitsu_79:5d:0e
Internet Protocol, Src: 160.217.1.10 (160.217.1.10), Dst: 160.217.208.142
User Datagram Protocol, Src Port: domain (53), Dst Port: 1337 (1337)
Domain Name System (response)
    Transaction ID: 0x000c
    Flags: 0x8180 (Standard query response, No error)
    Questions: 1
    Answer RRs: 3
    Authority RRs: 6
    Additional RRs: 6
    Queries
    Answers
        www.google.com: type CNAME, class IN, cname www.l.google.com
            Name: www.google.com
            Type: CNAME (Canonical name for an alias)
            Class: IN (0x0001)
            Time to live: 11 minutes, 32 seconds
            Data length: 8
            Primary name: www.l.google.com
        www.l.google.com: type A, class IN, addr 72.14.207.99
            Name: www.l.google.com
            Type: A (Host address)
            Class: IN (0x0001)
            Time to live: 4 minutes, 15 seconds
            Data length: 4
            Addr: 72.14.207.99
        www.l.google.com: type A, class IN, addr 72.14.207.104
            Name: www.l.google.com
            Type: A (Host address)
            Class: IN (0x0001)
            Time to live: 4 minutes, 15 seconds
            Data length: 4
            Addr: 72.14.207.104
    Authoritative nameservers
        l.google.com: type NS, class IN, ns d.l.google.com
            Name: l.google.com
```

```
                        Type: NS (Authoritative name server)
                        Class: IN (0x0001)
                        Time to live: 11 hours, 52 minutes, 32 seconds
                        Data length: 4
                        Name server: d.l.google.com
            l.google.com: type NS, class IN, ns e.l.google.com
                        Name: l.google.com
                        Type: NS (Authoritative name server)
                        Class: IN (0x0001)
                        Time to live: 11 hours, 52 minutes, 32 seconds
                        Data length: 4
                        Name server: e.l.google.com
            l.google.com: type NS, class IN, ns g.l.google.com
                        Name: l.google.com
                        Type: NS (Authoritative name server)
                        Class: IN (0x0001)
                        Time to live: 11 hours, 52 minutes, 32 seconds
                        Data length: 4
                        Name server: g.l.google.com
            l.google.com: type NS, class IN, ns a.l.google.com
                        Name: l.google.com
                        Type: NS (Authoritative name server)
                        Class: IN (0x0001)
                        Time to live: 11 hours, 52 minutes, 32 seconds
                        Data length: 4
                        Name server: a.l.google.com
            l.google.com: type NS, class IN, ns b.l.google.com
                        Name: l.google.com
                        Type: NS (Authoritative name server)
                        Class: IN (0x0001)
                        Time to live: 11 hours, 52 minutes, 32 seconds
                        Data length: 4
                        Name server: b.l.google.com
            l.google.com: type NS, class IN, ns c.l.google.com
                        Name: l.google.com
                        Type: NS (Authoritative name server)
                        Class: IN (0x0001)
                        Time to live: 11 hours, 52 minutes, 32 seconds
                        Data length: 4
                        Name server: c.l.google.com
    Additional records
            a.l.google.com: type A, class IN, addr 216.239.53.9
                        Name: a.l.google.com
                        Type: A (Host address)
                        Class: IN (0x0001)
                        Time to live: 13 hours, 30 minutes
                        Data length: 4
                        Addr: 216.239.53.9
            b.l.google.com: type A, class IN, addr 64.233.179.9
                        Name: b.l.google.com
                        Type: A (Host address)
                        Class: IN (0x0001)
                        Time to live: 13 hours, 30 minutes
                        Data length: 4
                        Addr: 64.233.179.9
            c.l.google.com: type A, class IN, addr 64.233.161.9
                        Name: c.l.google.com
                        Type: A (Host address)
                        Class: IN (0x0001)
                        Time to live: 13 hours, 30 minutes
                        Data length: 4
                        Addr: 64.233.161.9
            d.l.google.com: type A, class IN, addr 64.233.183.9
                        Name: d.l.google.com
                        Type: A (Host address)
                        Class: IN (0x0001)
```

```
                    Time to live: 13 hours, 30 minutes
                    Data length: 4
                    Addr: 64.233.183.9
                e.l.google.com: type A, class IN, addr 66.102.11.9
                    Name: e.l.google.com
                    Type: A (Host address)
                    Class: IN (0x0001)
                    Time to live: 13 hours, 30 minutes
                    Data length: 4
                    Addr: 66.102.11.9
                g.l.google.com: type A, class IN, addr 64.233.167.9
                    Name: g.l.google.com
                    Type: A (Host address)
                    Class: IN (0x0001)
                    Time to live: 13 hours, 30 minutes
                    Data length: 4
                    Addr: 64.233.167.9
```

The answer section and the additional information section in the previous example are in bold.

2.3.5 Compression

Compression is used to help in reducing the size of DNS packets. Domain names or their parts reoccur in DNS packets. The process is based on stating the name only once and substituting each occurrence of the name with a flag indicating the first occurrence of the name.

As has been said earlier, domain names are not in dot notation in DNS packets, but numbers defining the length of the next part are used to separate individual parts of domain names. The separator number is contained in one byte. Each part of a domain name can have up to 63 characters, which means that the maximum value of the length of the separating byte will be 63 in decimal notation or 00111111 in binary notation.

If the value of this byte is 192 or more, only a flag indicating the previous occurrence will be stated instead of the whole domain name. The flag is 16 bits long. The first two bits of the flag contain 1s, which distinguishes it from a separator. The remaining bits contain the position number of the byte (counted from the beginning of the DNS packet) where the domain name flag indicates the previous occurrence of the domain name starts.

0 would indicate the first byte, i.e., the ID field in the header section.

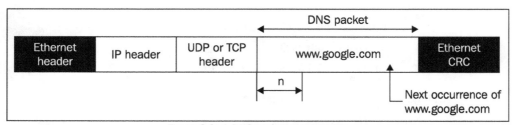

Figure 2.3: A DNS packet compression

The following code shows an example of a DNS packet with a compressed header. The DNS packet is shown in bold. The domain name www.google.com is repeated in the packet. Its first occurrence in the question section is underlined. The reference to this occurrence in other sections are underlined too.

```
Frame 2 (318 bytes on wire, 318 bytes captured)
Ethernet II, Src: Cisco_8e:1f:80 (00:15:63:8e:1f:80), Dst: Fujitsu_79:5d:0e
Internet Protocol, Src: 160.217.1.10 (160.217.1.10), Dst: 160.217.208.142
User Datagram Protocol, Src Port: domain (53), Dst Port: 1337 (1337)
Domain Name System (response)
    Transaction ID: 0x000c
    Flags: 0x8180 (Standard query response, No error)
    Questions: 1
    Answer RRs: 3
    Authority RRs: 6
    Additional RRs: 6
    Queries
        www.google.com: type A, class IN
            Name: www.google.com
            Type: A (Host address)
            Class: IN (0x0001)
    Answers
        www.google.com: type CNAME, class IN, cname www.l.google.com
        www.l.google.com: type A, class IN, addr 72.14.207.99
        www.l.google.com: type A, class IN, addr 72.14.207.104
    Authoritative nameservers
        l.google.com: type NS, class IN, ns d.l.google.com
        l.google.com: type NS, class IN, ns e.l.google.com
        l.google.com: type NS, class IN, ns g.l.google.com
        l.google.com: type NS, class IN, ns a.l.google.com
        l.google.com: type NS, class IN, ns b.l.google.com
        l.google.com: type NS, class IN, ns c.l.google.com
    Additional records
        a.l.google.com: type A, class IN, addr 216.239.53.9
        b.l.google.com: type A, class IN, addr 64.233.179.9
        c.l.google.com: type A, class IN, addr 64.233.161.9
        d.l.google.com: type A, class IN, addr 64.233.183.9
        e.l.google.com: type A, class IN, addr 66.102.11.9
        g.l.google.com: type A, class IN, addr 64.233.167.9
0000  00 0b 5d 79 5d 0e 00 15 63 8e 1f 80 08 00 45 00   ..]y]...c.....E.
0010  01 30 00 00 40 00 3f 11 27 72 a0 d9 01 0a a0 d9   .0..@.?.'r......
0020  d0 8e 00 35 05 39 01 1c 28 c5 00 0c 81 80 00 01   ...5.9..(.......
0030  00 03 00 06 00 06 03 77 77 77 06 67 6f 6f 67 6c   .......www.googl
0040  65 03 63 6f 6d 00 00 01 00 01 c0 0c 00 05 00 01   e.com...........
0050  00 00 02 b4 00 08 03 77 77 77 01 6c c0 10 c0 2c   .......www.l...,
0060  00 01 00 01 00 00 00 ff 00 04 48 0e cf 63 c0 2c   ..........H..c.,
0070  00 01 00 01 00 00 00 ff 00 04 48 0e cf 68 c0 30   ..........H..h.0
0080  00 02 00 01 00 00 a7 00 00 04 01 64 c0 30 c0 30   ...........d.0.0
0090  00 02 00 01 00 00 a7 00 00 04 01 65 c0 30 c0 30   ...........e.0.0
00a0  00 02 00 01 00 00 a7 00 00 04 01 67 c0 30 c0 30   ...........g.0.0
00b0  00 02 00 01 00 00 a7 00 00 04 01 61 c0 30 c0 30   ...........a.0.0
00c0  00 02 00 01 00 00 a7 00 00 04 01 62 c0 30 c0 30   ...........b.0.0
00d0  00 02 00 01 00 00 a7 00 00 04 01 63 c0 30 c0 90   ...........c.0..
00e0  00 01 00 01 00 00 bd d8 00 04 d8 ef 35 09 c0 a0   ............5...
00f0  00 01 00 01 00 00 bd d8 00 04 40 e9 b3 09 c0 b0   ..........@.....
0100  00 01 00 01 00 00 bd d8 00 04 40 e9 a1 09 c0 60   ..........@....`
0110  00 01 00 01 00 00 bd d8 00 04 40 e9 b7 09 c0 70   ..........@....p
0120  00 01 00 01 00 00 bd d8 00 04 42 66 0b 09 c0 80   ..........Bf....
0130  00 01 00 01 00 00 bd d8 00 04 40 e9 a7 09         ..........@...
```

The contents of the flag indicating the domain name in hexadecimal notation is $C00C_{16}=$ 1100000000001100_2 in binary notation. The position number of the byte in the packet where the domain name occurs for the first time is $12_{10}=00000000001100_2$. The position number of the first byte is 0, the domain name can thus be found in the 13th byte of the DNS packet. It is, however, necessary to bear in mind that the example refers not to a DNS packet only, but a whole frame that has been sent by the network. The DNS packet starts with the 11th byte on the 3rd line (00 0C 81 80 ...). You can try to find another example of compression in the packet for yourself. The clue is that it is a reference to the string www.l.google.com.

2.3.6 Inverse Query

Inverse queries must not be mistaken for reverse queries. With inverse queries, for example, the IP address is translated back to the name, but the search is based on an A type RR. Reverse translation is based on a PTR type RR. Not all name servers support inverse queries. They are specified in RFC 1035. Inverse query is an obsolete query.

2.3.7 Methods of RR Transfer via a DNS Packet

A single DNS packet may contain one or several RRs. If a DNS packet holds one RR, the format is a 'one-answer' format. The term 'many-answer' refers to the format in which one packet contains several RRs. Which format will be used by the server for communication is a matter of the name server implementation. While the many-answer format is obviously more efficient, it is only supported by the BIND version 8 implementation or higher and version 4.9.5 with patches implemented.

2.3.8 Communication Examples

We will illustrate this by several examples of DNS client-DNS server communication. The hexadecimal notation will be left out to make the examples more transparent. Note especially the headers of the individual packets.

Example of a Nonexistent RR Query and the Answer

The query for translation of the name aaa.abc.cz was raised using the nslookup program, and an ultimate (recursive) answer was required. The use of nslookup resulted in sending two packets, a query and an answer.

```
# nslookup
Default Server:  localhost
Address:  127.0.0.1

> aaa.abc.cz
Server:  localhost
Address:  127.0.0.1
*** localhost can't find aaa.abc.cz: Non-existent host/domain
>
```

DNS Query

```
+ FRAME: Base frame properties
 + ETHERNET: ETYPE = 0x0800 : Protocol = IP:  DOD Internet Protocol
 + IP: ID = 0x3186; Proto = UDP; Len: 56
 + UDP: Src Port: Unknown, (1258); Dst Port: DNS (53); Length = 36 (0x24)
   DNS: 0x14:Std Qry for aaa.abc.cz. of type Host Addr on class INET addr.
      DNS: Query Identifier = 20 (0x14)
      DNS: DNS Flags = Query, OpCode - Std Qry, RD Bits Set, RCode - No error
         DNS: 0............... = Query
         DNS: .0000.......... = Standard Query
         DNS: .....0......... = Server not authority for domain
         DNS: ......0........ = Message complete
         DNS: .......1....... = Recursive query desired
         DNS: ........0...... = No recursive queries
         DNS: .........000.... = Reserved
         DNS: ............0000 = No error
      DNS: Question Entry Count = 1 (0x1)
      DNS: Answer Entry Count = 0 (0x0)
      DNS: Name Server Count = 0 (0x0)
      DNS: Additional Records Count = 0 (0x0)
```

```
         DNS: Question Section: aaa.abc.cz. of type Host Addr on class INET addr.
            DNS: Question Name: aaa.abc.cz.
            DNS: Question Type = Host Address
                DNS: Question Class = Internet address class
```

DNS Answer

```
+ FRAME: Base frame properties
+ ETHERNET: ETYPE = 0x0800 : Protocol = IP:  DOD Internet Protocol
+ IP: ID = 0x9D43; Proto = UDP; Len: 56
+ UDP: Src Port: DNS, (53); Dst Port: Unknown (1258); Length = 36 (0x24)
   DNS: 0x14:Std Qry Resp. : Name does not exist
       DNS: Query Identifier = 20 (0x14)
       DNS: DNS Flags = Response, OpCode - Std Qry, AA RD RA Bits Set, RCode -
   Name does not exist
           DNS: 1............... = Response
           DNS: .0000.......... = Standard Query
           DNS: .....1......... = Server authority for domain
           DNS: ......0......... = Message complete
           DNS: .......1........ = Recursive query desired
           DNS: ........1....... = Recursive queries supported by server
           DNS: .........000.... = Reserved
           DNS: ............0011 = Name does not exist
       DNS: Question Entry Count = 1 (0x1)
       DNS: Answer Entry Count = 0 (0x0)
       DNS: Name Server Count = 0 (0x0)
       DNS: Additional Records Count = 0 (0x0)
       DNS: Question Section: aaa.abc.cz. of type Host Addr on class INET addr.
           DNS: Question Name: aaa.abc.cz.
           DNS: Question Type = Host Address
           DNS: Question Class = Internet address class
```

Example of Communication with a Root Server

You can use the nslookup program to request a recursive translation of the www.packtpub.com name from a root server. Root servers are configured not to carry out recursive translations. As a result, you will obtain names and IP addresses of the TLD.NET authoritative servers only.

```
# nslookup
Default Server:  localhost
Address:  127.0.0.1

> server a.root-servers.net
Default Name Server:  a.root-servers.net
Address:  198.41.0.4

> set recurse
> www.packpub.com.
Name Server:  a.root-servers.net
Address:  198.41.0.4
Name:    www.packpub.com
Served by:
- A.GTLD-SERVERS.NET
      192.5.6.30
      com
- G.GTLD-SERVERS.NET
      192.42.93.30
      com
- H.GTLD-SERVERS.NET
      192.54.112.30
      com
- C.GTLD-SERVERS.NET
      192.26.92.30
      com
```

```
 - I.GTLD-SERVERS.NET
       192.43.172.30
       com
 - B.GTLD-SERVERS.NET
       192.33.14.30

       com
 - D.GTLD-SERVERS.NET
       192.31.80.30
       com
 - L.GTLD-SERVERS.NET
       192.41.162.30
 >
```

Example of Communication with the ns1.volny.cz DNS Server

To give an example contrasting with the preceding one, the same query will be sent to a common name server (as opposed to a root server). The request sent to ns1.volny.cz is the reverse translation of www.packtpub.com. The query has been set in the nslookup program. To make the example interesting, the debug level is set. Look for the differences between the nslookup transcript with the DNS packet content.

```
>server ns1.volny.cz.
Default Name Server:  ns1.volny.cz
Address:  212.20.96.34

>set debug
> www.packpub.com.
Name Server:  ns1.volny.cz
Address:  212.20.96.34

------------
Got answer:
    HEADER:
        opcode = QUERY, id = 5185, rcode = NXDOMAIN
        header flags:  response, want recursion, recursion avail.
        questions = 1,  answers = 0,  authority records = 1,  additional = 0

    QUESTIONS:
        www.packpub.com.siemens.net, type = A, class = IN
    AUTHORITY RECORDS:
    ->  siemens.net
        ttl = 10800 (3 hours)
        origin = david.siemens.de
        mail addr = hostmaster.siemens.de
        serial = 2005102717
        refresh = 10800 (3 hours)
        retry   = 3600 (1 hour)
        expire  = 1209600 (14 days)
        minimum ttl = 43200 (12 hours)


------------
------------
Got answer:
    HEADER:
        opcode = QUERY, id = 5184, rcode = NOERROR
        header flags:  response, want recursion, recursion avail.
        questions = 1,  answers = 1,  authority records = 3,  additional = 3

    QUESTIONS:
        www.packpub.com, type = A, class = IN
    ANSWERS:
    ->  www.packpub.com
        internet address = 64.20.43.107
        ttl = 300 (5 mins)
```

```
            AUTHORITY RECORDS:
            ->   packpub.com
                 nameserver = ns1.my-name-server.com
                 ttl = 172800 (2 days)
            ->   packpub.com
                 nameserver = ns2.my-name-server.com
                 ttl = 172800 (2 days)
            ->   packpub.com
                 nameserver = ns3.my-name-server.com
                 ttl = 172800 (2 days)
            ADDITIONAL RECORDS:
            ->   ns1.my-name-server.com
                 internet address = 66.45.225.10
                 ttl = 110531 (1 day 6 hours 42 mins 11 secs)
            ->   ns2.my-name-server.com
                 internet address = 64.20.43.106
                 ttl = 110531 (1 day 6 hours 42 mins 11 secs)
            ->   ns3.my-name-server.com
                 internet address = 64.20.43.106
                 ttl = 110531 (1 day 6 hours 42 mins 11 secs)

        ------------
        Non-authoritative answer:
        Name:    www.packpub.com
        Address:  64.20.43.107

        >
```

Note that the client received two answers. The first one is a denial (rcode=NXDOMAIN). For justification see the QUESTIONS section. The first query is not concerned with www.packtpub.com, but with www.packpub.com.siemens.net. The reason is that from the www.packpub.com DNS name in the nslookup, the final dot was missing, and thus the local resolver added the domain set in the configuration of the local resolver, i.e., siemens.net.

The DNS Query

```
        Frame 64 (87 bytes on wire, 87 bytes captured)
        Ethernet II, Src: 160.217.208.142 (00:0b:5d:79:5d:0e), Dst: 160.218.208.254
        (00:15:63:8e:1f:80)
        Internet Protocol, Src: 160.217.208.142 (160.217.208.142), Dst: 212.80.74.20
        (212.80.74.20)
        User Datagram Protocol, Src Port: 1458 (1458), Dst Port: domain (53)
        Domain Name System (query)
            Transaction ID: 0x0013
            Flags: 0x0100 (Standard query)
            Questions: 1
            Answer RRs: 0
            Authority RRs: 0
            Additional RRs: 0
            Queries
                www.packpub.com.siemens.net: type A, class IN
                    Name: www.packpub.com.siemens.net
                    Type: A (Host address)
                    Class: IN (0x0001)
```

The DNS Answer (second answer only)

```
        Frame 69 (91 bytes on wire, 91 bytes captured)
        Ethernet II, Src: 160.218.208.254 (00:15:63:8e:1f:80), Dst: 160.217.208.142
        (00:0b:5d:79:5d:0e)
        Internet Protocol, Src: 212.80.74.20 (212.80.74.20), Dst: 160.217.208.142
        (160.217.208.142)
        User Datagram Protocol, Src Port: domain (53), Dst Port: 1459 (1459)
```

```
Domain Name System (response)
    Transaction ID: 0x0014
    Flags: 0x8180 (Standard query response, No error)
    Questions: 1
    Answer RRs: 1
    Authority RRs: 0
    Additional RRs: 0
    Queries
        www.packpub.com: type A, class IN
            Name: www.packpub.com
            Type: A (Host address)
            Class: IN (0x0001)
    Answers
        www.packpub.com: type A, class IN, addr 66.45.225.11
            Name: www.packpub.com
            Type: A (Host address)
            Class: IN (0x0001)
            Time to live: 5 minutes
            Data length: 4
            Addr: 66.45.225.11
```

An Example of TCP usage

You can use the nslookup program to obtain all the RRs that are associated with the name
aaa.pvtnet.cz. In this example, the name aaa.pvtnet.cz is used. The name is prepared only for
this example to demonstrate all of RRs.

```
# nslookup
Default Server:  localhost
Address:  127.0.0.1

> set q=any
> aaa.pvtnet.cz
Server:  localhost
Address:  127.0.0.1

aaa.pvtnet.cz    text = "Budejovice locality"
aaa.pvtnet.cz    text = "mail server"
aaa.pvtnet.cz    text = "32 MB operating memory"
aaa.pvtnet.cz    text = "an upgrade to 64 MB soon"
aaa.pvtnet.cz    CPU = PC         OS = Linux 1.3.20
aaa.pvtnet.cz    text = "e-mail: alena@pvt.net"
aaa.pvtnet.cz    text = "test node"
aaa.pvtnet.cz    text = "mail for aaa.pvtnet.cz"
aaa.pvtnet.cz    text = "not working yet"
aaa.pvtnet.cz    preference = 10, mail exchanger = info.pvt.net
aaa.pvtnet.cz    preference = 20, mail exchanger = cbu.pvtnet.cz
aaa.pvtnet.cz    preference = 100, mail exchanger = mail.pvtnet.cz
aaa.pvtnet.cz    preference = 200, mail exchanger = mail2.pvtnet.cz
aaa.pvtnet.cz    internet address = 195.47.55.55
pvtnet.cz        nameserver = ns.pvt.net
pvtnet.cz        nameserver = ns1.pvt.net
pvtnet.cz        nameserver = snmp0.pvt.net
pvtnet.cz        nameserver = ns0.pipex.net
pvtnet.cz        nameserver = ns1.pipex.net
info.pvt.net     internet address = 194.149.104.203
cbu.pvtnet.cz    internet address = 194.149.105.18
ns.pvt.net       internet address = 194.149.105.18
ns1.pvt.net      internet address = 194.149.103.201
snmp0.pvt.net    internet address = 194.149.103.34
ns0.pipex.net    internet address = 158.43.128.8
ns1.pipex.net    internet address = 158.43.192.7
>
```

The DNS Query sent by UDP

```
+ FRAME: Base frame properties
+ ETHERNET: ETYPE = 0x0800 : Protocol = IP:  DOD Internet Protocol
+ IP: ID = 0x5BA9; Proto = UDP; Len: 59
+ UDP: Src Port: Unknown, (1284); Dst Port: DNS (53); Length = 39 (0x27)
   DNS: 0xC:Std Qry for aaa.pvtnet.cz. of type Req. for all on class INET addr.
      DNS: Query Identifier = 12 (0xC)
      DNS: DNS Flags = Query, OpCode - Std Qry, RD Bits Set, RCode - No error
         DNS: 0............... = Query
         DNS: .0000.......... = Standard Query
         DNS: .....0......... = Server not authority for domain
         DNS: ......0........ = Message complete
         DNS: .......1....... = Recursive query desired
         DNS: ........0...... = No recursive queries
         DNS: .........000.... = Reserved
         DNS: ...........0000 = No error
      DNS: Question Entry Count = 1 (0x1)
      DNS: Answer Entry Count = 0 (0x0)
      DNS: Name Server Count = 0 (0x0)
      DNS: Additional Records Count = 0 (0x0)
    + DNS: Question Section: aaa.pvtnet.cz. of type Req. for all on class INET
    addr.
```

The DNS Answer

The complete answer exceeds 512 B. For this reason the resolver got an answer shortened by the UDP in which the truncation has been indicated by the TC (truncated) bit.

```
+ FRAME: Base frame properties
+ ETHERNET: ETYPE = 0x0800 : Protocol = IP:  DOD Internet Protocol
+ IP: ID = 0x6970; Proto = UDP; Len: 524
+ UDP: Src Port: DNS, (53); Dst Port: Unknown (1284); Length = 504 (0x1F8)
   DNS: 0xC:Std Qry Resp. for aaa.pvtnet.cz. of type Host Addr on class INET addr.
      DNS: Query Identifier = 12 (0xC)
      DNS: DNS Flags = Response, OpCode - Std Qry, AA TC RD RA Bits Set, RCode -
   No error
         DNS: 1............... = Response
         DNS: .0000.......... = Standard Query
         DNS: .....1......... = Server authority for domain
         DNS: ......1........ = Message truncated
         DNS: .......1....... = Recursive query desired
         DNS: ........1...... = Recursive queries supported by server
         DNS: .........000.... = Reserved
         DNS: ...........0000 = No error
      DNS: Question Entry Count = 1 (0x1)
      DNS: Answer Entry Count = 14 (0xE)
      DNS: Name Server Count = 5 (0x5)
      DNS: Additional Records Count = 0 (0x0)
    + DNS: Question Section: aaa.pvtnet.cz. of type Req. for all on class INET
    addr.
    + DNS: Answer section: aaa.pvtnet.cz. of type Host Addr on class INET addr.(14
    records present)
    + DNS: Authority Section = N/A
```

A DNS Query in TCP

```
+ FRAME: Base frame properties
+ ETHERNET: ETYPE = 0x0800 : Protocol = IP:  DOD Internet Protocol
+ IP: ID = 0x5FA9; Proto = TCP; Len: 71
+ TCP: .AP..., len:   31, seq:  31853005-31853035, ack: 320256001, win: 8760, src:
   1285  dst:   53
   DNS: 0x100:Std Qry for ¤ö_ of type Unknown Type on class Unknown Class
      DNS: TCP Length = 12 (0xC)
      DNS: Query Identifier = 256 (0x100)
```

```
DNS: DNS Flags = Query, OpCode - Std Qry, RCode - Server unable to interpret
query
        DNS: 0............... = Query
        DNS: .0000.......... = Standard Query
        DNS: .....0......... = Server not authority for domain
        DNS: ......0........ = Message complete
        DNS: .......0....... = Iterative query desired
        DNS: ........0...... = No recursive queries
        DNS: .........000.... = Reserved
        DNS: ............0001 = Server unable to interpret query
    DNS: Question Entry Count = 0 (0x0)
    DNS: Answer Entry Count = 0 (0x0)
    DNS: Name Server Count = 0 (0x0)
    DNS: Additional Records Count = 865 (0x361)
  + DNS: Additional Records Section:  of type Unknown Type on class Unknown
Class(865 records present)
```

The DNS Full Length Answer of 650 bytes retrieved by TCP

```
+ FRAME: Base frame properties
+ ETHERNET: ETYPE = 0x0800 : Protocol = IP:  DOD Internet Protocol
+ IP: ID = 0x697C; Proto = TCP; Len: 692
+ TCP: .AP..., len:  652, seq: 320256001-320256652, ack:  31853036, win:33580,
    src:   53  dst: 1285
  DNS: 0xC:Std Qry Resp. for aaa.pvtnet.cz. of type Host Addr on class INET addr.
        DNS: TCP Length = 650 (0x28A)
        DNS: Query Identifier = 12 (0xC)
        DNS: DNS Flags = Response, OpCode - Std Qry, AA RD RA Bits Set, RCode - No
    error
        DNS: 1............... = Response
        DNS: .0000.......... = Standard Query
        DNS: .....1......... = Server authority for domain
        DNS: ......0........ = Message complete
        DNS: .......1....... = Recursive query desired
        DNS: ........1...... = Recursive queries supported by server
        DNS: .........000.... = Reserved
        DNS: ............0000 = No error
    DNS: Question Entry Count = 1 (0x1)
    DNS: Answer Entry Count = 14 (0xE)
    DNS: Name Server Count = 5 (0x5)
    DNS: Additional Records Count = 7 (0x7)
  + DNS: Question Section: aaa.pvtnet.cz. of type Req. for all on class INET
addr.
  + DNS: Answer section: ._aaa_pv. of type Unknown Type on class Unknown
Class(14 records present)
  + DNS: Authority Section = N/A
  + DNS: Additional Records Section = N/A
```

An Example Illustrating the use of the nslookup Program to Find Out Communication Content

To monitor the communication between a client and a server, DNS server administrators usually do not use Microsoft Network Monitor, but use the nslookup program. The debug and d2 debug levels list the DNS packet content in a transparent form.

Compare the listing obtained by nslookup after the debug and d2 debug levels had been set. Both queries are concerned with the same RR (for more about the nslookup program, see Section 5.1.4).

The nslookup program is set to the debug debugging level.

```
>set debug
> www.packtpub.com.
Name Server:  ns1.volny.cz
Address:  212.20.96.34
```

```
Trying DNS
;; res_mkquery(0, www.packtpub.com, 1, 1)
------------
Got answer:
    HEADER:
    opcode = QUERY, id = 12203, rcode = NOERROR
    header flags:  response, want recursion, recursion avail.
    questions = 1,  answers = 2,  authority records = 4,  additional = 4

    QUESTIONS:
    www.packtpub.com, type = A, class = IN
    ANSWERS:
    ->  www.packtpub.com
    canonical name = packtpub.com
    ttl = 8190 (2 hours 16 mins 30 secs)
    ->  packtpub.com
    internet address = 217.207.125.58
    ttl = 8190 (2 hours 16 mins 30 secs)
    AUTHORITY RECORDS:
    ->  packtpub.com
    nameserver = remote1.easydns.com
    ttl = 8190 (2 hours 16 mins 30 secs)
    ->  packtpub.com
    nameserver = remote2.easydns.com
    ttl = 8190 (2 hours 16 mins 30 secs)
    ->  packtpub.com
    nameserver = ns1.easydns.com
    ttl = 8190 (2 hours 16 mins 30 secs)
    ->  packtpub.com
    nameserver = ns2.easydns.com
    ttl = 8190 (2 hours 16 mins 30 secs)
    ADDITIONAL RECORDS:
    ->  remote1.easydns.com
    internet address = 209.200.131.4
    ttl = 167351 (1 day 22 hours 29 mins 11 secs)
    ->  remote2.easydns.com
    internet address = 205.210.42.20
    ttl = 22123 (6 hours 8 mins 43 secs)
    ->  ns1.easydns.com
    internet address = 216.220.40.243
    ttl = 2966 (49 mins 26 secs)
    ->  ns2.easydns.com
    internet address = 209.200.151.4
    ttl = 453 (7 mins 33 secs)

------------
Non-authoritative answer:
Name:    packtpub.com
Address: 217.207.125.58
Aliases: www.packtpub.com
```

The nslookup **program is set to the** d2 **debugging level.**

```
#nslookup
> set d2
> www.packtpub.com.
Name Server:  ns1.volny.cz
Address:  212.20.96.34

Trying DNS
;; res_mkquery(0, www.packtpub.com, 1, 1)
------------
SendRequest(), len 34
    HEADER:
    opcode = QUERY, id = 12204, rcode = NOERROR
    header flags:  query, want recursion
```

```
        questions = 1,  answers = 0,  authority records = 0,  additional = 0

        QUESTIONS:
        www.packtpub.com, type = A, class = IN

    ------------
    ------------
Got answer (216 bytes):
        HEADER:
        opcode = QUERY, id = 12204, rcode = NOERROR
        header flags:  response, want recursion, recursion avail.
        questions = 1,  answers = 2,  authority records = 4,  additional = 4

        QUESTIONS:
        www.packtpub.com, type = A, class = IN
        ANSWERS:
        ->  www.packtpub.com
        type = CNAME, class = IN, dlen = 2
        canonical name = packtpub.com
        ttl = 8157 (2 hours 15 mins 57 secs)
        ->  packtpub.com
        type = A, class = IN, dlen = 4
        internet address = 217.207.125.58
        ttl = 8157 (2 hours 15 mins 57 secs)
        AUTHORITY RECORDS:
        ->  packtpub.com
        type = NS, class = IN, dlen = 18
        nameserver = remote1.easydns.com
        ttl = 8157 (2 hours 15 mins 57 secs)
        ->  packtpub.com
        type = NS, class = IN, dlen = 10
        nameserver = remote2.easydns.com
        ttl = 8157 (2 hours 15 mins 57 secs)
        ->  packtpub.com
        type = NS, class = IN, dlen = 6
        nameserver = ns1.easydns.com
        ttl = 8157 (2 hours 15 mins 57 secs)
        ->  packtpub.com
        type = NS, class = IN, dlen = 6
        nameserver = ns2.easydns.com
        ttl = 8157 (2 hours 15 mins 57 secs)
        ADDITIONAL RECORDS:
        ->  remote1.easydns.com
        type = A, class = IN, dlen = 4
        internet address = 209.200.131.4
        ttl = 167318 (1 day 22 hours 28 mins 38 secs)
        ->  remote2.easydns.com
        type = A, class = IN, dlen = 4
        internet address = 205.210.42.20
        ttl = 22090 (6 hours 8 mins 10 secs)
        ->  ns1.easydns.com
        type = A, class = IN, dlen = 4
        internet address = 216.220.40.243
        ttl = 2933 (48 mins 53 secs)
        ->  ns2.easydns.com
        type = A, class = IN, dlen = 4
        internet address = 209.200.151.4
        ttl = 420 (7 mins)

    ------------
Non-authoritative answer:
Name:     packtpub.com
Address:  217.207.125.58
Aliases:  www.packtpub.com
```

3

DNS Extension

Till now we have described common DNS functions that every DNS implementation should support. On the contrary, DNS extensions are other optional DNS functions. It is up to each particular application to choose which of them it will support and which not. For example, the DNS Update extension is widespread because of its successful implementation in Windows 2000 and consequently in the Windows 2003 operating system.

This book contains a lot of examples to demonstrate the functionality. All the given examples may not work by the time you read this book. Some of them would demonstrate negative output and some of them would demonstrate some specific parts of output. Sometimes you can get similar output, if you use new URLs.

3.1 DNS Update

The DNS Update mechanism is described in RFC 3007. The DNS Update operation enables dynamic correction of entries in the DNS database. Therefore, this is also referred to as **dynamic update**. DNS Update provides for adding/deleting one or more records to/from the zone file. BIND version 8 already uses DNS Update, therefore, we will take advantage of the BIND version 8 terminology, i.e., master/slave name server. DNS Update is also widely used by Windows 2000 as the fundamental features of DNS Update:

- The DNS database entries (RR) do not need to be statically corrected by the system administrator, but can be corrected dynamically by using DNS protocol.

- DNS Update does not provide support for creating new zones, it only enables the correction of already existing zones. DNS Update thus does not enable the addition of a new SOA record or its removal. The SOA record can only be modified.

- When using DNS Update, data in the zone can only be corrected in the primary master server. If the slave server receives a DNS Update request, it is forwarded to the primary master server.

DNS Update operations are also composed of requests and answers. By using one DNS Update request, we can correct one or several records in one particular zone.

Zone corrections using DNS Update can be carried out under specific conditions. The condition is the existence or nonexistence of the relevant RR records in the master zone before corrections. So, if you request to delete a record in the zone, this record has to exist in that particular zone before the correction. There can be several specified correction conditions. As for carrying out the correction, the conditions are treated as a whole, i.e., if one of the conditions is not fulfilled, then all conditions are considered unfulfilled and no requested corrections are done.

The DNS Update packet specifies separately the conditions of carrying out corrections and the RR records that are to be added or removed from the zone file.

DNS Update uses the DNS protocol specification as it is defined by RFC 1035 (see Chapter 2). The RFC 2136 standard, together with the new RFC 3007 standard, defines some extensions of this protocol, for example, new message types or new result codes. The DNS packet format for Update remains the same, consisting of five parts. Individual parts have specific contents and names. The DNS Update packet consists of sections as shown in the following figure:

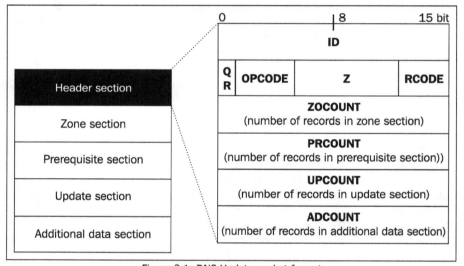

Figure 3.1: DNS Update packet format

Here is a brief description of each section of the DNS Update packet:

- **Header section:** Contains control information
- **Zone section**: Defines the zone to which corrections apply
- **Prerequisite section**: A set of RR records that must exist in the zone
- **Update section**: A set of RR records that are to be corrected or deleted
- **Additional data section**: Contains information that is not a part of the update, but is necessary for updating

3.1.1 Header Section

The header section, like DNS Query header section, contains identification in the first two bytes (ID field), followed by two bytes for control fields, and there are four two-byte fields for the length of the individual sections (each length is 2 bytes):

- **ZOCOUNT**: Number of records in the Zone section
- **PRCOUNT**: Number of records in the Prerequisite section
- **UPCOUNT**: Number of records in the Update section
- **ADCOUNT**: Number of records in the Additional data section

Field	Length (bytes)	Meaning
ID	16	Message identification is copied into the answer
QR	1	0 for DNS Update request 1 for DNS Update answer (DNS Update does not use other check bits.)
Opcode	4	Value is 5 (DNS Update); copied from the request into the answer
Z	7	Reserved for future use; should be zero (0) in all requests and responses
Rcode	4	Response code in an answer, unidentified in a request (see Table 3.2)

Table 3.1: The meaning of individual control fields

Error Code	Numeric Value	Error Description
NOERROR	0	No errors.
FORMERR	1	Message format error—the name server is unable to interpret the request.
SERVFAIL	2	An internal server error has occurred when processing the message (for example, OS error or the forwarding timeout exceeded.)
NXDOMAIN	3	The name that should exist does not exist.
NOTIMP	4	The name server does not support the specified Opcode.
REFUSED	5	The name server refuses to execute the message, for example, due to security reasons.
YXDOMAIN	6	Some name that should not exist does exist.
YXRRSET	7	Some RR records that should not exist do exist.
NXRRSET	8	Some RR records that should exist do not exist.
NOAUTH	9	The server is not an authority for that particular zone.
NOTZONE	10	A name used in the Prerequisite or Update section is not within the zone denoted by the Zone section.

Table 3.2: Answer result codes (the Rcode field)

3.1.2 Zone Section

The zone section defines the zone that will be updated. One DNS Update request can only be used for updating one zone, i.e., the zone section only authorizes one record to be used.

The section consists of three parts:

- **ZNAME**: zone name
- **ZTYPE**: must be SOA
- **ZCLASS**: zone class (IN)

3.1.3 Prerequisite Section

The Prerequisite section contains a set of RR records that must exist on the primary master server in a particular zone at the moment of delivering an Update packet. We have five choices (alternatives) in the prerequisite section:

- **There must be at least one RR record of a given NAME and TYPE** (*RR set exists, value independent*). The prerequisite section contains one record of a given NAME and TYPE that is expected in the zone. Other items are of no importance, therefore, we will use RDLENGTH=0, RDATA remains empty, CLASS=NY, TTL=0.

  For example, an A type record is requested with the domain name of aaa.company.com and with any RDATA that exists in the domain.

- **There must be a set of RR records of a given NAME and TYPE in the zone**, with the right side corresponding to the right side of the Update packet records (*RR set exists, value dependent*). The order of records is of no importance. The section contains a set of RR records of a given NAME and TYPE, and RDATA, TTL=0, CLASS is specified in the zone section.

  For example, a zone containing the following records is requested:

  ```
  mail.company.com.    A    195.47.11.11
  www.company.com.     A    195.47.11.12
  company.com.         MX   10   mail.company.com
  ```

- **The zone does not contain any RR record of a given NAME and TYPE** (*RR set does not exist*). The section contains one RR record of a given NAME and TYPE, RDLENGTH=0, RDATA is empty, CLASS=NONE, TTL=0.

  For example, the zone requested does not contain any type A record with the mail.company.com domain name.

- **The zone must contain at least one record of a given NAME and TYPE defined in the zone section** (*Name is in use*). The section contains one RR record of a given NAME, RDLENGTH=0, RDATA is empty, CLASS=ANY, TYPE=ANY, TTL=0.

  For example, the zone requested contains at least one record, the domain name of which contains the company.com field, i.e., it is not an empty zone.

- **There are no RR records of any TYPE with a given NAME** (*The name is not in use*). The section contains one RR record of a given NAME, RDLENTGHT=0, RDATA is empty, CLASS=NONE, TYPE=ANY, TTL=0.

  For example, the requested zone does not contain any record of the domain name that would contain the `company.com` string, i.e., it is an empty zone.

3.1.4 Update Section

The update section contains RR records that are to be added to or removed from the zone. Four different changes are possible:

- **Add RR records**: The update section contains several records. Records of a given NAME, TYPE, TTL, RDLENGTH, and RDATA are added to the file. CLASS is taken over from the zone section. Duplicate records in the list are ignored.

  For example, if you want to add the following records:

  ```
  company.com.      MX    20    mh.company.com.
  mh.company.com.   A     195.47.13.12
  ```

- **Remove a set of RR records of a given type**: The section contains one record with the given NAME and TYPE indicating which records should be removed. TTL=0, CLASS=ANY, RDLENGTH=0, RDATA is empty.

  For example, if you want to remove all records containing the domain name `mail.company.com`.

- **Remove all RR records of a given name**: The section contains one RR record; the given NAME indicates which records should be removed. TYPE=ANY, TTL=0, CLASS=ANY, RDLENGTH=0, RDATA is empty.

  For example, if you want to remove all MX type records containing the domain name `company.com`.

- **Remove one RR record**: The section contains a record that is to be removed (NAME, TYPE, RDLENGTH, RDATA). TTL=0, CLASS=NONE.

  For example, if you want to remove the following record:

  ```
  company.com.   IN  MX  10    mail.company.com.
  ```

3.1.5 Additional Data Section

The additional data section contains the RR records that have anything to do with the update itself or new records added by using the update. For example, it can contain a glue record for the zone if a new NS record is added to the zone.

3.1.6 Journal File

The changes carried out via the DNS Update operation do not update the zone files directly; the name server saves all the changes in the **zone journal files**. The contents of the zone journal file are then reflected in the zone files on a regular basis. The zone file updating according to the journal will be carried out at the time of stopping or restarting name servers.

Each zone uses its journal file, which is automatically created from the first operation in the DNS Update zone. This file has a name identical to the zone name and the standard extension of `.jnl`. Journal files have binary contents, which means that it is neither possible nor allowed to correct these files manually. The ban on manual correction applies also to the zone files that use the DNS Update operation. The reason for this is obvious: the zone files do not have to contain the most up-to-date information since part of the latest information on the zone can be stored in the journal file. If you need, for some reason, to manually adjust the dynamically corrected zone and you chose to break the ban, then proceed as follows:

1. Shut down the name server (using the `rndc stop` command).
2. Remove the journal file, since its content is already reflected in the zone files, and its content would be inconsistent after carrying out the changes in zones anyway.
3. Adjust the zone file.
4. Restart the name server.

3.1.7 Notes

It is recommended to use the DNS Update operations together with a security system. One of the possibilities is the Secure Dynamic Update specified by RFC 2137. If you choose not to use the Secure Dynamic Update, at least make sure that the server will accept only Update queries from a given IP address. This IP will be set up in the server configuration.

3.2 DNS Notify

The DNS Notify operation is described in RFC 1996. DNS Notify can inform the slave servers about data changes in the zone. If DNS Notify is used, a slave server can have actual zone data sooner than waiting for the expiration of the time interval in the refresh field, listed in the zone SOA record.

Communication between the master and slave servers concerning the zone is initiated, when using the DNS Notify operation, by the master server. The master server informs slave servers of any possible changes in zones; so if the zone is changed, the master tells slave servers *"Ask me for the transfer."* The slave server then requests the zone transfer immediately after receiving this notify message.

The DNS notify message will be received by all severs that are listed in the NS records for the given zone. The server indicated in the SOA record is not informed since it is presumed that it is this server that generates the messages. Some implementations enable master server administrators to add other IP addresses of other name servers to the set of the existing ones. The set of servers for which the DNS Notify is generated is called the **Notify Set**.

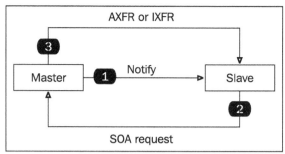

Figure 3.2: DNS Notify

3.2.1 Notify Message

The notify message uses the DNS packet format defined by RFC 1035. DNS Notify uses just one subgroup of fields in the packet; the fields not used must be filled by binary zeros. The message type (Opcode) is set to 4 (NOTIFY). The master server can send the NAME, CLASS, TYPE, and RDATA of the records changed in the zone as part of the notify message. Notify messages do not use the section of authoritative servers or the Additional data section.

An example of DNS Notify: the master zone of abcde.com has been corrected.

```
+ FRAME: Base frame properties
+ ETHERNET: ETYPE = 0x0800 : Protocol = IP:  DOD Internet Protocol
+ IP: ID = 0xD4; Proto = UDP; Len: 54
+ UDP: Src Port: Unknown, (1049); Dst Port: DNS (53); Length = 34 (0x22)
    DNS: 0x54C6:Std Qry for abcde.com. of type SOA on class INET addr.
       DNS: Query Identifier = 21702 (0x54C6)
       DNS: DNS Flags = Query, OpCode - Rsrvd, RCode - No error
          DNS: 0............... = Query
          DNS: .0100.......... = Reserved
          DNS: .....0.......... = Server not authority for domain
          DNS: ......0......... = Message complete
          DNS: .......0........ = Iterative query desired
          DNS: ........0....... = No recursive queries
          DNS: .........000.... = Reserved
          DNS: ............0000 = No error
       DNS: Question Entry Count = 1 (0x1)
       DNS: Answer Entry Count = 0 (0x0)
       DNS: Name Server Count = 0 (0x0)
       DNS: Additional Records Count = 0 (0x0)
       DNS: Question Section: abcde.com. of type SOA on class INET addr.
          DNS: Question Name: abcde.com.
          DNS: Question Type = Start of zone of authority
          DNS: Question Class = Internet address class
```

The opcode field in the DNS packet is set to 4. The software used for catching the packet on the network—MS Network Monitor version 4—interprets this value, though, as Rsrvd (reserved), since this version of MS Network Monitor does not yet support DNS Notify messages.

An example of a DNS Notify answer:

```
+ FRAME: Base frame properties
+ ETHERNET: ETYPE = 0x0800 : Protocol = IP:  DOD Internet Protocol
+ IP: ID = 0x84C9; Proto = UDP; Len: 40
+ UDP: Src Port: DNS, (53); Dst Port: Unknown (1049); Length = 20 (0x14)
    DNS: 0x54C6:Std Qry Resp. : This query not supported by name server
```

```
        DNS: Query Identifier = 21702 (0x54C6)
        DNS: DNS Flags = Response, OpCode - Rsrvd, RA Bits Set,
          RCode - This query not supported by name server
          DNS: 1............... = Response
          DNS: .0100........... = Reserved
          DNS: .....0.......... = Server not authority for domain
          DNS: ......0......... = Message complete
          DNS: .......0........ = Iterative query desired
          DNS: ........1....... = Recursive queries supported by server
          DNS: .........000.... = Reserved
          DNS: ............0100 = This query not supported by name server
        DNS: Question Entry Count = 0 (0x0)
        DNS: Answer Entry Count = 0 (0x0)
        DNS: Name Server Count = 0 (0x0)
        DNS: Additional Records Count = 0 (0x0)
        DNS: Frame Padding
```

Either UDP or TCP transport protocols are used for transmitting the Notify packet. If TCP protocol is used, the notify message is sent just once. There is a time interval set on the master server, during which time it waits for the answer. When using TCP, neither master nor slave servers are allowed to interrupt the provision of services during the transaction.

If UDP protocol is used, then the master server sends notify messages to the slave server periodically. The master server stops sending the notify message when a reply has been received. If the master server does not receive an answer, it stops the transmission of these messages after using up the set number of message repetitions or after ICMP protocol announces that the port is not accessible. The interval between transmitting individual messages can be specified as a parameter in the master server configuration (usually 60s). Similarly, the number of permitted repetitions can be set as well (usually 5).

The only event that activates the transmission of the notify message is a change in the SOA record. After the notify message has been received, the slave server should act as if the interval indicated in the refresh field of the SOA record in the zone indicated in QNAME has expired. The slave server should therefore ask the master server for the SOA of the relevant zone and check the serial number field and if the serial number has been increased, then also initiate AXFR or IXFR.

In the zone transfer message, the zone transfer should be carried out from the master that has sent the massage to the slave server.

The master server can also include the changed RR records (the changed name, class, type, and, optionally, also RDATA) in the notify message. This information (the changed RR records in the answer section) cannot be used in any case for correcting data on the slave server or as an indication that zone transfer should be carried out or that the zone refresh time should be changed. It is just information that the slave server could use in order to find out, for example, that it already has the up-to-date data and, therefore, does not need to initiate a zone transfer.

The notify answer does not contain any relevant information. What is important, however, is the fact that the master server receives this answer. If the slave server receives the notify message containing QNAME from a node that is not the master of the given zone, it should ignore it and generate an error message in the log. The server should send, upon starting, a notify message for each authoritative zone. When restarting the server, sending a notify message is optional. Each slave server will probably receive several copies of the same notify messages. The notify protocol must therefore support such multiplicity.

The master server tries to avoid an excessive number of zone transfers executed at the same time. Thus, it can send the notify messages with a certain delay. This delay will be selected on a random basis so each slave server will start its zone transfer at a different time. This delay cannot exceed the time indicated in the refresh field. The delay can be one of the adjustable master zone parameters (30–60s). A slave server that has received a notify message must, first of all, finish the already initiated transaction, and then it can send out messages to lower-level servers (to slave servers to which it is the master).

In BIND version 8.1 and higher, the DNS Notify mechanism is implemented by default.

3.3 Incremental Zone Transfer

Incremental zone transfer is specified by RFC 1995. **Incremental zone transfer (IXFR)** enables the transfer of only the data changed from the master server to the slave server, i.e., just a part of the relevant zone, should a change in the zone data occur. On the other hand, the classic zone transfer (AXFR) transfers the whole zone, should it be altered in any way.

The database history is needed in order for the master server to be able to provide the slave server with only the zone records that have been changed. The master server is thus obliged to keep track of the differences between the newest version of the zone and several older ones. The master server sends the zones that have been corrected on the master server by using DNS Update to the slave server via IXFR. Individual file versions differ in the serial number contained in the SOA record. If the slave server finds out that it needs new data for the zone and supports IXRF, it sends a request to the master server indicating that the latest zone version it has is, for example, 98052001 (serial). The master server then sends the changed records to the slave server, i.e., the records that are to be removed as well as new records. Alternatively, the server may send the whole zone as a reply. The whole zone is also sent when the client's SOA record is so old that the server is unable to send IXFR.

Once the zone in cache has been corrected, the slave server must save the changes in the file and then it is able to reply to IXFR requests. For entering changes in the zone files carried out via IXFR, the journal files, similar to DNS Update, are used. If the server receives a request with an SOA number higher than its own, then the server returns a reply in the form of its own current SOA record only.

For IXFR requests transfer both TCP and UDP can be used. If the client sends a request using UDP, then a UDP reply should be sent back. If the reply exceeds 512 bytes, the server uses UDP just for sending the SOA record, and the client is obliged to establish a connection via TCP.

The slave server that requests the incremental zone transfer is referred to as the **IXFR client**. The master of the slave server that provides the incremental zone transfer is referred to as the **IXFR server**.

IXFR uses DNS-formatted packets as defined by RFC 1035.

3.3.1 Request Format

IXFR is entered in the request type field (Opcode), and the authoritative name servers section contains an SOA record of the zone saved on the slave server.

3.3.2 Reply Format

Again, IXFR is indicated in the Opcode field of the reply. The first and last RR in the reply section is an SOA record of the zone that is to be updated.

In IXFR, it is possible to send one or more changes (the last version(s) of the zone) as an answer within one zone. In the answer section, the list of all changes within one version is bordered on both sides with SOA records.

Adding or removing a RR is considered a change. The old SOA record precedes the deleted records, while the new SOA RR precedes the added records. A correction of the record is considered as removing the original record and adding a new one.

An IXFR reply has the following characteristics:

- Again, IXFR is indicated in the Opcode field of the reply. The first and last RR in the reply section is an SOA record of the zone that is to be updated.

- IXFR provides for sending a reply in the form of one or several changes (the last or several last versions of the zone) within one zone. The list of all the changes within one version is closed on both sides with SOA records and is located in the reply section.

- Adding or removing an RR is considered a change. The records removed follow the old SOA records and the added records follow a new SOA RR. A correction of the record is considered as removing the original record and adding a new one.

- The changes are listed in the reply section in the order oldest to newest.

- The IXFR client can exchange an old version of the file for a new one only after all of the changes received have been executed successfully.

- The incremental reply differs from a nonincremental one by starting with two SOA records.

- It is not possible to return the whole zone as a reply in IXFR. If there are too many changes in the zone and it is not worth using IXFR, then the client has to repeat the request asking for the AXFR transmission.

3.3.3 Purging

The IXFR server does not have to contain all of the preceding zone versions; the old ones can be removed any time. As for a large and often changing zone, we can encounter a large space of cache for zone changes. The information contained in the files of older versions can be thrown away if the actual IXFR transmission takes a longer time than using AXFR.

3.3.4 Examples from RFC 1995

Let us take into account three versions of zone data, with version 3 being the most up-to-date.

```
Given the following three generations of data with the current serial
  number of 3,

    JAIN.AD.JP.           IN SOA NS.JAIN.AD.JP. mohta.jain.ad.jp. (
                              1 600 600 3600000 604800)
```

```
                         IN NS   NS.JAIN.AD.JP.
     NS.JAIN.AD.JP.      IN A    133.69.136.1
     NEZU.JAIN.AD.JP.    IN A    133.69.136.5
```

NEZU.JAIN.AD.JP. is removed and JAIN-BB.JAIN.AD.JP. is added.

```
     jain.ad.jp.         IN SOA ns.jain.ad.jp. mohta.jain.ad.jp. (
                                 2 600 600 3600000 604800)
                         IN NS   NS.JAIN.AD.JP.
     NS.JAIN.AD.JP.      IN A    133.69.136.1
     JAIN-BB.JAIN.AD.JP. IN A    133.69.136.4
                         IN A    192.41.197.2
```

One of the IP addresses of JAIN-BB.JAIN.AD.JP. is changed.

```
     JAIN.AD.JP.         IN SOA ns.jain.ad.jp. mohta.jain.ad.jp. (
                                 3 600 600 3600000 604800)
                         IN NS   NS.JAIN.AD.JP.
     NS.JAIN.AD.JP.      IN A    133.69.136.1
     JAIN-BB.JAIN.AD.JP. IN A    133.69.136.3
                         IN A    192.41.197.2
```

The following IXFR query

```
            +---------------------------------------------------+
Header      | OPCODE=SQUERY                                      |
            +---------------------------------------------------+
Question    | QNAME=JAIN.AD.JP., QCLASS=IN, QTYPE=IXFR          |
            +---------------------------------------------------+
Answer      | <empty>                                            |
            +---------------------------------------------------+
Authority   | JAIN.AD.JP.          IN SOA serial=1              |
            +---------------------------------------------------+
Additional  | <empty>                                            |
            +---------------------------------------------------+
```

could be replied to with the following full zone transfer message:

```
            +---------------------------------------------------+
Header      | OPCODE=SQUERY, RESPONSE                            |
            +---------------------------------------------------+
Question    | QNAME=JAIN.AD.JP., QCLASS=IN, QTYPE=IXFR          |
            +---------------------------------------------------+
Answer      | JAIN.AD.JP.          IN SOA serial=3              |
            | JAIN.AD.JP.          IN NS  NS.JAIN.AD.JP.        |
            | NS.JAIN.AD.JP.       IN A   133.69.136.1          |
            | JAIN-BB.JAIN.AD.JP. IN A   133.69.136.3           |
            | JAIN-BB.JAIN.AD.JP. IN A   192.41.197.2           |
            | JAIN.AD.JP.          IN SOA serial=3              |
            +---------------------------------------------------+
Authority   | <empty>                                            |
            +---------------------------------------------------+
Additional  | <empty>                                            |
            +---------------------------------------------------+
```

or with the following incremental message:

```
            +---------------------------------------------------+
Header      | OPCODE=SQUERY, RESPONSE                            |
            +---------------------------------------------------+
Question    | QNAME=JAIN.AD.JP., QCLASS=IN, QTYPE=IXFR          |
            +---------------------------------------------------+
Answer      | JAIN.AD.JP.          IN SOA serial=3              |
            | JAIN.AD.JP.          IN SOA serial=1              |
            | NEZU.JAIN.AD.JP.     IN A   133.69.136.5          |
            | JAIN.AD.JP.          IN SOA serial=2              |
```

```
                      | JAIN-BB.JAIN.AD.JP. IN A    133.69.136.4    |
                      | JAIN-BB.JAIN.AD.JP. IN A    192.41.197.2    |
                      | JAIN.AD.JP.          IN SOA serial=2        |
                      | JAIN-BB.JAIN.AD.JP. IN A    133.69.136.4    |
                      | JAIN.AD.JP.          IN SOA serial=3        |
                      | JAIN-BB.JAIN.AD.JP. IN A    133.69.136.3    |
                      | JAIN.AD.JP.          IN SOA serial=3        |
                      +------------------------------------------------+
       Authority      | <empty>                                        |
                      +------------------------------------------------+
       Additional     | <empty>                                        |
                      +------------------------------------------------+
```

or with the following condensed incremental message:

```
                      +------------------------------------------------+
       Header         | OPCODE=SQUERY, RESPONSE                        |
                      +------------------------------------------------+
       Question       | QNAME=JAIN.AD.JP., QCLASS=IN, QTYPE=IXFR       |
                      +------------------------------------------------+
       Answer         | JAIN.AD.JP.          IN SOA serial=3           |
                      | JAIN.AD.JP.          IN SOA serial=1           |
                      | NEZU.JAIN.AD.JP.     IN A   133.69.136.5       |
                      | JAIN.AD.JP.          IN SOA serial=3           |
                      | JAIN-BB.JAIN.AD.JP.  IN A   133.69.136.3       |
                      | JAIN-BB.JAIN.AD.JP.  IN A   192.41.197.2       |
                      | JAIN.AD.JP.          IN SOA serial=3           |
                      +------------------------------------------------+
       Authority      | <empty>                                        |
                      +------------------------------------------------+
       Additional     | <empty>                                        |
                      +------------------------------------------------+
```

or, if UDP packet overflow occurs, with the following message:

```
                      +------------------------------------------------+
       Header         | OPCODE=SQUERY, RESPONSE                        |
                      +------------------------------------------------+
       Question       | QNAME=JAIN.AD.JP., QCLASS=IN, QTYPE=IXFR       |
                      +------------------------------------------------+
       Answer         | JAIN.AD.JP.          IN SOA serial=3           |
                      +------------------------------------------------+
       Authority      | <empty>                                        |
                      +------------------------------------------------+
       Additional     | <empty>                                        |
                      +------------------------------------------------+
```

It can be expected that IXFR will be used in large domains in the future (for example, .com, .org, and so on).

3.4 Negative Caching (DNS NCACHE)

Keeping negative replies to DNS requests is defined by RFC 1034 and RFC 2308.

Negative caching means that into the name server cache is entered information that authoritative name server bear out that the requested RR record not existing in DNS.

Resolvers used in the past did not generate the same negative answers to the same request. In order for us to use negative replies correctly, we need to exactly define the content of a negative reply and the time for which it should be kept in cache.

RFC 1034 defines negative caching as optional. Some BIND implementations like BIND version 4.9.2 support negative caching. RFC 2308 defines negative caching as an obligatory feature of the resolver and defines the content of a negative reply.

Windows 2000 uses negative caching. The time is kept implicitly at 5 minutes. If we want to change this time period, we have to adjust the NegativeCacheTime key (of the REG_DWORD type) in the HKEY_LOCAL_MACHINE\SYSTEM\CurrentControlSet\Services\Tcpip\Parameters. This key indicates the time in seconds.

Which of the negative replies are to be kept in cache? RFC 2308 defines saving negative replies with RCODE set to NXDOMAIN and NOERROR_NODATA as obligatory.

Error	Error Description
Name error (NXDOMAIN)	The domain name entered in QNAME in the request does not exist. RCODE is set to NXDOMAIN. The authoritative section can contain SOA and NS records.
NOERROR_NODATA	RCODE set to NOERROR, but the reply section contains no RR record. The authoritative section may contain an SOA record and NS records.

Table 3.3: Compulsorily saved negative replies

Other negative replies are optional. These can comprise negative answers caused by a name server error (see Table 3.4).

Error	Error Description
Server failure	The server does not provide the zone data due to a zone configuration error. The server does not provide any zone data due to the master server being inaccessible for the zone.
Dead / Unreachable server	The server does not exist, is out of order, or is unavailable.

Table 3.4: Optionally saved negative replies

If the server supports saving replies other than NXDOMAIN and NOERROR_NODATA, these cannot be kept in cache for more than 5 minutes. The server IP address of the reply must also be saved as part of the stored information.

3.4.1 How Long are Negative Answers Stored in Memory?

All RR records saved in cache are considered valid if their TTL is greater than 0. TTL is therefore the decisive item with respect to cache. Also, negative answers have to have their TTL defined if they are to be kept in cache.

Now, where to define the TTL of a negative answer if the negative answer does not usually contain any RR record in the reply section (as shown in the first example of Section 2.3.8)? The TTL for the negative answer is defined in the way that the zone SOA record is inserted into the authoritative section of the answer.

3.4.2 The MINIMUM Field in an SOA Record

There have been three different interpretations of the MINIMUM field:

1. Minimum TTL for all RR records in the zone (this has never been used).
2. Implicit TTL for all RR records in the zones that do not contain the TTL field. (applies to primary name servers only). After carrying out a zone transfer, all RR records have the TTL field filled out.
3. TTL of a negative reply for the zone.

From now on, the MINIMUM field in an SOA record will prevail according to interpretation in point 3. TTL for individual RR records must be defined directly in RR records or by using the new $TTL command in the file zone.

Command syntax:

```
$TTL ttl commentary
```

All RR records listed after the $TTL command in the file that do not have their own ttl explicitly defined take over the ttl from the $TTL command.

The real TTL is defined as a minimum of the TTL field in the SOA record and the MINIMUM field. In case of negative answers, the TTL is reduced in cache the same way as in case of positive answers. If the TTL of a negative answer equals zero, the information in cache is invalid.

3.4.3 Saving Negative Reply Rules

The rules for saving negative replies are as follows:

- Saving negative answers is obligatory. If the resolver saves replies directly in cache, it must also save negative answers.
- Unauthorized negative answers cannot be saved.
- The SOA record from the authoritative section of the answer must be saved in cache as well.
- Negative answers without the SOA answer must not be saved.
- The SOA record saved in memory must be attached to the reply.
- The NXDOMAIN answer must be saved together with QNAME and QCLASS.
- The NOERROR_NODATA must be saved together with QNAME, QTYPE, and QCLASS.
- The $TTL command must be contained in the master file.

3.5 DNS IP version 6 Extension

DNS extension for IP version 6 is defined by RFC 1886, which was later amended and partially replaced by RFC 2874.

3.5.1 AAAA Records

IP version 4 uses the A record for the translation of a name into an IP address. The AAAA record was initially introduced for IP version 6. The difference is that the AAAA record has in the IP address field a 16-byte IP version 6 address and not a 4-byte address. The use of the AAAA record will not prevail in the future, though.

3.5.2 A6 Records

RFC 2874 replaces the AAAA record with the A6 record.

The A6 record is used for interfaces using IP version 6 addressing. Where an A record has an IP address, the RDATA field of the A6 record has, for example, the following form:

```
64   ::1244:67E3:589A:9ABC   subnet.isp.com
```

with 64 being the prefix length (number of prefix bits), ::1244:67E3:589A:9ABC being the final part of the address suffix, and subnet.isp.com being the prefix name. Therefore the complete A6 record may look as follows:

```
www          IN  A6  64   ::1244:67E3:589A:9ABC   subnet.isp.com
```

> How it work? If you would like to search IP version 6 address of the DNS name www, then you take IP version 6 address of prefix. Cut first part of this address in prefix length. Result of this is prefix. By concatenating prefix and suffix you will obtain searching IP version 6 address of www.

Let us now have a look at the new parts of the A6 record:

The **Address suffix** is the IP version 6 address. Unimportant parts of this address are fulfilled by zeros. For example ::1244:67E3:589A:9ABC have first 64 bits fulfilled by zero.

The **Prefix name** is a DNS name of the prefix (DNS name of left part of IP version 6 address). This prefix name is defined by another A6 record of the relevant zone—in the isp.com domain zone name, in our case:

```
subnet       IN  A6  0    36AB:12:90A4:56::
```

The **Prefix length** is a number ranging from 0 to 128, referring to the number of prefix bits of the address that corresponds to the prefix name.

If the prefix length equals to 0, the prefix name is not indicated in the record, with the A6 record resulting in the following:

```
www          IN  A6  0    36AB:12:90A4:56:1244:67E3:589A:9ABC
```

As is shown by the example above, one IP version 6 address is saved in DNS by using several A6 records, with each of the records containing a part of the IP address. If the resolver wants to translate a DNS name into an IP version 6 address, it must take out not only one record, as it does in A and AAAA types, but several A6 records. The information contained in these records must then be put together by the resolver so as to receive the valid IP address as a result. The mechanism used by the resolver to do this is referred to as **A6 record chains**, i.e., building chains of the pieces of information contained in A6 records.

To make the issue of A6 record chains even clearer, let us have a look at one more example. A company named Company Ltd. is connected to the Internet via an ISP provider that has been assigned the 2435:00A1:BA00::/40 subnetwork. The provider then assigns the 2435:00A1:BA01:: /48 subnetwork to the company.

The company has its name server (ns.company.com) with the address of 2435:00A1:BA01:1:1: 1234:5678:1 and a www server with the address of 2435:00A1:BA01:1:1:1234:5678:2. The company uses the company.com domain.

The DNS will contain the following records:

```
$ORIGIN company.com
    ns          IN  A6  48  ::1:1:1234:5678:1        company-net.isp.com
    www         IN  A6  48  ::1:1:1234:5678:2        company-net.isp.com

$ORIGIN isp.com
    company-netIN  A6  40  0:0:0001::               prague.isp.com
    prague      IN  A6  0   2435:00A1:BA00::
```

Also note that the glue record in the superior domain has the same form as well. Including a full IP address without using A6 record chains is recommended for name server A6 records. If the node uses an IP version 4 address, then it is not suitable to map it into IP version 6, but, on the contrary, including an IP version 4 record of the A-type directly in DNS is recommended.

Example:

```
NS1 IN  A6  0   4EE8::55:6:78E:1234:6578
NS2 IN  A       195.168.16.1
```

3.5.3 Reverse Domains

The IP6.INT domain was introduced for reverse translations at first. Subsequently, in November 2001, the IANA registered IP6.ARPA for reverse translations. This domain corresponds to IN-ADDR.ARPA for IP version 4.

IP6.INT

Items in the IP6.INT domain are entered in nibble format. Individual bytes of an IP address are recorded backwards, not with the whole bytes, but only their halves being reversed. One half of a byte is represented by one hexadecimal digit. Individual hexadecimal bytes are separated with dots (i.e., with a *delimiter* in the domain name.)

Example:

An IP address of 4321::1:2:3:4:567:89AB will be recorded as (an IP6.INT domain item):

```
B.A.9.8.7.6.5.0.4.0.0.0.3.0.0.0.2.0.0.0.1.0.0.0.0.0.0.0.1.2.3.4.IP6.INT.
```

(An IP address of 4321::1:2:3:4:567:89AB is an abridged version of 4321:0000:0001:0002:0003:0004:0567:89AB).

IP6.ARPA

Items in IP6.ARPA are entered in the bit-string format.

Example:

The IP address of `4321::1:2:3:4:567:89AB` will be, as an IP6.INT domain item, recorded as:

`\[x43210000000010002000300004056789AB/128].IP6.ARPA.`

Note that records in IP6.ARPA begin with a backslash, and the digit sequence of an IP address is enclosed in brackets [ ] and introduced by the *x* character. The order of digits in the item is the same as in an IP address. The backslash is followed by brackets with the number of bytes of the IP address.

The following record also represents the reverse domain from the example shown previously:

`\[x43210000/32].\[x0001/16].\[000200030004056789AB/80].IP6.ARPA.`

3.5.4 DNAME Records

The DNAME record is analogous to the CNAME record. The DNAME record enables you to label subtrees in the tree structure of domain names.

We have the following DNAME records:

```
prague.company.isp.com     IN  DNAME        company.com
\[x43210000/32]            IN  DNAME   pilsen-rev.ispb.com
```

NS records are no longer used for delegating reverse domains, but the sequence of the DNAME record is used instead of the classic delegations. The use of DNAME records also decreases the number of zone files used for reverse delegations.

The mechanism for using DNAME records for delegating reverse domains will be explained in the example of the Company Ltd. introduced in Section 3.5.2.

The DNS must contain the following entries for reverse translation:

```
$ORIGIN IP6.ARPA
\[x243500A1BA /40]         IN  DNAME   ip6-rev.isp.com

$ORIGIN ip6-rev.isp.com
\[01/8]                    IN  DNAME   company-rev.company.com

$ORIGIN company-rev.company.com
\[00010001123456780001/80]IN  PTR     ns.company.com
\[00010001123456780002/80]IN  PTR     www.company.com
```

The following steps have been taken by the resolver when trying to translate the IP address of `2435:00A1:BA01:1:1:1234:5678:2` into a name.

```
Request: \[x243500A1BA0100010001123456780002/128].IP6.ARPA
To the server of the IP6.ARPA domain
Reply: \[x243500A1BA /40].IP6.ARPA        DNAME   ip6-rev.isp.com

Request: \[x0100010001123456780002/88].ip6-rev.isp.com
To the server of the ip6-rev.isp.com domain
Reply: \[01/8]          DNAME   company-rev.company.com

Request: \[x00010001123456780002/80]. company-rev.company.com
To the server of the company-rev.company.com domain
Reply:
\[x00010001123456780001/128]. company-rev.comany.com PTR ns.company.com
```

3.6 DNS Security Protocols

This section will deal with the protocols specifying DNS security. An important thing is that currently the most widely used BIND version 9 DNS server (the name server) supports the majority of these protocols. DNSsec and TIG are the basic mechanisms.

3.6.1 DNSsec

DNSsec is an extension of DNS specified in RFC 2535 that deals with the basic issues of DNS security. Within the domain tree, we can secure certain domains of lower class by using DNSsec. The ideal case would be if security began at the root name servers going up through the whole DNS tree, all the way to the names of individual computers, mail proxies (MX records), or other names listed in DNS. But this is a promise of the future.

We have to realize that DNSsec is not, for operational purposes, divided into domains, but into zones. The zone is an area administered by a particular name server. Since security will be provided for certain name servers with their respective administrators, the relevant public keys are valid within a particular zone and not generally within the whole domain.

DNSsec uses asymmetrical cryptography. It does not use certificates; public keys are inserted into KEY records. It may appear at first that the keys are placed into DNS independently of any certification according to X.509 provided by certification authorities.

But, similarly to having an impression that DNS is primitive, we are also proven wrong when taking a more detailed look at KEY records (i.e., inserting public keys into DNS), where public keys are certified indirectly. To be more specific: the administrator of the superior domain will sign the key for the subordinate domain.

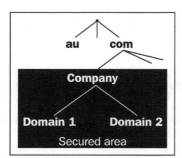

Figure 3.3: company.com domain secured by DNSsec

If DNSsec provides security to the DNS of the company.com domain and lower, we will insert the KEY record for the company.com zone that contains a public key, the relevant private key of which is used for signing information concerning the company.com domain. If we set up a subordinate zone of, let us say department.company.com, then we will include another KEY record in the name server of the department.company.com zone that will include the public key used for verifying the data of this subdomain. In general, this is a different public key, but it cannot be inserted in DNS completely as we choose.

In order for the subdomain of `department.company.com` to be seen from the Internet, the `company.com` administrator has to carry out a delegation to the `department.company.com` zone. By delegation it is understood that the administrator has to indicate relevant NS records that delegate authority 'downward' (as an option, glued A records can be added as well). If DNSsec is used, not only the NS and (optionally) A records containing the zone public key are defined, but also the KEY records. The zone administrator electronically signs the zone and places this signature into the SIG record. Indicating the KEY record in the zone from which authority is delegated downwards is an analog of public key certification. If we get an authorized reply containing a public key for a lower-level zone, then the public key for the relevant lower-level zone is trustworthy.

The question is, however, how to distribute the public keys for the highest domains since these are not certified by any higher-level key. The solution is simple—they are manually written in the resolver configuration file.

3.6.2 KEY Record

The KEY record contains the public key maintained in the DNS system. The KEY record has a specific RDATA field described in Figure 3.4. Other fields are analogous to other RR records.

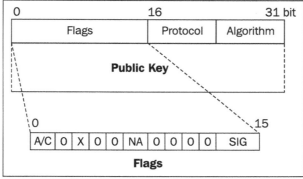

Figure 3.4: KEY record RDATA field

The RDATA field of the KEY record consists of the following items:

- For the **Flags** item, individual bits have the following meaning:
    - The **A/C** bits have the following values:
      10: Use of the key is prohibited for authentication.
      01: Use of the key is prohibited for confidentiality (DNS security makes use of keys for authentication only).
      11: Both bits are set, the "no key" value. There is no key information and the RR stops after the algorithm octet. A signed KEY RR can authenticatably assert that, for example, a zone is not secured.
      00: Use of the key for authentication and/or confidentiality is permitted.
    - Setting the **X** bit specifies that the KEY record contains an extended Flags field, i.e., the Algorithm field is followed by another 16 bits of the Flags field.

- o The **NA** bits specify what purpose the key has:
  00: The record contains a user key, which can be used for authentication in application protocols (for example, Telnet, FTP, etc.).
  01: The record contains a zone key, i.e., the key that the primary DNS server will use for signing the zone data electronically.
  10: The record contains a key for a different purpose (for example, securing routing, time administration like NTP protocol, and so on).
  - o The last 4 bits referred to as **SIG** are dedicated to labeling the key that can be used for DNS Update.
- The **Protocol** item contains the protocol aimed at the key:
  - o 1: Reserved for TLS protocol
  - o 2: Reserved for electronic mail
  - o 3: DNSsec
  - o 4: Reserved for IPsec
- The **Algorithm** item contains a cryptographic algorithm dedicated to the key:
  1: RSA/MD-5

  2: Diffie-Hellman

  3: DSA

  4: ECC

The tools for the generation of the relevant keys are also part of the distribution in the Version 9 BIND server. We can generate public/private key pairs by using the `dnssec-keygen` application.

Example:

```
dnssec-keygen -a DSA -b 768 -n ZONE company.com
```

with -a specifying the cryptographic algorithm that we use for generating the keys, -b specifying the key length, and with -n specifying if generating should result in a zone key (ZONE), individual record key (HOST), or user key (USER). The zone name (i.e., the DNS name) is the last parameter.

The previous command has generated two files (+003 being the key of the DSA algorithm, +03719 being the key ID):

- `Kcompany.com.+003+03719.private` containing the relevant private key.
- `Kcompany.com.+003+03719.key` containing the KEY type with a generated public key:

```
company.com. IN KEY 256 3 3 BI/K+szyYtKfJP5GS7wORDt9toeJ2xPmv8SSMy+qtXBThOQKsbgqyc2
O yA5aKZ1pHJo92w//MJlXO7Z2TwgUOTW6TMAY34hU5c1cquSUpPgK/yBi f/jqfLy1xQar5kRxgOyn7
hg9GKT7nlFThMAqL9SWvxFTcEzb2GOuxD7u LZz5/MZk8YzuWqXSXq495HUy22rjp/x8TRlIYmTss3EX
/hKtF7fo2L1C KTN+997feTvqLXQ71UOPrsmFNj3qO7atDJTPEMUbwheZdIUnVC5poOJI E6NMbARsod
NaaI2Hka9+iFo47uIP8ISc+DACJGITaXBkRP+iNkjyrGU+ w29FTH3zZ4ahEk26JvxtEUhWDvaqJYO6S
8n2N2RqR/Qhd08UsvwLyCEs hIffBqPtFMzm/IvJf+TB
```

The meaning of the individual RDATA field items in the generated KEY record:

- 256_{10} (0 0 0 0 0 0 01 0 0 0 0 0 0 0 0_2): Only the two NA bits are set to the value of 01, i.e., the key cannot be used for encrypting (the DSA algorithm is not suitable for encrypting).
- 3: The key is aimed at DNSsec.
- 3: The key is a key of the DSA algorithm.

Similarly, we can also generate the keys for the department.company.com domain. We will receive a file named Kdepartment.company.com.+003+23457 containing a KEY record with the public key:

```
department.company.com. IN KEY 256 3 3 BP+lDE7W5LpEr7djd26pQGd6wctJ+8aICq1BMuCupKIOOC
NPVDR64sHW Pionq3QO7t884DeA9vOb4b3k14dazmBRKINfqvBF/hintoTqJH2jENUs LxNk23CTBgi2
fIQuzbKZXSdJan4GUGGMQjFjdf8VSlHLNcOYaWB4hXqf ZuQRRgbWUFA4CZXOSgSOpNAm4h6jk7S1qnv
8EL+MUdnVOg3wT82qj7ma xAdEPOY5Q6fORIJ+QHEsl6xuGoWYEjYmyGlH+r9r/NOKLxf9O4Xesziz r
3lloPnuXTC/LO3gA6OViJYYQXeuCGldjcLP6AK2rm16svx/sTM+v+Ff SdI7pkqBOQoq28bfd3qgRioj
FIWbeBhk14vjBn5INbwxcErGmKXtdbpl GHxDukSykxrQBZNRNmG8
```

3.6.3 SIG Record

The SIG record is used for saving a digital signature in DNS, i.e., DNSsec uses SIG records for the authentication of its data.

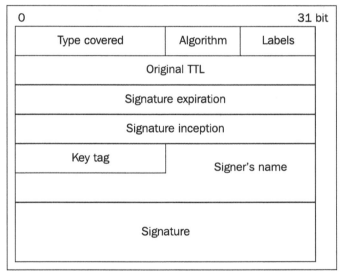

Figure 3.5: The RDATA field of the SIG record

Figure 3.5 shows the shape of the RDATA field schema. The meaning of individual data fields is as follows:

- **Type covered** contains the type of the record signed.
- **Algorithm** contains the algorithm number (see the KEY record in Section 3.6.2).
- **Labels** contains the number of labels (chains) that form the DNS name, for example:
  - In the DNS name . labels=0
  - In com. labels=1
  - In company.com labels=2, and so on
- The **Original TTL** contains the original value of the TTL of the RR record. The problem is that TTL values are automatically decreased in the cache of individual DNS servers. If the RR record is digitally signed, then it is necessary to keep two TTL fields: one is the value when originally signed and cannot be changed (or the signature would become invalid) and the second is the current value.
- The digital signature is valid during the period form the **Signature inception** time until **Signature expiration** time.
- The **Key tag** field contains a key identification that has been used for the signature. This field is especially useful when there are several keys serving the same purpose. DNS can contain several keys because for example we need to use several cryptographic algorithms at the same time. The 2 lowest bytes of the public key module are used as the identification, for example, of the RSA/MD-5 algorithm.
- The **Signer's name** field contains domain name of the signer who created the signature.
- The last field contains the digital signature itself.

Again, BIND version 9 has several tools for generating SIG records. The first is the dnssec-make-keyset application that we can subscribe to ourselves by the generated KEY record:

```
dnssec-makekeyset  -t 259200 -e +500000 Kcompany.com.+003+03719
```

with -t indicating the TTL assigned to the generated KEY and SIG records, -e specifying the expiry time of the digital signature (from that moment), and the last parameter being the shared name of the files containing the public and private keys generated by the dnsec-keygen command.

The keyset-company.com file containing the KEY record signed by the private key of the relevant public key will be created. This file can be compared to a certificate request, though it is not handed over to the certification authority, but to an administrator of the higher-level domain (with the smaller label item). The file contains the following:

```
$ORIGIN .
$TTL 259200      ; 3 days
company.com              IN KEY  256 3 3 (
                         BI/K+szyYtKfJP5GS7wORDt9toeJ2xPmv8SSMy+qtXBT
                         h0QKsbgqyc2OyA5aKZ1pHJo92w//MJlX07Z2TwgUOTW6
                         TMAY34hU5c1cquSupPgK/yBif/jqfLy1xQar5kRxgOyn
                         7hg9GKT7nlFThMAqL9SWvxFTCEzb2G0uxD7uLZz5/MZk
                         8YzuWqXSXq495HUy22rjp/x8TR1IYmTss3EX/hKtF7fo
                         2L1CKTN+997feTvqLXQ71U0PrsmFNj3qO7atDJTPEMUb
                         wheZdIUnVC5poOJIE6NMbARsodNaaI2Hka9+iFo47uIP
```

```
                         8ISc+DACJGITaXBkRP+iNkjyrGU+w29FTH3zZ4ahEk26
                         JvxtEUhWDvaqJYO6S8n2N2RqR/Qhd08UsvwLyCEshIff
                         BqPtFMzm/IvJf+TB ) ; key id = 3719
              SIG        KEY 3 2 259200 20010607033618 (
                         20010601084258 3719 company.com.
                         BHrEtaQBiMpVRxVQgl3i4Nf7LAPXfftgFiqH6EGI64Fp
                         BhuuVu/GipM= )
```

Note that the KEY record has not changed except the key ID derived from the key value. Also note the SIG record that contains the following items in the generated file:

- The signed record type is the KEY, i.e., a KEY record is signed

- Algorithm=3, i.e., DSA

- The label field contains 2 since the DNS name of company.com consists of two chains, i.e., the company chain and the com chain

- The original TTL is 259200

- The signature expires on 20010607033618, i.e., June 7, 2001 at 03:36:18 (UTC)

- The signature is valid until 200110601084258, i.e., June 1, 2001 at 08:42:58 (UTC)

- The key ID is 3719.

- The signature was created by company.com

Similarly, the department.company.com key can be signed as well:

```
dnssec-makekeyset  -t 259200 -e +500000 Kdepartment.company.com.+003+23457
```

thus creating the keyset-department.company.com. file containing the relevant digital signature:

```
$ORIGIN .
$TTL 259200      ; 3 days
department.company.com     IN KEY  256 3 3 (
                           BP+lDE7W5LpEr7djd26pQGd6wctJ+8aICq1BMuCupKIO
                           OCNPVDR64sHWPionq3Q07t884DeA9vOb4b3k14daZmBR
                           KINfqvBF/hintoTqJH2jENUsLxNk23CTBgi2fIQuZbKZ
                           XSdJan4GUGGMQjFjdf8VSlHLNcOYawB4hXqfZuQRRgbW
                           UFA4CZXOSgSOpNAm4h6jk7S1qnv8EL+MUdnVOg3wT82q
                           j7maxAdEPOY5Q6fORIJ+QHEsl6xuGoWYEjYmyGlH+r9r
                           /NOKLxf904XesziZr3lloPnuXTC/LO3gA6OViJYYQXeu
                           CGldjcLP6AK2rm16svx/sTM+v+FfSdI7pkqBOQoq28bf
                           d3qgRiojFIWbeBhk14vjBn5INbwxcErGmKXtdbplGHxD
                           ukSykxrQBZNRNmG8 ) ; key id = 23457
              SIG          KEY 3 3 259200 20010607040154 (
                           20010601090834 23457 department.company.com.
                           BAre8ynWlPvA version
                           6hhe69mbVmAGm24dxwJUqcpHE2PvXwq
                           +V23HHqZWQo= )
```

The signature can be sent to the administrator of the higher domain, i.e., company.com.

The higher-level domain administrator has a tool for signing keys from subordinate domains:

```
dnssec-signkey  keyset-department.company.com. Kcompany.com.+003+03719
```

The first parameter is the file name received from the administrator of the subordinate domain, and the second parameter is the common beginning of the names of files containing both the public and private keys of the signing authority.

This will result in the creation of the `signedkey-department.company.com.` file with signed public key (signed KEY record):

```
$ORIGIN .
$TTL 259200      ; 3 days
department.company.com        IN KEY  256 3 3 (
                              BP+lDE7W5LpEr7djd26pQGd6wctJ+8aICq1BMuCupKIO
                              OCNPVDR64sHWPionq3Q07t884DeA9vOb4b3k14daZmBR
                              KINfqvBF/hintoTqJH2jENUsLxNk23CTBgi2fIQuZbKZ
                              XSdJan4GUGGMQjFjdf8VS1HLNcOYawB4hXqfZuQRRgbW
                              UFA4CZXOSgSOpNAm4h6jk7S1gnv8EL+MUdnVOg3wT82q
                              j7maxAdEPOY5Q6fORIJ+QHES16xuGoWYEjYmyGlH+r9r
                              /NOKLxf904xeszizr3lloPnuXTC/L03gA60ViJYYQXeu
                              CGldjcLP6AK2rm16svx/sTM+v+FfSdI7pkqBOQoq28bf
                              d3qgRiojFIWbeBhk14vjBn5INbwxcErGmKXtdbplGHxD
                              ukSykxrQBZNRNmG8 ) ; key id = 23457
                      SIG     KEY 3 3 259200 20010607040154 (
                              20010601090834 3719 company.com.
                              BIusFqCyPwcBIVhWq6LP+QuLk0usd2SUpQ26D9dDf7iO
                              NBIepCyze7Y= )
```

It is worth mentioning that the `department.company.com` zone key (KEY record) is already signed by a different key—the key of the superior `company.com` zone (SIG record). The KEY record signed by the SIG record that has been signed by the superior domain will be saved in the DNS database.

So, if we have not supported DNSsec so far and we have the following zone file for the `department.company.com` zone, then we can insert the public zone key by using the KEY record and, as an option, the digital signature of this public key acquired from the superior domain administrator (`company.com`):

```
$TTL 99999
@       IN      SOA     ns.company.com. dostalek.company.com. (
                        1          ; Serial
                        3600       ; Refresh
                        300        ; Retry
                        3600000 ; Expire
                        3600 )     ; Minimum
        IN      NS      ns.company.com.
computer IN     A       10.1.1.2
```

This will give us the following:

```
$TTL 99999
@       IN      SOA     ns.company.com. dostalek.company.com. (
                        1          ; Serial
                        3600       ; Refresh
                        300        ; Retry
                        3600000 ; Expire
                        3600 )     ; Minimum
        IN      NS      ns.company.com.
$TTL 259200
        IN KEY  256 3 3 (
                        BP+lDE7W5LpEr7djd26pQGd6wctJ+8aICq1BMuCupKIO
                        OCNPVDR64sHWPionq3Q07t884DeA9vOb4b3k14daZmBR
                        KINfqvBF/hintoTqJH2jENUsLxNk23CTBgi2fIQuZbKZ
                        XSdJan4GUGGMQjFjdf8VS1HLNcOYawB4hXqfZuQRRgbW
                        UFA4CZXOSgSOpNAm4h6jk7S1gnv8EL+MUdnVOg3wT82q
                        j7maxAdEPOY5Q6fORIJ+QHES16xuGoWYEjYmyGlH+r9r
                        /NOKLxf904xeszizr3lloPnuXTC/L03gA60ViJYYQXeu
                        CGldjcLP6AK2rm16svx/sTM+v+FfSdI7pkqBOQoq28bf
                        d3qgRiojFIWbeBhk14vjBn5INbwxcErGmKXtdbplGHxD
```

```
                              uksYkxrQBZNRNmG8 ) ; key id = 23457
            SIG      KEY 3 3 259200 20010607040154 (
                         20010601090834 3719 company.com.
                         BIusFqCyPwcBIVhWq6LP+QuLkOusd2SUpQ26D9dDf7i0
                         NBIepCyze7Y= )
computer   IN     A       10.1.1.2
```

3.6.4 NXT Record

Individual records in DNS are not ordered in sequences. The NXT record, however, makes up for this drawback. Using this record, we can specify what object follows the current object in DNS.

Let us take a hypothetical example of DNS record:

```
department.company.com.    IN SOA ...
                           IN NS ns.company.com.
ftp                        IN A 10.1.1.1
computer                   IN A 10.1.1.2
```

In this case, when transferring a zone, an attacker could not remove a record beginning `computer IN A ...`, causing the `computer.department.company.com` server to be unavailable.

By using NXT records, we can find out which record;

```
1 department.company.com. IN   SOA ...
2                         IN   NS ns.company.com.
3                         IN   NXT ftp.department.company.com. NS SOA NXT
4 ftp                     IN   A 10.1.1.1
5                         IN   NXT computer.department.company.com. A NXT
6 computer                IN   A 10.1.1.2
7                         IN   NXT department.company.com A NXT
```

In this example, the initial SOA and NS records (lines 1 and 2) are followed by the `ftp.department.company.com` record. This interconnection is described by the NXT record on the third line. Also, the fact that the `computer.department.company.com` follows the `ftp.department.company` record is expressed by the NXT record on line 5.

The question is how to specify the fact that the `computer.department.company.com` is the last record of the given zone. The solution is simple. Imagine that the zone is a cycle, i.e., the first record follows the last one. This way it is easy to understand the meaning of the NXT record on the last line.

The RDATA field of the NXT record is shown in the following figure:

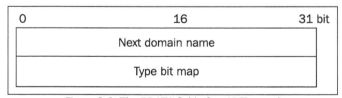

Figure 3.6: The RDATA field of an NXT record

The RDATA field consists of only two items. The first one contains the DNS name and the second one a type bit map specifying which types or records are used to describe the current object in the database. The sequence number of the bit map corresponds to the record type. The bit for the NXT record is always set.

The most commonly used types are shown in the following table:

Record	Type	Record	Type
A	1	ISDN	20
NS	2	RT	21
CNAME	5	NSAP	22
SOA	6	SIG	24
WKS	11	KEY	25
PTR	12	PX	26
HINFO	13	GPOS	27
MINFO	14	AAAA	28
MX	15	NXT	30
TXT	16	SRV	33
RP	17	CERT	37
ASFDB	18	A6	38
X.25	19		

Table 3.5: Record names and their types

So, if an object has its NS and SOA records set, then the mask contains bit 2 (NS), 6 (SOA), and 30 (NXT—always set).

If a request for nonexistent DNS records is sent, the authoritative section contains an interval of two consecutive names between which the requested DNS record was to be located, thus informing us that there is no such name in DNS.

In the following example, DNS made a request, by using the `dig` command, for the `server.department.company.com` record. This was the very last record of the zone. The authoritative section contains the NXT record of the last zone record, which means there is nothing more in the zone.

```
$ dig @195.47.37.196  server.department.company.com A

; <<>> DiG 9.1.3rc1 <<>> -p 5353 server.department.company.com A
@195.47.37.196 +adflag
;; global options:  printcmd
;; Got answer:
;; ->>HEADER<<- opcode: QUERY, status: NXDOMAIN, id: 49597
;; flags: qr aa rd ra; QUERY: 1, ANSWER: 0, AUTHORITY: 4, ADDITIONAL: 0

;; QUESTION SECTION:
;server.department.company.com.   IN   A

;; AUTHORITY SECTION:
department.company.com.    3600    IN   SOA ns.company.com. dostalek.company.com.
 1 3600 300 3600000 3600
department.company.com.    3600    IN   SIG SOA 3 3 99999 20010701112735
20010601112735 23457 department.company.com.
BHd7h+zUJL4sJ9sRH4wGsQMTNdfTRpo16237f30jEKe4cNHnOonbfOI=
computer.department.company.com. 99999 INNXT department.company.com. A SIG NXT
```

```
computer.department.company.com. 99999 INSIG NXT 3 4 99999 20010701112735
20010601112735 23457
                    department.company.com.
                    BF5ESPyUtLrBlUEaJvt5L01JPSijFtvUI/2SThgmu+pGUc39wx4rR40=

;; Query time: 11 msec
;; SERVER: 195.47.37.196#5353(195.47.37.196)
;; WHEN: Fri Jun  1 14:41:30 2001
;; MSG SIZE  rcvd: 317
```

3.6.5 Zone Signature

BIND version 9 also contains a tool for signing zones. By entering the following command, we sign the department.company.com zone:

```
dnssec-signzone department.company.com
```

As a parameter, the name of the file containing the data of the relevant zone has been used. The following department.company.com field has been created:

```
; File written on Fri Jun  1 13:27:35 2001
; dnssec_signzone version 9.1.3rc1
department.company.com. 99999 IN SOA  ns.company.com dostalek.company.com. (
                                1        ; serial
                                3600     ; refresh
                                300      ; retry
                                3600000  ; expire
                                3600     ; minimum
                                )
                259200    SIG      SOA 3 3 99999 20010701112735 (
                                   20010601112735 23457
                                   department.company.com.
                                   BHd7h+zUJL4sJ9sRH4wGsQMTNdfTRpo16237
                                   f30jEKe4cNHnOonbfOI= )
                99999     NS       ns.company.com.
                99999     SIG      NS 3 3 99999 20010701112735 (
                                   20010601112735 23457
                                   department.company.com.
                                   BH3zSccdOPD5CEDdEy+LNSlRG9pEKdwHFxGe
                                   q9BSH8wYt9qmiGMDJRw= )
                259200    KEY      256 3 3 (
                                   BP+lDE7W5LpEr7djd26pQGd6wctJ+8aICq1B
                                   MuCupKI00CNPVDR64sHWPionq3QO7t884DeA
                                   9vOb4b3k14daZmBRKINfqvBF/hintoTqJH2j
                                   ENUsLxNk23CTBgi2fIQuzbKZXSdJan4GUGGM
                                   QjFjdf8VSlHLNcOYawB4hxqfZuQRRgbWUFA4
                                   CZXOSgSOpNAm4h6jk7S1qnv8EL+MUdnVOg3w
                                   T82qj7maxAdEPOY5Q6fORIJ+QHEsl6xuGOWY
                                   EjYmyGlH+r9r/NOKLxf904XesziZr3lloPnu
                                   XTC/LO3gA6OViJYYQXeuCGldjcLP6AK2rm16
                                   svx/sTM+v+FfSdI7pkqBOQoq28bfd3qgRioj
                                   FIWbeBhk14vjBn5INbwxcErGmKXtdbplGHxD
                                   ukSykxrQBZNRNmG8 ) ; key id = 23457
                259200    SIG      KEY 3 3 259200 20010607040154 (
                                   20010601090834 3719 company.com.
                                   BIusFqCyPwcBIVhWq6LP+QuLkOusd2SUpQ26
                                   D9dDf7iONBIepCyze7Y= )
                99999     NXT      computer.department.company.com. NS SOA SIG
                KEY NXT
                99999     SIG      NXT 3 3 99999 20010701112735 (
                                   20010601112735 23457
                                   department.company.com.
                                   BBUQYeZljDZYmw7Cd/c18eTNQKDO605u+rIy
                                   P4mJFcV8RigX2symCsg= )
```

```
computer.department.company.com. 259200 IN A  10.1.1.2
                259200  SIG    A 3 4 259200 20010701112735 (
                               20010601112735 23457
                               department.company.com.
                               BGwiQc/MoX6pK89fGC4IvH/cAhI6ElYuXySZ
                               AcToehusK7P/HBTIMcM= )
                99999   NXT    department.company.com. A SIG NXT
                99999   SIG    NXT 3 4 99999 20010701112735 (
                               20010601112735 23457
                               department.company.com.
                               BF5ESPyUtLrBlUEaJvt5LO1JPSijFtvUI/2S
                               Thgmu+pGUc39wx4rR40= )
```

Note that for all records (except for SIG) a digital signature is generated. This makes signing the zone a considerably time consuming operation, especially in cases of zones containing many thousands of entries, such as .com or another TLD.

We set the configuration file of /etc/named.conf so the data are read from the file with the signed suffix, i.e., from the department.company.com.signed file.

```
options {
        directory  "/usr/users/dostalek/run";
        listen-on port 5353 { 195.47.37.196;};
        pid-file "/usr/users/dostalek/run/pid";
};
zone "0.0.127.in-addr.arpa" { type master; file "127.rev";};
zone "."                    { type hint;   file "named.ca";};
zone "company.com" { type master; file "company.com.signed";};
zone "department.company.com" { type master; file
"department.company.com.signed";};
```

3.6.6 Display Data

The dig application can now display the data for the zone signed by us. In the first example, we display NS records, and in the second example, we display KEY records. (The DNS server used in the example runs on port 5353.)

```
dig @195.47.37.196 -p 5353 department.company.com NS

; <<>> DiG 9.1.3rc1 <<>> -p 5353 department.company.com NS @195.47.37.196
+adflag
;; global options:  printcmd
;; Got answer:
;; ->>HEADER<<- opcode: QUERY, status: NOERROR, id: 49597
;; flags: qr aa rd ra; QUERY: 1, ANSWER: 2, AUTHORITY: 0, ADDITIONAL: 1

;; QUESTION SECTION:
;department.company.com.        IN  NS

;; ANSWER SECTION:
department.company.com.    99999   IN  NS ns.company.com.
department.company.com.    99999   IN  SIG NS 3 3 99999 20010701112735
        20010601112735 23457 department.company.com.
        BH3zSccdOPD5CEDdEy+LNSlRG9pEKdwHFxGeq9BSH8wYt9qmiGMDJRw=

;; ADDITIONAL SECTION:
department.company.com.    259200 IN  KEY 256 3 3
```

```
BP+1DE7W5LpEr7djd26pQGd6wctJ+8aICq1BMuCupKI00CNPVDR64sHW
Pionq3Q07t884DeA9vOb4b3k14daZmBRKINfqvBF/hintoTqJH2jENUs
LxNk23CTBgi2fIQuzbKZXSdJan4GUGGMQjFjdf8VSlHLNcOYawB4hxqf
ZuQRRgbWUFA4CZXOSgSOpNAm4h6jk7S1qnv8EL+MUdnVOg3wT82qj7ma
xAdEPOY5Q6fORIJ+QHEsl6xuGoWYEjYmyGlH+r9r/NOKLxf904XesziZ
r3lloPnuXTC/LO3gA60ViJYYQXeuCGldjcLP6AK2rm16svx/sTM+v+Ff
SdI7pkqBOQoq28bfd3qgRiojFIWbeBhkl4vjBn5INbwxcErGmKXtdbpl
GHxDukSykxrQBZNRNmG8
```

```
;; Query time: 16 msec
;; SERVER: 195.47.37.196#5353(195.47.37.196)
;; WHEN: Fri Jun  1 14:10:29 2001
;; MSG SIZE  rcvd: 471


$ dig @195.47.37.196 -p 5353 department.company.com KEY

;; Truncated, retrying in TCP mode.
;; Got answer:
;; ->>HEADER<<- opcode: QUERY, status: NOERROR, id: 41218
;; flags: qr aa rd ra; QUERY: 1, ANSWER: 2, AUTHORITY: 2, ADDITIONAL: 0

;; QUESTION SECTION:
;department.company.com.       IN  KEY

;; ANSWER SECTION:
department.company.com.    259200  IN  KEY 256 3 3
BP+1DE7W5LpEr7djd26pQGd6wctJ+8aICq1BMuCupKI00CNPVDR64sHW
Pionq3Q07t884DeA9vOb4b3k14daZmBRKINfqvBF/hintoTqJH2jENUs
LxNk23CTBgi2fIQuzbKZXSdJan4GUGGMQjFjdf8VSlHLNcOYawB4hxqf
ZuQRRgbWUFA4CZXOSgSOpNAm4h6jk7S1qnv8EL+MUdnVOg3wT82qj7ma
xAdEPOY5Q6fORIJ+QHEsl6xuGoWYEjYmyGlH+r9r/NOKLxf904XesziZ
r3lloPnuXTC/LO3gA60ViJYYQXeuCGldjcLP6AK2rm16svx/sTM+v+Ff
SdI7pkqBOQoq28bfd3qgRiojFIWbeBhkl4vjBn5INbwxcErGmKXtdbpl
GHxDukSykxrQBZNRNmG8
department.company.com.    259200  IN  SIG KEY 3 3 259200
        20010607040154 20010601090834 3719 company.com.
        BIusFqCyPwcBIVhWq6LP+QuLkOusd2SUpQ26D9dDf7i0NBIepCyze7Y=

;; AUTHORITY SECTION:
department.company.com.    99999   IN  NS  ns.company.com.
department.company.com.    99999   IN  SIG NS 3 3 99999
        20010701112735 20010601112735 23457 department.company.com.
        BH3zSccdOPD5CEDdEy+LNSlRG9pEKdwHFxGeq9BSH8wYt9qmiGMDJRw=

;; Query time: 9 msec
;; SERVER: 195.47.37.196#5353(195.47.37.196)
;; WHEN: Fri Jun  1 14:10:21 2001
;; MSG SIZE  rcvd: 552
```

3.6.7 DNS Protocol

Figure 3.7 shows the DNS QUERY packet header. This header occupies the three reserved bits labeled as **Z**, which should be set to zero. Extending DNS will use two reserved bits. These bits are labeled as **AC** and **CD** in Figure 3.7.

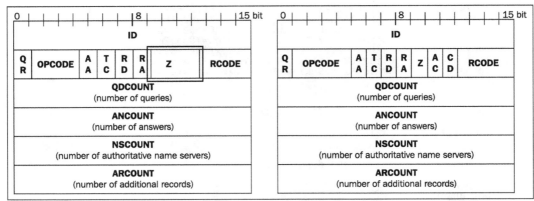

Figure 3.7: Original packet of DNS query (left) and packet with DNSsec extension (right)

The **AD** (**Authenticated Data**) bit in the reply of the name server indicates that the data in the reply section and the authoritative name servers' section are authenticated by the server. The **CD** (**Checking Disabled**) bit indicates that the server accepts also unauthenticated data.

The previous sections have shown how to electronically sign RR records using SIG records. This mechanism, however, does not secure a reply of the DNS server as a whole, i.e., it does not secure the transaction. It is very simple for an aggressor to change the DNS packet header bits, while taking out some RR records from certain sections or switching records between individual sections. When doing this, they can also take out or switch SIG records, i.e., the digital signature.

The solution to this is to add a special SIG record to the end of the server reply. This SIG record digitally signs the server reply including the request section (i.e., the resolver's request). A similar SIG record can be theoretically added to the end of the resolver's request that is sent to the server.

A disadvantage of the system of adding SIG records to the end of additional information is that we need to have the relevant online private key used for creating the digital signature.

You have probably noticed, when signing the zone, that signing extensive zones can be a demanding task. The private key is expected to be held in a special appliance. The zone administrator signs the zone using this appliance, and then transfers the signed zone onto the name server. The security of the private key is increased this way.

Additionally, signing with the private key is not automatic, but can be done only when the administrator is present. The replies of the name server vary so much that they cannot be prepared in advance and must be calculated by the online server.

3.7 TSIG

DNSsec, described in the previous section, has several drawbacks. Asymmetrical cryptography is so demanding that using this mechanism for DNS Update is difficult. RFC 2845 specifies an alternative mechanism referred to as **TSIG** (**Transaction Signatures**).

TSIG is aimed at authorizing between two systems. Both systems mutually exchange shared secrets. The data transferred between these two systems are then authorized by the HMAC-MD5 algorithm, i.e., the shared secrets create concatenate with the data to be transferred and the result is then used for calculating the hash with the MD-5 algorithm.

This cryptographic checksum is transferred in the TSIG record. This record is recreated for any data transferred; so there is no reason to keep it in the database.

The shared secret can also be created by the already mentioned `dnssec-keygen` tool:

```
dnssec-keygen -a hmac-md5 -b 128 -n HOST computer1-computer2
```

Again, this program will create two files, `Kcomputer1-computer2.+157+38038.key` and `Kcomputer1-computer2.+157+38038.private`. In this case, however, is not use asymmetrical cryptograpy so both files contain the same key (although each file has a slightly different format). For example, the `Kcomputer1-computer2.+157+38038.private` file contains:

```
Private-key-format: v1.2
Algorithm: 157 (HMAC_MD5)
Key: QsylTZpRInmNwGqB4yUOrQ==
```

From the file, we will use just a Base64 encoded shared secret of `QsylTZpRInmNwGqB4yUOrQ==`, saving it into configuration files in the `/etc/named.conf` file of both computers:

```
key computer1-computer2. {
    algorith hmac-md5;
    secret QsylTZpRInmNwGqB4yUOrQ==;
};
```

Additionally, we have to indicate in the configuration files of both servers that they are expected to use the relevant shared secret. If the other computer's IP address is `10.1.1.1`, then we indicate the following in the `/etc/named.conf` file:

```
server 10.1.1.1  {
    keys {computer1-computer2. ;};
};
```

Now, dynamic DNS Update can only be enabled if it is authorized by the shared secret:

```
allow-update { key computer1-computer2. ;};
```

3.7.1 TKEY

In order for TSIG to work correctly, an exchange of shared secrets is necessary. It has already been mentioned that the shared secret can be exchanged in a different way and can be entered manually in the `/etc/named.conf` file.

The **Diffie-Hellman algorithm** can be used for establishing a shared secret manually. The TKEY algorithm specified by RFC 2930 uses this option. If there is a need for an exchange of Diffie-Hellman public numbers, the client sends a request (TKEY record) containing a KEY record with the relevant public Diffie-Hellman number in the additional information section. In its reply, the server indicates its public Diffie-Hellman number. Based on both public Diffie-Hellman numbers, both parties are able to calculate the shared secret.

Another mechanism that can be optionally supported is using an **asymmetric encrypting algorithm**. In this case, the resolver sends a request to the name server asking it to generate the shared secret. A KEY record with a client public key is a part of the request. The server then generates the shared secret encrypting it with the public key received. The encrypted shared secret is sent to the client, which decrypts it using its private key.

Similarly, it is possible for the client to generate the shared secret, encrypting it with the public key for the server.

3.8 Saving Certificates to DNS

RFC 2538 specifies the method used for saving certificates and CRL in DNS. Certificates and CRL are saved in **CERT records**. Saving certificates and CRL according to X.509 as well as saving PGP and SPKI certificates is supported. It is important to stress that DNS here is aimed at distributing the certificates and CRL. CERT records are not aimed at securing DNS.

4

Name Server Implementation

As of now, you should have all the information about the DNS system, its functionality, and the DNS protocol. Let's see how to implement a DNS system and try to set up your own DNS server. Nowadays there are several versions of DNS implementation. The oldest DNS implementation is BIND version 4. This implementation is very simple so we will describe basic principles on it.

4.1 DNS Database

The basic assets of DNS are DNS databases and well configured name servers that manage these databases. The DNS protocol, which uses Resource Records (hereinafter RRs) in its queries and responses, was described in Chapter 2. RRs are primarily managed by hostmasters in disk files in primary name servers in a text format. These disk files are called **DNS databases**.

DNS databases are stored in files in the primary name server. Their content is loaded into memory at startup as shown in the following figure:

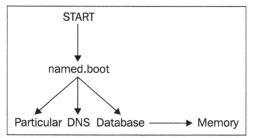

Figure 4.1: Program named finds out information about
DNS databases in the named.boot file during startup

A DNS database consists of individual files that are specified as the last parameters of the individual commands of the named.boot configuration file. A database on a disk may contain the following types of data:

- Authoritative data for the administered zone: This must start with the SOA record. This data can only be kept in the primary name server. A secondary name server receives this data from the primary or other secondary name servers through a zone transfer query.

- Data enabling access to root name servers (cache/hint zone): This does not start with a SOA record. The TTL field must therefore be stated explicitly in the individual records. This is nonauthoritative data for the local name server. It has to be in every name server with the exception of the slave and root servers.

- Data that the name server uses when delegating authority for subdomains to other name servers: NS records are used for delegating authority. This data is a part of a superordinate zone to which the local name server is the authority. If the authority is delegated to a name server whose domain name is a part of the delegated subdomain, it is necessary to add an A record specifying the IP address of this name server to the NS record. This A record is called a 'glue A record'.

The general syntax of the individual database lines (i.e., DNS records) is as follows:

```
[name] [TTL]    class   type    data_dependent_on_the_type_of_a_record
```

Fields in [ ] are optional; their values are taken from the previous record (for example, from the SOA record). Comments are separated by semicolons.

Description of individual fields:

- The **name** field contains the domain name. There are a number of possibilities:
  o The field is not filled in, and its value is taken from the name field of the previous record.
  o The name field can have the value @ in the SOA record. This value means that the name of the domain stated in the relevant command of the named.boot (or named.conf) configuration file should be inserted in the name field.
  o The domain name is stated in the name field without a dot at the end. In this case the name of the domain stated in an SOA record is automatically attached to this name. If the $ORIGIN command is stated in front of the record (without a dot at the end), the name of the domain stated in the $ORIGIN command is added.
  o The domain name is stated in the name field with a dot at the end. This is referred to as an absolute name, and is used exactly as is written.

- The **TTL** field contains the lifespan of a record (in seconds) in the non-authoritative name server's cache memory. The non-authoritative name server decreases this value automatically. When this value reaches zero, the record is thrown away. The default value of the field is zero. However, if the record is preceded by an SOA record, the default value of the field is taken from the Minimum TTL field of the SOA record. The SOA record is always stated at the beginning of the file, i.e., it may not immediately precede our record.

- The **class** can be IN (Internet), HS (Hesiod), or CH (Chaos). We are going to focus exclusively on IN records. (Implementations of the named program supporting Hesiod do exist; however, we will not be involved with them here.)

- The **type** is one of the types stated in Table 2.1 (for example, NS, CNAME, etc.).

- The last field includes data dependent on the type of the record. If the domain name is used, then the domain name should end with a dot; otherwise, the name of the domain would be added to it automatically. And vice versa, if an IP address is used, the fourth digit in the IP address must not end with a dot.

For more details, see RFC 1035.

4.2 RR Format

Names in the database must start on the first position. If the first character in the line is a space, the name from the previous line is used. A file consists of RRs (Resource Records), listed in Table 2.1.

4.2.1 SOA Records

The **Start Of Authority** (**SOA**) record determines the name server that is an authoritative source of information for the particular domain. There is always only one SOA record in the file, and it is placed at the beginning of the file of authoritative resource records.

Example 1: The record for the server of the company.com zone:

```
@   IN SOA ns.company.com  .hostmaster.company.com (
                                 1            ;Serial
                                 86400        ;Refresh after 24 hours
                                 600          ;Retry after 5 min.
                                 120960       ;Expire after 2 weeks
                                 86400)       ;Minimum TTL of 1 day
```

The explanation of the code is as follows:

- The name must start immediately on the first position of the line and must have a dot at the end. It specifies the name of a zone. Usually @ is used instead of the name of the zone, which means the name of the zone should be taken from the DNS configuration files (named.boot, named.conf etc.).
- IN specifies the type of address (IN=Internet).
- SOA specifies type of record.
- The first name after SOA (ns.company.com) is the name of the primary name server, and the second name (hostmaster.company.com) defines the mailing address of the person responsible for the data of zone. Because the @ symbol has a special meaning in a SOA record, a dot must be used in the mailing address in place of it, i.e., the address will be hostmaster.company.com instead of hostmaster@company.com.
- The parenthesis shown allows the record to continue into the following lines.
- serial states the serial number of the database file version. If you change the file, you have to increase this serial number too. It is highly recommended to use the number in the yyyymmddnn format (year, month, day, and update number within this day).

  The secondary name server asks the primary name server only about an SOA record. It compares the value in the serial field of the SOA record with its own and, providing the primary name server has a serial value in the SOA record higher than the secondary name server, the zone from the primary name server is transferred to the secondary name server too.

This means that if the administrator modifies the DNS database of the primary name server and forgets to increase the value of the serial field, no secondary data will be transferred and changes will not be done in the secondary server. If you find out that the administrator of the primary name server has made this type of a mistake, the only option to repair it is to cancel the file for the particular zone in the secondary name server, terminate the named program in the secondary name server, and start it again.

The value of the serial field does not influence actions of the primary name server; i.e., if you forget to increase the value of the field in the primary name server, the changes will be made to the primary name server after restarting the name server.

- The following items state time parameters in seconds:

  o Refresh states how often secondary servers should check their data. If they discover during this check that they have data with a lower serial, they will carry out a zone transfer using the TCP protocol.

  o Retry states that if the secondary server cannot contact the primary server at the end of the refresh interval, it will keep trying to do so every x seconds (x=retry interval).

  o Expire states that if the secondary server does not manage to contact the primary server within y seconds (y=expire interval), it will stop providing information (the data is too old). The rule Expire > Refresh must be observed.

  o Minimum TTL applies to all records in the database file (as a default value), and the name server provides this value in each answer. It asks how long the other servers (nonauthoritative servers) can keep the particular record in their cache memory (zero prevents the records from being saved into the cache).

If you do not know the values usually used in the SOA record, then see RFC 1537. It recommends the following values:

For top-level domains:

```
86400    ;  Refresh          24 hours
7200     ;  Retry            2 hours
2592000  ;  Expire           30 days
345600   ;  Minimum TTL      4 days
```

For other domains:

```
28800    ;  Refresh          8 hours
7200     ;  Retry            2 hours
604800   ;  Expire           7 days
86400    ;  Minimum TTL      1 day
```

4.2.2 A Records

A (Address) records assign IP addresses to domain names of computers. The IP address cannot have a dot at the end.

Example 1:

```
company.com           IN  SOA   ...
...
www                   IN  A     172.17.14.1
www.branch            IN  A     172.17.18.1
my.branch.company.com. IN  A    172.17.14.2
your                  IN  A     10.1.1.3
...
```

In these A records, IP addresses are assigned to the following computers: `www.company.com`, `www.branch.company.com`, `my.branch.company.com`, and `your.company.com`.

4.2.3 CNAME Records

Synonyms to domain names can be created using CNAME records. This is often referred to as 'creating aliases for computer names'.

Example 2:

```
company.com           IN  SOA   ...
...
mail                  IN  A     192.1.1.2
www                   IN  CNAME mail.company.com.
...
```

Example 2 describes a situation where a company has one `mail.company.com` computer, which it also wishes to use as a WWW server. On the right side of the CNAME record must be the domain name. The IP address is assigned to this domain name by an A record. The synonym must not appear on the right side, i.e., CNAME must not point to CNAME. Example 3 shows an incorrect delegation of names.

Example 3 (incorrect):

```
company.com    IN   SOA   ...
...
mail           IN   A     192.1.1.2
www            IN   CNAME mail.company.com.
server         IN   CNAME www.company.com.
...
```

We should always write the full domain name with a dot at the end on the right side in CNAME records. If the dot is not included, the name of the domain is added. This could be used in small databases, but as the database grows, it becomes confusing, and any potential mistakes of this kind are sometimes very difficult to trace.

4.2.4 HINFO and TXT Records

HINFO and TXT records are for information only. An HINFO record has two items in its data part. The first item is information about hardware, and the second one is information about software. A TXT record contains a general data string in its data part.

Example 4:

```
company.com    IN   SOA   ...
...
mail           IN   A     192.1.1.2
               IN   HINFO AlphaServer UNIX
               IN   TXT   my favorite server
...
```

4.2.5 NS Records

NS records define authoritative name servers for a zone. The right side must include a name to which an IP address is assigned by an A record. The right side must not include a synonym, i.e., an NS record must not point to a CNAME record.

There are always identical NS records in two databases:

1. In the database of a superordinate zone. These NS records delegate authority to a subordinate name server.

2. In the database of subordinate zone. Database on subordinate zone contains authoritative data for zone only.

> If the domain name of the subordinate name server is in a subordinate domain, a glue A record with the IP address of the name server must follow this NS record. This is necessary because the superordinate name server has to know a link to the IP address of the subordinate name server. This link is included as additional information in its DNS response.

The same NS records are in the database in an authoritative name server for the zone, i.e., according to the terminology of the previous paragraph in the lower-level name server.

Example 5:

An authoritative name server of a higher-level zone, company.com, delegates authority for the domain, branch.company.com, to the ns.branch.company.com server. As the subordinate name server is a part of the subordinate domain, it is necessary to add a glue A record (nonauthoritative) in the superordinate zone for the ns.branch.company.com computer:

```
company.com        IN  SOA    ...
                   IN  NS     ns.provider.net.
                   IN  NS     ns.company.com.
ns                 IN  A      11.1.1.1
branch             IN  NS     ns.company.com.
                   IN  NS     ns.branch.company.com.
ns.branch          IN  A      11.2.2.2
...
```

The name server of the branch.company.com domain, i.e., the authoritative name server of a lower-level domain has the following database available:

```
branch.company.com IN  SOA    ...
                   IN  NS  ns.company.com.
                   IN  NS  ns.branch.company.com.
ns                 IN  A   11.2.2.2
...
```

Again, it is necessary to point out that it is a good idea to type the full domain address with a dot at the end on the right side of NS records.

4.2.6 MX Records

MX records specify the mailing server of the domain. The reason for this is that in most cases, we do not want an email address in the format `user@computer.company.com`; instead it is preferred to use `user@company.com`, i.e., we wish to hide the name of the mail server.

An MX record shows to which computer a mail of a particular domain should be sent. The MX record also includes a priority number, which can be used to determine several computers where the mail for the domain can be sent. The first attempt is to deliver the mail to the computer with the highest priority (lowest value). If this attempt fails, the mail goes to the next computer (with a higher priority value), and so on.

Example 6 describes a situation where the mail for the `company.com` domain should be sent to the `mail.company.com` computer. If this computer is not accessible, the mail is sent to the `mail1.provider.net` computer, where it waits until the `mail.company.com` computer is accessible. If the `mail1.provider.net` computer is not accessible either, the mail is sent to the `mail2.provider.net` computer.

Example 6:

```
company.com      IN  SOA    ...
                 IN  MX     30 mail2.provider.net
                 IN  MX     20 mail1.provider.net
                 IN  MX     10 mail.company.com
mail             IN  A      11.1.1.8
...
```

4.2.7 PTR Records

A **Pointer Record (PTR)** is used to translate an IP address into a domain name, i.e., to translate items from `in-addr.arpa` domain to the computer name.

Example 7:

PTR records for the `ns.company.com` computer with IP address 195.47.200.1 and for the `www.company.com` computer with IP address 195.47.200.201:

```
200.47.195.in-addr.arpa.  IN  SOA    ....
1                         IN  PTR    ns.company.com.
201                       IN  PTR    www.company.com.
```

(Do not forget to add a dot (.) at the end of the record otherwise, you will produce a mistake `'ns.company.com.200.47.195.in-addr.arpa.'`.)

However, this example is completely out of context. In practice, it is necessary to take into consideration a whole sequence of delegations. This example is described in more detail in example 8.

Example 8:

Let us assume that our company (`company.com`) has assigned IP address interval 195.47.200.0/24, i.e., the whole class C network. In this case for reverse translation:

1. A delegation of 195.in-addr.arpa zone to name servers for Europe (RIPE), ns.ripe.net, is implemented in Internet root servers. If the root servers used named version 4 program, the delegation would be carried out in the following manner:

   o The following line would be placed in the named.boot file:
   ```
   primary.    root.db
   ```

   o The root.db file among other lines would include:
   ```
   195.in-addr.arpa  IN  NS    ns.ripe.net
   ns.ripe.net       IN  A     193.0.0.193
   195.in-addr.arpa  IN  NS    ns.apnic.net
   ns.apnic.net      IN  A     203.37.255.97
   195.in-addr.arpa  IN  NS    munnari.oz.au
   munnari.oz.au     IN  A     128.250.22.2
                     IN  A     128-.250.1.21
                     IN  AAAA  2001:388:c02:4000::1:21
   ...
   ```

   (Zone 195.in-addr.arpa is so important that it currently has 12 authoritative servers spread worldwide.)

2. In the ns.ripe.net name server, i.e., a higher-level name server for Europe (the Netherlands, Amsterdam):

   o Example of a line that would be placed in the named.boot file:
   ```
   primary    195.in-addr.arpa    195.rev
   ```

   o Example of lines that would be placed in 195.rev file:
   ```
   195.in-addr.arpa.  IN  SOA       ...
   ...
   200.47             IN  NS    ns.company.com.
                      IN  NS    ns.provider.net.
   ```

3. In the ns.company.com name server (primary name server):

   o Example of a line that would be placed in the named.boot file:
   ```
   primary 200.47.195.in-addr.arpa    200.47.195.rev
   ```

   o Example of lines that would be placed in the file 200.47.195.rev:
   ```
   200.47.195.in-addr.arpa   IN  SOA     ...
                             IN  NS    ns.company.com.
                             IN  NS    ns.provider.net.
   1                         IN  PTR   ns.company.com.
   201                       IN  PTR   www.company.com.
   ...
   ```

4. In the name server ns.provider.net (secondary name server):

   Example of a line that would be placed in the named.boot file:
   ```
   secondary    200.47.195.in-addr.arpa    195.47.200.1 200.47.195.rev
   ```

It is necessary to point out once more that dots after the name of the computer (on the right side) must not be omitted, because if the dot is omitted, the domain ending in-addr.arpa is added and the name cannot be used.

You are probably expecting that it will be pointed out that the synonym (CNAME) must not be on the right side, i.e., the PTR record cannot point to a CNAME record. However, this is not true. This was considered a mistake in the BIND system for many years, but after some time, it became a useful tool and later became even a norm (RFC 2317). Chapter 7 deals with the use of this mechanism.

4.2.8 SRV Records

The SRV record was implemented as an experiment in RFC 2052 and then definitely established in RFC 2782. The main difference between these two norms is the fact that RFC 2782 uses an underscore (_) before the name of the service and protocol. Windows 2000 prefers to use SRV records.

The purpose of the SRV record is not only to keep the names of computers, but also the names of services in the DNS database. We have already encountered a similar example before—it was in MX records with electronic mail as a service. MX records specify the mailing servers to which the mail should be sent. The priority defines which mailing server should be contacted first and which mailing servers should follow.

Let us look closer at an example of a WWW server. When we want to see information about some firm, for example, Company Ltd., we type `http://www.company.com/` into the address field of our browser, i.e., we want to use HTTP to contact a WWW server from the `company.com` domain. However, it is only an unwritten rule (a custom) that web servers are called WWW.

The SRV record systematically enters into DNS the information necessary for the detection of the particular web server. In this case, we are looking for a name in DNS (HTTP uses the TCP protocol for its transport):

`_http._tcp.www.company.com`

SRV record syntax is as follows (the code in the DNS protocol has a value 33 for the SRV record):

`_Service_Protocol.domain name [TTL] IN SRV Priority Weight Port Target-computer.`

Each element from this syntax is explained as follows:

- `Service` specifies a symbolic name of the service (server) such as LDAP, HTTP, SMTP, and so on.

- `Protocol` specifies the protocol such as TCP or UDP.

- `Priority` determines the priority. The company can operate a number of WWW servers to make sure that if any failure occurs, one of the servers will be accessible. The company will want to determine the priority, i.e., which server the client should try to contact first and which it should try to contact next.

- The company's server may be heavily loaded and the company therefore operates a number of parallel web servers of the same priority. Every one of these will be running on a computer with a different output. That is why the `weight` is introduced (weight in the sense of weighted average). DNS includes records such as:

  ```
  _http._tcp.www.company.com    IN  SRV 10    1  80  server1.company.com.
                                IN  SRV 10    3  88  server2.company.com.
  ```

  As both records have the same priority (10), if both of them are accessible, the client can contact either of them randomly. However, the `server2.company.com` has higher output than `server1.company.com`. Therefore the `weight` says that the servers should be contacted randomly, but if a great number of connections are made, 25% of the connections should be made with `server1.company.com` and 75% of the connections should be made with `server2.company.com`, i.e., server 2 has three times as high an output as server1.

Zero weight is for administrators, i.e., no load balancing of the computers is made.

- `Port` specifies the port the server is running on.

- `Target-computer` specifies the name of the computer (link to an A record) on which the service is provided (on which the server is running). If only a dot is inserted instead of the computer name, the service is not provided.

Here is an example:

```
$ORIGIN company.com
@         IN        SOA ...
          IN        NS ...
...
; the following lines specify that the telnet protocol should be used to
; contact ether
; server1 or server2. Server2 has three times as high of an output.
_telnet_tcp  IN    SRV 0   1   23  server1.company.com.
             IN    SRV 0   3   23  server2.company.com.
; if neither server1, nor server2 are accessible, the administrator should
; contact
; server3:
             IN SRV 10  0   23  server3.company.com.
; Two www-servers are being operated. A client should contact server1 on port
; 80 and
; if the computer server1 is inaccessible,
; he should contact server2 on port 88:
_http._tcp   IN SRV 0   0   80  server1.company.com.
             IN SRV 5   0   88  server2.company.com.
; As it is a convention to write www before the name of the domain in HTTP
protocol
; we will add:
_http._tcp.www IN  SRV 0   0   80  server1.company.com.
               IN  SRV 5   0   88  server2.company.com.
; We mustn't forget A records. We will use @ to specify the current
; domain (to make sure that its name is not taken from the previous record):
@         IN    A    10.1.1.2
          IN    A    10.1.1.2
; Of course, we will also state A records of the individual servers:
server1 IN   A    10.1.1.1
server2 IN   A    10.1.1.2
server3 IN   A    10.1.13
; Other services are not supported:
*._tcp IN SRV 0   0   0
*._tcp IN SRV 0   0   0
```

A description of the asterix (*) is given in Section 4.2.11.

4.2.9 $ORIGIN

The domain name is stated in the name parameter of a database record either absolutely (with a dot at the end) or relatively (without a dot at the end). The default domain is added automatically after a relative domain name. The $ORIGIN command is used to change the default domain. The DNS database may contain the following command:

$ORIGIN default_domain

In this case the default domain is modified according to the value stated as the first parameter of the $ORIGIN command.

If a relative name is stated, it is changed into a complete name by adding the domain specified in the SOA record or defined by a parameter of the $ORIGIN command that precedes the database record. The $ORIGIN command then changes the default domain.

If the default domain is not changed by the $ORIGIN command, the domain from the SOA record is used. If the SOA record has the @ symbol instead of the domain, the first parameter of the primary or secondary command from the etc/named.boot file is used.

4.2.10 $INCLUDE

Another file can be inserted into the source file on the disk using the following command:

`$INCLUDE file`

The file is inserted in the same location as a command. It is also possible to state:

`$INCLUDE file default_domain`

This way you both insert a file and change the default domain. The change in the default domain is only valid for the lines of the inserted file.

4.2.11 Asterix (*) in a DNS Name

We can use an asterix (*) as a wild card character in a DNS name. But how does an asterix work? Let's look at an example using an A record:

`*.company.com  IN  A   10.1.1.10`

DNS will answer any query about an item of the company.com domain not explicitly stated in DNS that its address is 10.1.1.10, i.e., computer1.company.com has the address 10.1.1.10, computer2.company.com also has the address 10.1.1.10, and so on. Even if we want it to be so and if we make a mistake and write compter1.company.com instead of computer1.company.com, DNS will not answer that we made a mistake, but it will give us an address, which is most likely to be a different address to the one we would have expected.

> Throughout the book, we have consistently tried to avoid the use of an asterisk in domain names. Our experience has proven that the use of an asterisk in domain names lead to unexpected errors. Therefore, they are only used in MX records, and they might be used in the future for SRV records.

4.3 Name Server Implementation in BIND

The format of individual records in DNS databases was established by the BIND system. Name servers appeared later, but the original DNS database format remained unchanged. Windows 2000 also uses this format. (Of course, if Windows 2000 stores primary text database files into the Active Directory, everything is transformed into the standard format of Active Directory.)

First, let us examine version 4 of the BIND system, which should not be ignored.

4.3.1 named Program in BIND Version 4 System

The name server of the BIND system is implemented by the named program. We are now going to focus on version 4, which is easy to understand and forms the basis of the succeeding versions. The configuration of this version is very simple. It is also recommended for administrators of Windows 2000 networks to familiarize themselves with this version because the name server implemented in Windows 2000 server can be operated not only by using Windows, but also by editing configuration files, whose format is based on the BIND system version 4.

The named program first reads the named.boot configuration file at startup. At startup it also reads the DNS databases from the disk and loads them into the cache memory according to instructions specified in the named.boot file. By default, the named.boot configuration file is located in the /etc directory. Any different location of the configuration file must be specified by a parameter in the command line starting the named program. The named.boot configuration file contains the following commands:

- directory: Specifies a directory on the disk, where the DNS databases are stored. Within commands, the names of files are specified without their paths. For example:

  directory   /etc/namedb

- primary: Specifies that the name server will be the primary name server for the zone stated as the first parameter in the command and the relevant database is in the text file stated as the second parameter. For example:

  primary company.com db.company.com

  Every name server (including caching-only name servers) must be a primary name server at least for the 0.0.127.in-addr.arpa domain. For example, even when caching the name server, only the configuration file must include a command such as the following:

  primary   0.0.127.in-addr.arpa   db.0.0.127

- secondary: Specifies that the name server will be a secondary name server for the zone specified by the first parameter. The following parameters (must be stated as IP addresses) are IP addresses of servers, from which data will be transferred with the help of the named-xfer program. If the last parameter is included (which cannot be stated in the IP address format), it is then understood as the name of the file in which the data should be saved after it has been transferred. For example:

  secondary   branch.company.com 172.17.14.1   172.17.18.1   branch.company
  .com.tmp

  This example tells us that authoritative data of branch.company.com domain should be acquired by the zone transfer query from the server 172.17.14.1 and saved in file branch.company.com.tmp. If this server is inaccessible, the data will be copied from server 172.17.18.1.

  If the name of a file is not stated (the last parameter is omitted), the transferred data is not saved into a disk (it is only saved into the cache).

- `cache`: Determines the file from which the information about root name servers should be copied into the memory. For example:

  `cache        cache.db`

  This says that information about root name servers from the `cache.db` file should be loaded into the memory. This file does not include authoritative data, i.e., it does not include the SOA record at the beginning so all data must be explicitly stated in every record—especially, the TTL field.

  However, it is important to realize that the root name server itself does not have the `cache` command in the configuration file. Instead of that the following command is used:

  `primary db.root`

  In this case the `db.root` file will include the data similar to the `cache.db` file. At the beginning it will include an SOA record. The particular records of the file may not include a TTL field; its value will be taken from the SOA record.

- `forwarders`: Specifies that the local name server should hand queries over to the forwarder server. Other parameters stated are IP addresses of name servers accessible on the Internet, which will carry out the translation themselves. For example:

  `forwarders 193.85.240.40 193.85.240.40`

No, it was not a mistake when the same IP address was typed twice. This is a common trick in the case of forwarders. This increases the timeout for which the local server waits for a reply from a forwarder before it starts contacting root name servers itself.

- `slave`: Follows after the `forwarders` command if we want the local server to work as a slave server, i.e., in any case, the name server must not contact root name servers. For example:

  ```
  forwarders 193.85.240.40 193.85.240.40
  slave
  ```

Here is an example of a configuration file for the primary name server of the `company.com` domain:

```
directory   /etc/namedb
primary     company.com         db.company.com
primary     17.172.in-addr.arpa db.172.17
primary     0.0.127.in-addr.arpa db.127.0.0
cache       .                   db.cache
```

4.3.2 New Generation BIND

BIND has changed completely from version 8. The new versions of BIND support some new DNS mechanisms.

Versions from 8.1 onwards support:

- Dynamic update (RFC 2136)
- DNS notify (RFC 1996)
- Incremental zone transfer, IXFR (RFC 1995)

Versions from 8.2 onwards support:

- Negative caching (RFC 2308)
- DNS clarifications (RFC 2181)
- DNSsec (RFC 2065); for more detail see Section 3.6
- Support of virtual name servers

Versions from 8.2.2 onwards support interoperability with Windows 2000.

Versions from 9 onwards support:

- View support, known as split DNS
- New types of RR for the translation of domain names to IPv6
- Reverse domain `ip6.arpa` and bit-string format for transcription of the IPv6 reverse domain

Now, an overview of the main changes in implementation of BIND 8.x compared to BIND 4.x is as follows:

- BIND 8 uses the new `/etc/named.conf` configuration file; this configuration file has both new names and new syntax
- BIND 8 enables configure message logging in detail
- BIND 8 enables access control according to ACL
- BIND 8 uses a new master/slave architecture

And an overview of the main changes in implementation of BIND 9.x compared to BIND 8.x is as follows:

- Method of dealing with mistakes in zone files and `named.conf` configuration file
- `$TTL` command
- BIND 9 uses 'many-answer format' for the zone transfer as default
- Administrative tools, `program.rndc`
- BIND 9 is a multithread application
- Support for checking the domain names
- A new library for the resolver known as the **Lightweight resolver**
- Full support for IPv6

There are distributions of the BIND system for various operating systems. We tested the distribution for UNIX as well as for Windows. The distribution for Windows even had a number of additional advantages:

- The distribution is already compiled. (However, compilation of version 9 is complicated by the fact that its distribution, unlike the previous versions, does not include OpenSSL; so if you want to activate DNSsec, you have to compile OpenSSL first.)

- This name server can also run in Windows versions that are not servers themselves, i.e., in Windows 2000 Professional or Windows XP.

- Testing programs (such as dig) are a part of the distribution. These programs are practical even if you are using an original name server from Microsoft.

The Internet Systems Consortium releases new versions of BIND and informs about potential attacks and bugs. This information can be found at http://www.isc.org/.

4.3.2.1 Configuration File

The configuration file of BIND version 8 and higher is usually called /etc/named.conf. This file has a completely new syntax. The configuration file consists of statements and comments. Statements are ended by a semicolon (;). Statements and comments are the only elements that can appear without enclosing braces. Many statements contain a block of substatements, which are also ended by a semicolon.

Configuration files used in BIND 4.9.x can be converted into the new format using a Perl script named bootconf.pl, which is a part of the BIND 8 source kit.

If the named.conf file has mistakes, the startup of BIND 9 will end with a fatal error. The previous BIND versions usually started up even though some of their functions did not work correctly.

Although the syntax of the configuration file of the new generation BIND is completely different from the configuration file in version 4, the DNS database syntax (SOA, A, PTR, NS, and other resource records) is unchanged in versions 8 and 9 (see Section 4.2). The database files for BIND version 9 are extended, for example, by new RR types of records. Descriptions of these extensions can be found in Section 4.3.2.2.

Configuration File Statements

A list of configuration file statements is as follows:

- acl: Defines a named IP address matching list for access control and other uses.

- control: Defines the control channels used by the rndc utility. (This statement is used from version 9 onwards.)

- include: Includes a file.

- key: Specifies key information for use in authentication and authorization using TSIG.

- logging: Specifies what the server logs and where the log messages are stored.

- options: Controls global server configuration options and sets defaults for other statements.

- server: Sets certain configuration options on a per server basis.

- trusted-keys: Defines trusted DNSsec keys. (This statement is used from version 9 onwards.)

- view: Defines a view. (This statement is used from version 9 onwards.)

- zone: Defines a zone.

The logging and option statements can only be used once in the configuration file.

Some statements of the configuration file can have a great number of parameters. However, a description of all parameters would probably make this chapter the most boring part of this book. Therefore it was decided to describe in detail only the most commonly used parameters. To make sure that readers do not feel that they are missing out, the full syntax for every statement is included.

Examples of Name Server Configuration

For a start, let's look at a couple of examples of configurations for different types of servers.

Example 1: Caching-only name server

```
#
# caching-only name server
#
// Two corporate subnets we wish to allow queries from
acl "my-networks" {195.47.37.0/24; 195.47.31.0/24; };      // definition of the
                                                           // IP addresses group
options {
    directory "/etc/namedb";     // Working  directory, in which also zone
                                 // files are stored
    pid-file "named.pid";        // Put pid file in working dir
    allow-query {"my-networks";}; // The server will deal with queries from
                                 // IP addresses from the my-networks group
};
//root name servers - hint zone
zone "." {type hint; file "root.hint";};
//reverse mapping for 127.0.0.1
zone "0.0.127.in-addr.arpa"{
    type master;
    file "localhost.rev";
    notify no;
};
```

Example 2: An authoritative-only name server

```
#
#first named.conf
#

options {
        directory /etc/master"; // Working directory
    pid-file "named.pid";       // Put pid file in working dir
    allow-query { any; };       // This is the default
    recursion no;               // Do not provide recursive service
    } ;
    logging {
    channel protocol {          // Definition of the channel for recording
errors
        file "log/protocol.txt" versions 5 ;
            severity debug;
        } ;
    channel output {
        file "log/output.log";
    category default {          // Assigning category default to the channel
protocol
        protocol;
        } ;
    category ncache {
        output;
        } ;
    category db {
        output;
        } ;
        } ;
```

```
    zone "." in {                    // Zone hint
        type hint;
        file "named.cache";
    } ;
    zone "abcde.com" in { // Name server is primary for the abcde.com domain
        type master;
        notify yes;
        file "abcde.com.zone";
    } ;
    zone "company.com" in {    // Name server is secondary for the company.com
        domain   type slave;
        masters {194.149.105.18;} ;
        file "company.com.zone";
    } ;
```

Comments

Comments in the configuration file can be in three formats:

```
/* in a format identical to C */
```

```
// in a format identical to C++
```

```
# in a format identical to Perl
```

A comment in the C style format (/*...*/) can mark a commentary text in a part of the line or a text of several lines. On the other hand, a comment in the C++ or Perl style format always means a one line comment. To be more specific, the text from // or # to the end of the line is considered a comment.

> Careful! Do not use a semicolon in comments because it has the meaning of the end of a statement here.

Example:

```
/* A multiple-line C style comment
   is enclosed in brackets from symbols
   asterisk and slash */

// A multiple-line C++ style comment has to start
//on every line with two slash symbols
this line is not a comment and therefore it will cause an error
//

# A comment in the Perl style
# The following line of the comment
```

acl Statement

Syntax:

```
acl name {
    address_match_list
} ;
```

Description:

The acl statement assigns a symbolic name to an address match list, primarily used for the **Access Control List (ACL)**. This list must be defined before it is used anywhere.

The following ACLs are built-in:

- `any`: Matches all hosts
- `none`: Matches no hosts
- `localhost`: Matches the IPv4 addresses of all network interfaces on the system
- `localnets`: Matches any host on an IPv4 network for which the system has an interface

address_match_list

Address match lists are primarily used to determine access control for various server operations. The elements that constitute an address match list can be any of the following:

- an IP address (IPv4 or IPv6)
- an IP prefix (in the / notation)
- a key ID as defined by the `key` statement
- the name of an address match list previously defined with the `acl` statement
- a nested address match list enclosed in brackets

Elements can be negated with a leading exclamation mark (`!`), and the match list names any, `none`, `localhost`, and `localnets` are predefined.

Every list is searched from left to right. If a suitable item is found, the process of searching ends. Positive comparisons enable access, negative comparisons deny access. If a particular IP address is not found in the list, access is denied for the computer accessing from this particular IP address.

An IP list defined in this manner can be used in `allow-query`, `allow-transfer`, `allow-update`, and `listen-on` parameters of other statements.

Example:

```
1.2.3/24;! 1.2.3.13;    # 1.2.3.13 is completely redundant
! 1.2.3.13; 1.2.3/24;   # Correct, the access is denied only for IP 1.2.3.13,
                        # other addresses from 1.2.3 have enabled access.
```

controls Statement

Syntax:

```
controls {
inet (ip_adr | *) [port.ip_port] allow {address_match_list} keys {key_list};
```

Description:

The `controls` statement declares control channels used by the `rndc` administrator utility for sending signals to the name server. The channel is defined in the `inet` attribute by an IP address and port. By default, port 953 will be used. Signals from the network can be sent using this channel. The use of this channel is enabled for hosts stated in the `allow` clause using a key stated in the `keys` clause.

`allow`: A list of IP addresses (ACL list) that have access to the channel. If the name of the key is a part of the ACL list, this name is ignored.

`keys`: List of names of keys that can be used for authentication of the access to the channel. Keys are used to sign a message sent into the channel.

If the `controls` statement is not present in the configuration file, the name server defines the default channel defined by IP address 127.0.0.1 or ::1 (IPv6) and port 953. A key stored in the `/etc/rndc.key` file can be used to sign the message. The `rndc-confgen-a` utility ensures the creation of the `/etc/rndc.key` key.

The `named.conf` configuration file without the `controls` statement can be used in transition from BIND version 8 to version 9. The default channel we just described earlier is then used for the `rndc` utility. The only thing that needs to be done is to ensure that the relevant key is created. After the transition to BIND 9, the key can be generated using the `rndc-keygen-a` utility. Example of using the `controls` statement is included in Section 5.2.

include Statement

Syntax:

```
include path;
```

Description:

The `include` statement includes the specified file into the place where the include statement is situated. The `include` statement cannot be used inside another statement. An example of *incorrect* usage:

```
acl int_host { "include ost_host_acl"} ;
```

Example:

```
include "/etc/security/keys.bind";
include "/etc/acls.bind";
```

key Statement

Syntax:

```
key key_id {
    algorithm algorithm_id;
    secret secret_string;
} ;
```

Description:

The `key` statement defines shared secret keys used with TSIG. The `key` statement can occur at the top level of the configuration file or inside a `view` statement. Keys defined in top-level `key` statements can be used in all views. Keys intended for use in a `controls` statement must be defined at the top level.

Keys are identified using the `key_id` identifier (also known as the key name), which is in domain name format. The `key` statement will also be used to define the key used by the `rndc` program.

`Algorithm_id` is a string that specifies the authentication algorithm. The only supported algorithm with TSIG is HMAC-MD5. `secret_string` is a secret used by the algorithm and is treated as a Base-64 encoded string. A key defined in this manner can be used in the `server` statement or as an item in the ACL list. An example for using the `controls` statement is given in Section 5.2.

logging Statement

Syntax:

```
logging {
    [channel channel_name {
      (file path_name
        [versions ( number | unlimited )]
        [size size_spec]
      | syslog(kern | user | mail | daemon | auth | syslog | lpr |
            news | uucp | cron | authpriv | ftp |
            local0 | local1 | local2 | local3 |
            local4 | local5 | local6 | local7 )
      | stderr
      | null );

      [ severity ( critical | error | warning | notice |
                   info | debug [ level ] | dynamic ); ]
      [ print-category yes_or_no; ]
      [ print-severity yes_or_no; ]
      [ print-time yes_or_no; ]
    } ;]

    [ category category_name {
      channel_name; [ channel_name; ...]
    } ;]

    ...
} ;
```

Description:

The logging statement configures a wide variety of logging options for the name server. It defines the types of events that should be logged, in what format, and where the individual types of messages should be logged. Theoretically, it is possible to use more logging statements in the configuration, but only the first logging statement will be used.

The name server divides the types of messages into groups called categories (category). Let's look at some examples of a category. The config category contains error messages relating to the configuration file. The category called default has a special position. It includes all other categories with the exception of those that are stated directly in the logging statement. A list of all categories of error messages can be found in the name server documentation, which is a part of every distribution.

Messages of a certain category are logged through **channels**. The channel defines where and in what format the message should be logged. Like categories, channels too have their own names.

The logging statement defines which category should log into which channel. If a category is not directed to any channel, this category will be logged in the same channel as the default category. If the logging statement does not include the default category or if the logging statement is not stated at all, the following default setting will be used:

category "default" {"default_syslog";"default_debug";};

One logging statement can define any number of channels and categories.

The `logging` statement is activated in BIND 9 after running the whole `named.conf`. This is different from the previous version 8, where the statement was activated at the moment it appeared in `named.conf`, i.e., it was activated sooner. Therefore, your search for error messages that occurred during the BIND 9 startup in the special channels will be in vain. Messages about the server startup are always logged in the default channel or, if you use the -g switch, in the standard system error file.

Now let's look at the channel definition in detail.

For every channel, you have to define where the events should be logged, what severity of an error the channel should log, and whether or not you require logging time stamps.

The channel can log messages:

- in a file (`file` option). You can define the maximum size and number of versions for the file.

- in a system log (`syslog` option). Logging is controlled by the `syslog.conf` configuration file.

- in an error system log (`stderr` option).

- nowhere (`null` option).

Here is an example of a channel definition called `test_channel`:

```
logging {
  channel "test_channel" {
    file "test.log"versions 4;
    print-time yes;
    print-category yes;
    print-severity yes;
    severity warning;
  };
  category default {
    test_channel;
  };
};
```

The channel named `test_channel` used in this example will log messages into the `test.log` file. A new file will be opened while restarting the server and the old file will be renamed. The current version has number 0. Four versions of the file will be stored; older versions will be automatically deleted. The size of a file is not limited. Time stamps, the category of the particular message, and the severity of the error will be logged in the file. Errors of warning and higher severity will be recorded in the channel. All types of messages will be logged into this channel, i.e., messages of all categories.

The `named` program has four predefined channels, which are as follows:

```
channel "default_syslog" { #  Send to syslog's daemon facility.
    severity info;          #  Only send priority info and higher.
    syslog daemon;          #  (Syslog daemon is part of the operating
                            #  system)
} ;

channel "default_debug" {
    file "named.run";  # Messages are logged in the named.run file
                       #  in the working directory.
    severity dynamic;  # Messages according to the currently
                       #  set debug level are logged.
```

```
    } ;

    channel "default_stderr" {# Messages are logged in stderr
        stderr;
        severity info;
    } ;
    channel "null" {
        null;               # All messages sent to this
                            # channels are thrown away.
    } ;
```

Apart from these four predefined channels, the DNS server administrator can define other channels as well. However, once the channel is defined, it is impossible to change its definition.

However, the use of the channels can be modified by changing the assignment of categories to the individual channels.

By default, all messages generated by the program are sent to the `default_syslog`; and `default_debug`; channels, i.e., into the system log and the `named.run` file in the work directory respectively.

options Statement

Syntax:

```
options {
    [version version_string]
    [directory path_name]
    [tkey-domain domainname; ]
    [tkey-dhkey key_name key_tag]
    [dump-file path_name]
    [memstatistics-file path_name]
    [pid-file path_name]
    [statistics-file path_name]
    [zone-statistics yes_or_no]
    [auth-nxdomain yes_or_no]
    [dialup dialup_option]
    [minimal-responses yes_or_no]
    [multiple-cnames yes_or_no]
    [notify yes_or_no | explicit; ]
    [recursion yes_or_no; ]
    [forward ( only | first );]
    [forwarders { ip_addr [port ip_port] ; [ip_addr [port ip_port] ; ...] };]
    [check-names ( master | slave | response )( warn | fail | ignore ); ]
    [allow-notify { address_match_list };]
    [allow-query { address_match_list };]
    [allow-transfer { address_match_list };]
    [allow-recursion { address_match_list };]
    [allow-v6-syntetics { address_match_list };]
    [blackhole { address_match_list };]
    [listen-on [port ip_port] { address_match_list };]
    [listen-on-v6 [port ip_port] { address_match_list };]
    [query-source [ address (ip_addr | *)][port (ip_port | *)];]
    [max-transfer-time-in number; ]
    [max-transfer-time-out number; ]
    [max-transfer-idle-in number; ]
    [max-transfer-idle-out number; ]
    [tcp-clients number; ]
    [recursive-clients number; ]
    [serial-query-rate number; ]
    [serial-queries number; ]
    [transfer-format ( one-answer | many-answers ); ]
    [transfer-in number; ]
```

```
        [transfer-out number; ]
        [transfers-per-ns number; ]
        [transfer-source (ip4_addr | *) [port ip_port] ; ]
        [transfer-source-v6 (ip6_addr | * [port ip_port] ; ]
        [notify-source (ip4_addr | *) [port ip_port] ; ]
        [notify-source-v6 (ip6_addr | *) [port ip_port] ; ]
        [also-notify { ip_addr [port ip_port] ; [ip_addr [port ip_port] ; ...] };]
        [max-ixfr-log-size number; ]
        [coresize size_spec ; ]
        [datasize size_spec ; ]
        [files size_spec ; ]
        [stacksize size_spec ; ]
        [cleaning-interval number; ]
        [heartbeat-interval number; ]
        [interface-interval number; ]
        [sortlist { address_match_list };]
        [lame-ttl number; ]
        [max-ncache-ttl number; ]
        [max-cache-ttl number; ]
        [sig-validity-interval number ; ]
        [use-ixfr yes_or_no; ]
        [provide-ixfr yes_or_no; ]
        [request-ixfr yes_or_no; ]
        [treat-cr-as-space yes_or_no ; ]
        [min-refresh-time number ; ]
        [max-refresh-time number ; ]
        [min-retry-time number ; ]
        [max-retry-time number ; ]
        [port ip_port; ]
        [additional-from-auth yes_or_no; ]
        [additional-from-cache yes_or_no; ]
        [random-device path_name; ]
        [max-cache-size size_spec ; ]
        [match-mapped-addresses yes_or_no; ]
    };
```

Description:

The options statement sets global options for the named program. This statement can be used in the configuration file only once. If this statement is not used, the default settings are used.

Parameters of the options Statement
This section discusses the parameters of the options statement.

File Specification
directory: This is the server's working directory. The directory must be stated in the absolute path format. Every relative directory path stated in the configuration file is evaluated in relation to the server's working directory. Most of the server's outgoing files are placed by default in this directory. If this directory is not specified, the directory from which the server was started is considered the default directory.

named-xfer: This is a path to the named-xfer program, which the server uses for incoming zone transfers. If the path is not specified, it is taken from the system. BIND version 9 system doesn't use the special named-xfer program for incoming zone transfers. All functions of the named-xfer program are implemented in the named program version 9; therefore, this parameter is no longer used in version 9.

dump-file: This is the pathname of the file the server dumps the database to when instructed to do so with the rndc dumpdb program. If it is not specified, the default is named_dump.db.

pid-file: This is the pathname of the file to which the server writes its process ID. If it is not specified, the default is /etc/named.pid or /var/run/named.pid. The .pid file is used by programs that want to send signals to the running name server.

statistics-file: This is the pathname of the file to which the server appends statistics. The server writes statistics after receiving a **SIGKILL** signal or a signal from the rndc stats program. If the pathname is not specified, named.stats is used by default.

Boolean Options

auth-nxdomain: If this parameter is set to the yes value, the AA bit is always set in the NXDOMAIN answer (negative answer) even if the server is not an authority. The default value for version 8 is yes, whereas for version 9 it is no.

fetch-glue: The default value is yes. If the set value is yes, the server adds glue records. The no setting can be used in connection with 'recursion no'. This parameter is not used in version 9.

multiple-cnames: If the yes value is set for this parameter, multiple RR CNAMEs are allowed.

notify: If the yes value is set for this parameter, the server sends the *notify* message when the zone for which the server is an authority changes. This message is sent to all servers specified in NS records and in the also-notify parameter. The default value for this parameter is yes. A subordinate server that receives and understands this message contacts the main server for the particular zone and, if it finds out that a zone transfer is necessary, it will immediately perform the action. The use of notify speeds up the convergence between the main server and its subordinate servers. The no value needs to be set for this parameter if the notify messages cause errors or cause the slave server to crash. This option can also be set in the zone statement, in which case it has priority before the setting in the option statement.

recursion: If the yes value is set for this parameter and a DNS query requests a recursion, the server will try to solve this query. If the no value is set for this parameter and the server does not know the answer directly, it will refer the client to a higher authority. The default value for this parameter is yes.

Forwarding

Forwarding decreases the traffic on lines leading to external name servers. Forwarding only occurs if the server is not an authority for the particular query and does not have the particular response to the query in its cache memory.

forward: This parameter is used with a list of servers to which the queries should be forwarded in the forwarders parameter. The default value for this parameter is first. The value first means that the server first contacts the forwarder server to solve the query and only if the forwarder does not manage does the server try to solve this query itself. The value only means that the server contacts the forwarder to solve the query and does not try to solve it itself.

forwarders: This parameter specifies the IP addresses of servers for forwarding. By default, the list is empty (no forwarding is carried out).

Name Check

check-names: This option was used in BIND 8 to restrict the character set of domain names in master files and/or DNS responses received from the network. The allowed characters are letters, numbers, and a dash.

BIND 9 does not restrict the character set of domain names and does not implement the check-names option.

Access Control

Individual types of access to the server such as a query, zone transfer, etc. can be enabled for some IP addresses only.

allow-query: This parameter defines which hosts are allowed to ask a common query. If this parameter is not specified, a common query from all hosts is permitted by default. allow-query can also be stated in the zone statement, in which case this setting has priority before the setting in the option statement.

allow-transfer: This parameter defines which hosts are permitted to do a zone transfer from the server. If this parameter is not specified, a zone transfer from all hosts is permitted by default. allow-transfer can also be stated in the zone statement, in which case this setting has priority before the setting in the option statement.

Interfaces

listen-on: Interfaces and ports from which the server accepts and answers queries can be stated in this parameter. This parameter can be used many times. If the listen-on parameter is not specified, the server listens on port 53 at all interfaces.

Example:

```
listen-on { 194.149.100.33; } ;
listen-on port 2323 { !195.47.127.44; 195.47/16 } ;
```

listen-on-v6: This parameter specifies those interfaces and ports on which the server accepts and answers queries using IPv6. If this parameter is not specified, the server does not react to queries using IPv6.

Zone Transfer

max-transfer-time-in: This parameter states the number of minutes for which the zone transfer can last. If a certain zone transfer is longer, it is terminated. The default value for this parameter is 120 minutes.

transfer-format: The server supports two methods of zone transfer, namely, one-answer (one DNS message for the transfer of one RR record) and many-answer (as many RR records packed into one DNS message as possible).

BIND 9 uses the many-answer format as the default format for zone transfers. This change may cause problems if you use old versions of BIND that do not support the many-answer format as slave servers.

transfers-in: This parameter states the maximum number of parallel inbound zone transfers. The default value for this parameter is 10.

`transfers-out`: This parameter states the maximum number of parallel outbound zone transfers. The default value for this parameter is 10. This parameter is a new one in BIND version 9.

`transfers-per-ns`: This parameter states the maximum number of inbound zone transfers that can be carried out at the same time from a particular remote name server. The default value for this parameter is 2.

Periodic Task Intervals

`clean-interval`: This parameter specifies a certain number of minutes (n). The server removes invalid records from the cache every n minutes. The default value for this parameter is 60 minutes. If the parameter is set at 0 minutes, invalid records are never removed.

`statics-interval`: This parameter specifies a certain number of minutes (n). The statistics about the main server will be logged in every n minutes. The default value for this parameter is 60 minutes. If the parameter is set at 0 minutes, the statistics are not logged.

server Statement

Syntax:

```
server ip_addr {
        [bogus yes_or_no; ]
        [provide-ixfr yes_or_no; ]
        [request-ixfr yes_or_no; ]
        [edns yes_or_no; ]
        [transfer number; ]

    [transfer-format ( one-answer | many-answers ); ]

    [keys { key_id [key_id... ]} ;]
} ;
```

Description:

The `server` statement defines characteristics to be associated with a remote name server. The statement can be stated in the configuration file level or inside the `view` statement. A statement stated in `view` is decisive for the particular view.

A server that provides incorrect data can be marked as *bogus*. This will disable further queries to this server. The default value for bogus is `no`.

The name of a key used to sign a request sent to a remote server is stated in the `keys` clause. One key is defined for one server.

Other parameters in this statement have the same meanings as parameters with identical names in the `options` statement. If a particular parameter is specified in the `server` statement, the value of the parameter specified in the `options` statement is not used for that particular server.

trusted-key Statement

Syntax:

```
trusted-keys {
string number number number string;
[string number number number string; [...] ]
};
```

Description:

This statement defines the DNSsec security root. The security root is defined if the public key for a nonauthoritative zone is known, but it is not possible to acquire this key safely using DNS. As soon as this key is marked trusted, it is used as a valid key for DNSsec. The resolver requires a DNSsec validation for all data in subdomains.

The `trusted-keys` statement can contain more keys. Every key is created by a domain name of the key, characteristics, protocol, algorithm, and Base-64 encrypted key.

view Statement

Syntax:

```
view view_name [class] {
match-clients {address_match_list};
match-destinations {address_match_list};
match-recursive-only {yes_or_no}
[view option; ...]
[zone-statistics yes_or_no;]
[zone_statement; ...]
};
```

Description:

The `view` statement allows you to configure the name server in such a manner that it answers to the same DNS query differently, depending on who is asking. In this case, the server can return information for the `company.com` domain about hosts in this domain that are a part of the internal network as a response to a query from an internal network and return only information about hosts in this domain that are a part of the external network as a response to queries from an external network. Therefore, the `view` statement allows you to easily solve two different needs of one domain without needing to use two real servers and maintaining two name servers.

Each `view` statement defines a view of one DNS namespace that can be seen by a group of clients. Groups of clients are defined using ACL. The server uses the view for the translation if the IP address of the client requiring the translation, matches the list in the `match-clients` clause, and the target address is a part of the list in the `match-destinations` clause. By default, all IP addresses are set for both clauses.

The `match-recursive-only` clause means that the view will be used only for recursive translations from clients listed in the `match-client` clause.

Zones defined within a `view` statement will only be accessible to clients that match the view. By defining a zone of the same name in multiple views, different zone data can be given to different clients, for example, 'internal' and 'external' clients in a split DNS setup. Within the view, the zones are defined by the `zone` statement.

The order in which the `view` statements are placed in the `named.conf` file is important. A client's DNS query is solved within the first view the client matches in the `match-clients` and `match-destinations` clauses. Therefore, the client only sees the zones defined within this view.

One zone can be defined within several views, and it can have different contents in each view.

Most choices from the `option` statement can be used in the `view` option.

> Caution! If you decide to define a view within the `named.conf` file, then all zones must be a part of some view, i.e., the `named.conf` file will be divided between the individual views.

Example: Configuration using `view`.

```
// Name server is for two networks; a different version of the comapny.com
// domain can be seen from each network.
acl "exnet" { 194.17.165.0/24;};
acl "intent" {172.17.14.0/24;};
acl "extPM" { 172.17.14.1;};        //indication of the primary server for an
                                    external network
acl "intPM" { 172.17.14.2;};        //indication of the primary server for an
                                    internal network

options {
    directory "d:\bind\bind_exe\etc\namedb"; // working directory
    pid-file "named.pid";           //  file containing PID process
    recursion no;                   //  ban of recursive queries
allow-query { "exnet"; "intent";};// The access to the server is permitted
                                    //  for networks 194.17.165.0/24
                                        and 172.17.14.0/24

view int {                          //  zones visible for hosts from the
                                        network 172.17.14.0/24only
match-clients {172.17.14.0/24;};
option {recursion yes;};            //  permission for recursive queries for
                                        hosts in an internal network

zone "0.0.127.in-addr.arpa" {
    type master;
    file "localhost.rev";
    notify no;
};
zone "company.com" {
    type slave;                     //  for this zone the server works as a slave
                                        server
    file "int/company.zone";
    masters { intPM ;};
    notify no;
};
};

view ext {                          //  zones visible for hosts in an external
network
// from IP address 194.17.165.14. The server will not translate, for example,
// a query about company.com from IP 194.17.165.30

match-clients {!172.17.14.0/24;};
options {recursion no; };
zone "company.com" {
    type slave;
    file "ext/company.zone";
    masters {extPM};
    notify no;
};
zone "0.0.127.in-addr.arpa" {
    type master;
    file "localhost.rev";
    notify no;
};
};
```

Example: Configuration of the intPM and extPM primary servers.

```
acl "sekNS" { 172.17.57.10;}; // indication of the secondary name server
options {
    recursion no;
    allow-query { none; };  // The server does not react to any DNS queries
// for translation.
    allow-transfer { none; }; // The server does not permit zone transfer.
    notify yes;    // The server sends notification messages.
    };
zone "company.com" {
    type master:
    file "company.zone";
allow-query { sekNS; };   //The server answers to DNS queries for
// translation from the secondary server only.
allow-transfer { sekNS; };//The server permits zone transfer to
// the secondary server only.
};
```

Configuration of the extPM and intPM primary servers differs only in the contents of the company.zone database file.

In this case, the secondary server is common for both views, but each primary name server has a different IP address. Both primary servers can run in one computer. However, this computer must have two IP addresses and each name server must use its own instance of the named program with its own IP address. Are you wondering why? It's because of the way the zone.transfer query works. In the case of two identical zones in different views the zone.transfer query cannot distinguish which view to use. Therefore, it is necessary to link the primary server for each one of these views with a unique IP address.

```
Company.zone file
$ttl 86400
@       IN  SOA company.comkabelova.company.com (3 86400 600 120960 86400)
        IN  NS  ns.company.com
ns      IN  A   172.17.14.23
www     IN  A   194.17.165.31
ftp     IN  A   194.17.165.32
u1      IN  A   172.17.14.30
u2      IN  A   172.17.14.35

company_ext.zone file
$ttl 86400
@       IN  SOA company.comkabelova.company.com (6 86400 600 120960 86400)
        IN  NS  ns.company.com
ns      IN  A   172.17.14.23
www     IN  A   194.17.165.31
ftp     IN  A   194.17.165.32
```

Only the zone stored in the company.zone file is visible for hosts in network 172.17.14.0/24, but not the zone in the company_ext.zone file. Therefore, it is important in this example to state the WWW and FTP hosts (running, for example, in a demilitarized zone and therefore accessible from both the Internet and the intranet) in both zone files.

zone Statement
Syntax:

The zone statement uses three types of syntax.

Type 1:

```
zone domain_name [( in | hs | hesoid | chaos )] {
    type master;
    file path_name;
    [check-names ( warn | fail | ignore );]
    [allow-update { address_match_list } ;]
    [allow-query { address_match_list } ;]
    [allow-transfer { address_match_list } ;]
    [notify yes_or_no;]
    [also-notify { ip_addr; [ip_addr; ...] } ;
} ;
```

Type 2:

```
zone domain_name [ ( in | hes | hesoid | chaos )] {
    type (slave | stub );
    [file path_name; ]
    masters { ip_addr; [ip_addr; ...]} ;
    [check-names ( warn | fail | ignore );]
    [allow-update { address_match_list } ;]
    [allow-query { address_match_list } ;]
    [allow-transfer { address_match_list } ;]
    [max-transfer-time-in number; ]
    [notify yes_or_no;]
    [also-notify { ip_addr; [ ip_addr; ...] } ;
} ;
```

Type 3:

```
zone . [(in | hs | hesoid | chaos )] {
    type hint;
    file path_name;

    [check-names (warn | fail | ignore );]
};
```

Description:

The zone statement defines particular zones.

Let's look at a brief description of the particular zone types once more.

master: The server has a master copy of the data for the zone and will be able to provide authoritative answers for it. (Primary zone in the previous version of BIND.)

slave: A subordinate zone that is a replica of a master zone. (Secondary zone in the previous version of BIND.) The list of masters specifies one or more IP addresses of master servers the slave contacts to update its copy of the zone. If the file parameter is stated, a copy is logged into a file. The use of this file parameter is recommended.

stub: The stub zone is similar to a slave zone, except that it replicates only the NS records of a master zone instead of the entire zone. stub zones are not a standard part of the DNS; they are a feature specific to the BIND implementation.

hint: The initial set of root name servers is specified using a hint zone. When the server starts up, it uses the root hints to find a root name server and get the most recent list of root name servers. If no hint zone is specified for class IN, the server uses a compiled default set of root server hints. Classes other than IN have no built-in default hints.

forward: This is not a real zone, but a method for forwarding queries on a per-domain basis. The name server has the role of a forwarder for the forward zone. A zone statement of type forward can contain a forward and/or forwarders statement, which will apply to queries within the domain given by the zone name.

The name of a zone can be followed by a class. If the class is not specified, in (Internet) is used.

Parameters:

Most parameters of the zone statement have the same meanings as the parameters of the options statement with identical names. If a certain parameter is specified in the zone statement, its value has a higher priority than the value of the parameter in the options statement.

allow-update: This parameter defines those hosts that are permitted to carry out a dynamic update of the server. By default, the dynamic update is prohibited from all hosts.

update-policy: This parameter provides the option to set rules for the dynamic update in greater detail compared with the allow-update parameter. The permission/ban of a dynamic update can be set not only for the whole zone, but also at a domain name level or for groups of names as it is in the case of the allow-update parameter. This parameter is only implemented in version 9 and higher.

Only one of allow-update and update-policy can be used in the zone statement.

4.3.2.2 DNS Database

BIND version 9 has also brought changes in zone files. Some of the most significant changes are the $TTL and $GENERATE statements.

$TTL Statement

Every zone file must include either the $TTL statement, which defines the default TTL value for the particular zone, or every RR record must include a TTL value. If this condition is not fulfilled, the server announces an error during startup. BIND 8 was still able to use the TTL value from the SOA record.

$GENERATE Statement

This statement is used to create an RR set that provides the reverse delegation of a subnet. Every DNS administrator who has at least once defined a reverse delegation for a subnet of, for example, 128 IP addresses, would be grateful for this statement. Chapter 7 tells you that a zone file must include a number of CNAME records for the reverse delegation of a subnet. For example, in the case of a subnet of 128 IP addresses, exactly 128 records have to be stated. These CNAME records, however, only differ in one position in the IP address (in the last byte), and this number is increased in each successive record by 1. Using this statement can solve the delegation quite nicely. Let's look at an example on how to use this statement.

Example:

Sequence of statements in the zone file:

```
$ORIGIN 37.47.195.IN-ADDR.ARPA.
$GENERATE 1-2 0 NS server$.company.com.
$GENERATE 1-127 $ CNAME $.0
```

This is equivalent to a set of 128 CNAME records and 2 NS records for a reverse delegation:

```
0.37.47.195.IN-ADDR.ARPA NS server1.company.com.
0.37.47.195.IN-ADDR.ARPA NS server2.company.com.
1.37.47.195.IN-ADDR.ARPA CNAME 1.0.37.47.195.IN-ADDR.ARPA.
2.37.47.195.IN-ADDR.ARPA CNAME 2.0.37.47.195.IN-ADDR.ARPA.
...
127.37.47.195.IN-ADDR.ARPA CNAME 127.0.37.47.195.IN-ADDR.ARPA.
```

4.3.2.3 Lightweight Resolver

In connection with the support of IPv6, BIND 9 has a new solution for the translation of DNS queries. It has a new resolver library.

Older applications that needed to translate an IP into a name and vice versa used a stub resolver. These applications had compiled libraries with a resolver and therefore sent requests for translation to the local name server as described in Sections 1.9 and 1.10. However, a stub resolver does not support the translation of A6 records for the IPv6 protocol (see Section 3.5.2).

BIND 9 replaces the stub resolver with a new solution. For DNS translations, it offers the *lightweight* resolver and *lightweight resolver* daemon pair. This pair communicates together using the lwres protocol.

How does this Mechanism Function?

An application using IPv6 is compiled with an lwres library, which is an implementation of an lwres client. Applications send requests for IP address translation to the lwres daemon (`lwresd`), which is an implementation of the lwres server.

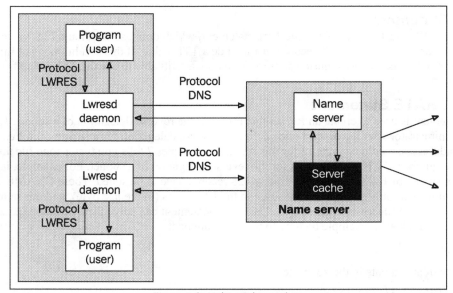

Figure 4.2: Lightweight resolver

Lwres is a simple caching-only name server. This server accepts queries from an application in the lwres protocol, transforms the queries into a DNS protocol, and sends them to a name server for resolution. Then it transforms the answer from the name server into the lwres protocol and sends it to the application. Lwres can translate both IPv4 and IPv6.

By default, Lwres accepts queries from IP 127.0.0.1 on the UDP port 921. The daemon sends queries to the name server stated in the nameserver statement in the /etc/resolv.conf file. If no server is specified in the file, or the attempt to send the query is not successful, Lwres is able to solve a DNS query independently. The /etc/resolv.conf file can be extended by the lwserver statement, which defines the IP address of the lwres daemon if it is running on a remote computer.

The lwres daemon uses its own configuration file /etc/lwres.conf. A name server can also be configured as an lwres daemon using the lwresd statement in the named.conf file.

lwres Statement
Syntax:

```
lwres {
    [listen-on { ip_addr [port ip_port] ; [ip_addr [port ip_port]; ...] };]
    [view view_name;]
    [search {domain_name ; [domain_name ; ...] }; ]
    [ndots number; ]
};
```

Description:

The most important parameter in this statement is listen-on, which defines a list of IP addresses from which the daemon accepts queries. The question is how successful this new mechanism will be in practice. BIND version 9.2 already offers a traditional stub resolver that supports IPv6.

4.4 Microsoft's Native Implementation of DNS in Windows 2000/2003

The DNS server is implemented in Windows servers as the 'DNS Server' service. It is controlled by a snap-in DNS module from the console (Microsoft Management Console—mmc command).

DNS server can be operated in Windows 2000/2003 separately (similar to the named program, which was described in Section 4.3.1) or together with the Active Directory. First, we will focus on a DNS server that runs separately.

When you start the snap-in DNS module for the first time after the installation of the DNS server, a text recommending that you configure the DNS server will appear. You can start it after you have configured the DNS server. The configuration of the chosen server can be started from the menu activated by a right-click or by choosing the Action option.

During the configuration, you are asked whether your server should work as a root server. A root server is established, for example, on an intranet if we do not want to translate the whole Internet, but only names from our internal network (for more details, see Chapter 9). If you answer that your server should work as a root server, a domain '.' will be established. We can also establish zones for an individual domain during the configuration.

In this case, it was selected that the server should not work as a root server, and the company.com and marta.cz zones were also established. An A record was added for my-computer.company.com by right-clicking on the zone. (The ld.company.com record was created automatically because this is my computer's name.) The result is shown in Figure 4.3.

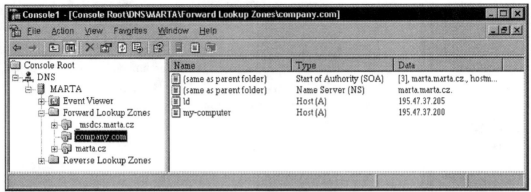

Figure. 4.3: Snap-in DNS Module (zone _msdcs.marta.cz was displayed in consequence that computer is a member of ActiveDirectory marta.cz domain)

The DNS server starts running. The server can be stopped, started, restarted, and so on using right-click and the All tasks option.

The following files with DNS databases were created in the %SystemRoot%\system32\dns directory:

- The cache.dns file for the cache/hint zone
- The company.com.dns file for the company.com zone
- The marta.cz.dns file for the marta.cz zone.

The syntax of these files is identical to the files described in the Section 4.2. Let us look at the company.com.dns file as an example (the comments have been omitted):

```
@               IN   SOA ld.company.com.   administrator.company.com (
                2    ; serial number
                900  ; refresh
                600  ; retry
                86400 ; expire
                600  ) ; minimum TTL
@               NS   ld.company.com.
ld              A    195.47.37.205
my-computer     A    195.47.37.200
```

You can display the properties of your DNS server by right-clicking the snap-in module:

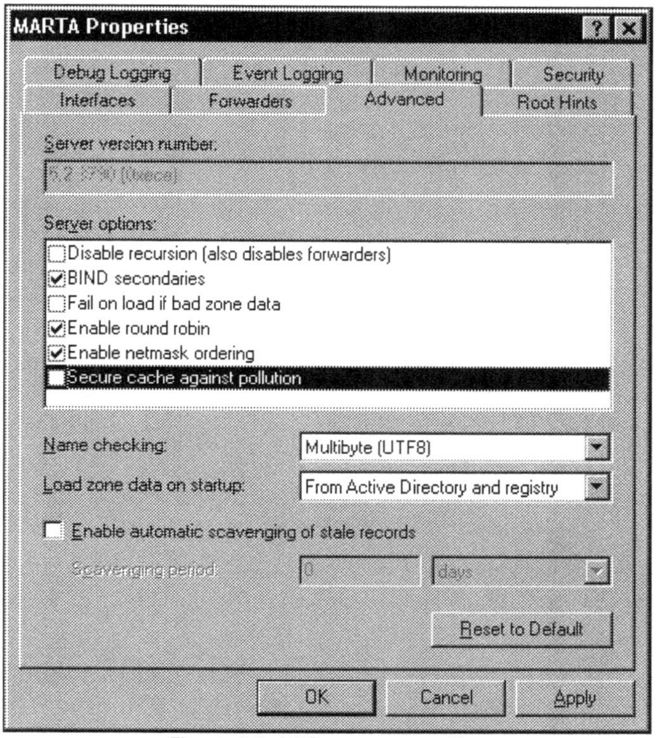

Figure 4.4: DNS server properties

Root Hints: This tab enables you to edit the cache.dns file.

Event Logging: This tab allows you to log individual actions of the server into the file. A text log file is created in the %SystemRoot%\system32\dns directory.

Interfaces: This tab allows you to specify network interfaces where your server will expect queries (where it will listen).

Advanced: The tab is chosen in Figure 4.4. The Load zone data on startup option can be used to choose if the data should be read from the %SystemRoot%\system32\dns directory or from the Active Directory. If reading from the file (From file) is selected, a file called boot with a syntax identical to the named.boot file of the BIND system version 4 (see Section 4.3.1) can be inserted into the particular directory. The DNS server then starts according to this file.

Another interesting feature in the Advanced tab is the Server options box that allows you to set some of the following server options:

- Disable recursion: The server will not deal with recursive queries (such as queries from resolvers).

- BIND secondaries: This option will allow zone transfer even for older DNS servers (for example, BIND versions older than 4.9.4), which do not use record compression.

- Fail on load if bad zone data: The server logs errors in the zone files that have been read. The question is whether it should continue to read the zone into the cache after the error has occurred or not. This is controlled through this option, which is saved in the strictFileParsing register.

- Enable round robin: See Section 1.7.1.

- Enable netmask ordering: This is different technique from 'round robin' (for arrangement of IP addresses in cases where one name has several IP addresses) is different from 'round robin' technology. When using this technique, the list of IP addresses is arranged according to the distance of the individual addresses from the client (the nearest IP address is the first on the list).

  Determining the distance is a problem. That is why the network mask is used. The distance can be explained in the following way: it is the distance of the particular IP address from the client's network IP address in the routing table to the network the client is connected to.

- Secure cache against pollution: The server will only save into cache those answers that come from the name servers in the domain whose items have been queried.

The individual DNS server parameters are stored in the HKEY_LOCAL_MACHINE\SYSTEM\ CurrentControlSet\Services\DNS\Parameters register folder. Some of the parameters are shown as follows:

- The BootMethod (REG-DWORD type) specifies from where the DNS databases should be read, i.e., from a file (1), from Windows registers (2), or from Active Directory (3).

- DatabaseDirectory (REG-SZ type) specifies the directory in which the DNS databases are located (by default, %SystemRoot%\system32\dns).

- DisableAutoReverseZone (REG_DWORD type) opens (value 0) or closes (value 1) the automatic generation of reverse domains 0.in-addr.arpa (reverse translation 0.0.0.0), 127.in-addr.arpa (reverse translation 127.0.0.1), and 255.in-addr.arpa (reverse translation 255.255.255.255).

- EventLogLevel (REG_DWORD type) specifies the importance of the logged events, where 0 means nothing is logged, 4 means maximum logging, and 2 and 3 are the levels in between.

- Forwarders (REG_SZ type) contains a list of forwarders separated by commas.

- IsSlave (REG_DWORD type). 0 means the server is not a slave server and 1 means the server is a slave server.

- ListenAddress (REG_BINARY type) contains a list of IP addresses on which the server listens.

- `LogFileMaxSize` (`REG_DWORD` type) contains the maximum length of a protocol (log).

- `LogFilePath` (`REG_DWORD` type) contains the name and path to a protocol.

- `LogLevel` (`REG_DWORD` type) contains a binary map of events to be logged.

- `NoRecursion` (`REG_DWORD` type). 0 means the server deals with DNS queries according to their identification (recursive queries are processed recursively and nonrecursive queries are processed nonrecursively) and 1 means all queries are processed nonrecursively.

- `UpdateOptions` (`REG_DWORD` type) contains a bit mask. A dynamic update is limited by setting the value 1 for individual bits of the mask. The lowest bit limits dynamic update of SOA records. The second lowest bit limits dynamic update of NS records and so on. Dynamic update can be completely limited by setting the maximum value of hexadecimal 80000000.

Apart from the DNS snap-in module, the `dnscmd.exe` command-line utility is available in Windows 2000. It is easy to control. For example, information about a local server can be obtained using the following command:

`dnscmd . / info`

This command will display detailed information about the server setting. Another program that can be used to control the DNS server is the `net` command. For example, the following command can be used to stop the DNS server:

`net stop dns`

When you want to activate the Active Directory in Windows 2000/2003, it is necessary to take into consideration that Active Directory will use DNS to search for its own services. These services are also maintained in SRV records. Therefore, Active Directory expects that the DNS server will support this type of record. Active Directory would also like to register these services into DNS dynamically (dynamic update). If the server does not support the dynamic update, the domain controller includes the `%systemroot%\System32\config\netlogon.dns` file, which contains a batch of SRV records that are entered into DNS statically. Active Directory can now be installed using the `dcpromo` command.

When using Active Directory, it is necessary to bear in mind that Active Directory uses a name space that happens to be divided in domains just like the DNS name space. Name servers of this name space are called **domain controllers**. These are two name spaces that have nothing in common. They are only integrated in the same database, Active Directory. However, it would be impractical if the name of the same `computer.company.com` computer was different in Windows from its name in the TCP/IP world. That is why both spaces happen to use the same names (the same sequences in names). This was only noticed when there was a need to issue the certificates for objects of these name spaces. The names of objects are stated in the certificates. The DNS name is written in the form `computer.company.com`, but name for the Active Directory name space is written as `DC=computer`, `DC=company`, and `DC=com`.

5

Tools for DNS Debugging and Administration

In this chapter, we will discuss tools for debugging DNS such as `nslookup`, `dnswalk`, and `dig`, how to control a name server using the `rndc` program, and the common errors that might occur while configuring DNS.

5.1 Tools for DNS Debugging

After the configuration and startup of a name server, it is necessary to check whether the name server works correctly. Mistakes in DNS are very unpleasant. When a mistake in DNS occurs, applications sometimes do not start at all, but more often, the whole system seems to work very slowly. This applies especially to the configuration of a firewall. If the firewall has long response intervals, it is most likely due to an incorrectly functioning DNS.

There are some informative RFCs that focus on DNS problems. For example, RFC 1537 focuses on frequent mistakes in DNS and RFC 1713 focuses on tools for debugging.

There are two methods that can be used to check the configuration, which are as follows:

1. The first method is based on assuming the resolver's role and sending DNS queries to your DNS server in the same way that the resolver does. In this case, you are testing whether the name server answers your queries as you expect it to. For such testing we will manage with very easy tolls as `ping` or `nslookup`. Some of these tools have at each systems disposal (which have installed TCP/IP protocol stack). The only we need good knowledge of DNS.

2. The second option is a complete check (DNS debugging) using a program that knows DNS rules and checks adherence to these rules in the domain on your name server. The result of this kind of a check is a list of mistakes that occurred in the configuration of the particular domain.

However, both of these methods assume that you have managed to start your name server, and the testing programs used can send their queries to the running name server. BIND version 9 offers administrator utilities that can be used for checking the configuration before starting the name server.

If you suspect that your DNS is not functioning correctly, always check accessibility of the Internet first. The following steps should be followed to check:

1. Whether TCP/IP on your PC works correctly using the `ping 127.0.0.1` command.

2. Whether you have connection to the router on the LAN (usually default gateway) using the `ping IP-address_of_the_router` (not the name of the router!) command.

3. Whether you have a connection to the local name server by using the `ping IP-address_of_the_name_server` (not the name of the name server!) command. If no connection exits try `tracert` command instead of `ping` command (in UNIX use `traceroute` command).

4. Whether you have connection into the Internet (outside LAN) using the `ping IP-address_in_the_world` command.

5. Whether you can access the Internet directly from the name server. Log in to the name server and use the `ping IP-address_in_the_world` command directly from the name server.

5.1.1 Check Configuration Files

If you are using BIND version 9, it is recommended that you start the name server check by using two very useful utilities that check the correctness of the configuration files and detect a number of small as well as serious mistakes. Some of the detected mistakes can even prevent the server from starting up and are therefore very difficult to find in any other way. These programs have the advantage that they can check the data files directly without having to start the server. The `named-checkconf` and `named-checkzone` utilities are a part of the name server distribution kit.

5.1.2 named-checkconf Utility

The `named-checkconf` utility checks the syntax of the `named.conf` configuration file.

Syntax:

```
named-checkconf [-t directory][filename]
```

5.1.3 named-checkzone Utility

The `named-checkzone` utility checks the syntax and consistency of the zone file.

Syntax:

```
named-checkzone [-dgv][-c class] zone [filename]
```

5.1.4 nslookup Program

The `nslookup` program is the program most often used for DNS checks. This program has one important advantage. It is a part of the TCP/IP package both in UNIX and in Windows, and therefore you do not have to look for it anywhere and compile it.

The `nslookup` program is used to send DNS queries to the DNS server and check whether the DNS server is answering correctly. The `nslookup` program allows you to act as a resolver and requires a final answer to your query from the name server. The `nslookup` program can also be used to simulate actions of a name server communicating with another name server (i.e., require partial answers only). This depends on the purpose of the test.

The `nslookup` program sends DNS queries by default to the name server that is a resolver for the particular system. For example, in UNIX, it sends queries to a name server specified in the `/etc/resolv.conf` file.

The `nslookup` program is started in the interactive mode by the `nslookup` command without any parameters. After this we obtain nslookup command prompt (which is > sign):

```
Default Server: ns.pvt.net
Address: 194.149.105.18
>
```

This answer means that the `ns.pvt.net` server is defined in the resolver configuration as the default name server in this test system. This name server has the IP address 194.149.105.18. You type your query into the prompt (>). You can ask about, for example, an IP address or the name of some host.

If you type the name of a host such as `www.company.com` at the prompt, the `ns.pvt.net` name server will try to find out the IP address of this host.

Query:

```
>www.company.com
Server: ns.pvt.net
Address: 194.149.105.18
```

Answer:

```
Name: www.company.com
Address: 194.149.104.206
>
```

If you type at the prompt an IP address such as 194.149.104.206, the default server will try to find out the domain name of the host with this IP address.

Query:

```
>194.149.104.206
Server: ns.pvt.net
Address: 194.149.105.18
```

Answer:

```
Name: www.company.com
Address: 194.149.104.206
>
```

As the above lines show, the `nslookup` program is by default looking for a suitable A or PTR record in DNS. However, the `nslookup` program can also be used to ask a name server about any RR record.

The type of record we would like to find must be defined in the `nslookup` program using the following command:

```
set querytype=type_of_a_record
```

```
This command can also be used in its shortened form:
set q=type_of_a_record
```

Again, we will use an example to look at the usage. This time we would like to see a list of servers to which the mail for the `whitehouse.gov` domain is directed. We already know that directing mail is defined by MX records in the zone file of the particular domain. Therefore, we are interested in all MX records. The required type of records is set to MX in the following way:

Query:

```
>set q=mx
> whitehouse.gov
...
```

Answer:

```
whitehouse.gov   MX preference = 200, mail exchanger = wh.eop.gov
whitehouse.gov   MX preference = 100, mail exchanger = mailhub-wh.eop.gov
whitehouse.gov   nameserver = dnsauth1.sys.gtei.net
whitehouse.gov   nameserver = dnsauth2.sys.gtei.net
whitehouse.gov   nameserver = dnsauth3.sys.gtei.net
dnsauth1.sys.gtei.net    internet address = 4.2.49.2
dnsauth2.sys.gtei.net    internet address = 4.2.49.3
dnsauth3.sys.gtei.net    internet address = 4.2.49.4
>
```

The mail for the White House is directed to the `mailhub-wh.eop.gov`. If this host in ureacheble, then mails will be directed to wh.eop.gov host. (This example was prepared only as a demonstration. You can use your own mail domain or URLs and compare the output.)

Note that the `nslookup` program displays not only the answer itself, but also additional information from the DNS packet received from the server. Apart from the answer, we can also see the authoritative servers for the `whitehouse.gov` domain and IP addresses of all servers in the answer. This additional information has been left out in the following examples to keep them clear and simple.

The `nslookup` program is also often used to find out the authoritative servers for a particular domain. This time, we would like to know the names of name servers that administer the particular domain. We can acquire this information by simply setting the type of records to NS:

Query:

```
>set q=ns
> whitehouse.gov
...
```

Answer:

```
whitehouse.gov   nameserver = dnsauth1.sys.gtei.net
whitehouse.gov   nameserver = dnsauth2.sys.gtei.net
whitehouse.gov   nameserver = dnsauth3.sys.gtei.net

dnsauth1.sys.gtei.net    internet address = 4.2.49.2
dnsauth2.sys.gtei.net    internet address = 4.2.49.3
dnsauth3.sys.gtei.net    internet address = 4.2.49.4
```

The domain whitehouse.gov is delegated to 3 authoritative name servers.

Exercises:

1. Find out authoritative name servers for some domain.
2. Find out root name servers for the Internet (i.e., authoritative name servers for a dot).

If you do not know whether a certain domain name is a canonical name or an alias, you can use the setting set q=any and find out all records relating to the particular domain server.

Query:

```
>set q=any
>info.provider.net
Server: localhost
Address: 127.0.0.1
```

Answer:

```
info.provider.net  CPU = AlphaServer 100  OS = OSF/1
info.provider.net  text = "email: libor.dostalek@pvt.cz"
info.provider.net  internet address = 194.149.104.203
```

In this case, the info.provider.net domain name is defined in three records, in an A record, a TXT record, and an HINFO record.

5.1.4.1 Debugging Mode

When looking for a mistake in the configuration, often the information that can be displayed using the nslookup program is not sufficient and we would like to know more. In this case, you can use the debugging mode of the program. Two levels of debugging mode can be set for the nslookup program, debug mode and d2 mode. Debugging levels are set by the set command.

5.1.4.2 Debug Debugging Level

The debug debugging level displays detailed information coming from DNS packets. To set the debug debugging level, use the set debug command.

If you look at Section 2.3.2, you will be able to read the output of the debugging mode quite easily. The individual sections of the extract start with a heading. Comments are added to the extract for your better understanding.

We will use an example to look at the usage. We are interested in the IP address of the test100.provider.net host.

Query:

```
>set debug
>test100.provider.net
Server: ns.company.com
Address: 0.0.0.0
```

Answer:

```
--------
Got answer: The first answer does not include the translated address yet.
HEADER: Section heading
opcode = QUERY, id = 1, rcode = NXDOMAIN
```

```
    header flags: response, auth. answer, want recursion, recursion avail.
    Questions = 1, answers = 0, authority records = 1, additional = 0

    QUESTIONS: Section containing the query
        test100.provider.net.company.com, type = A, class = IN
    AUTHORITY RECORDS: Section about authoritative servers
    ->company.com
        ttl = 129600 (1day 12hours)
        origin = mh.company.com
        mail addr = hostmaster.company.com
        serial = 1996020802
        refresh = 10800 (3hours)
        retry = 3600 (1hour)
        expire = 360000 (4days 4hours)
        minimum ttl = 129600 (1day 12hours)
    -----------
```

In this case, the second packet contains the answer:

```
    -----------
    Got answer:
        HEADER:
            opcode = QUERY, id = 2, rcode = NOERROR
            header flags: response, want recursion, recursion avail.
            questions = 1, answers = 1, authority records = 4, additional = 4

    QUESTIONS:
        Test100.provider.net, type = A, class = IN
    ANSWERS:
    -> test100.provider.net
        internet address = 194.149.100.1
        ttl = 129175 (1day 11hours 52mis 55secs)
    AUTHORITY RECORDS:
    -> provider.net
        nameserver = NS0.PIPEX.net
        ttl = 122697 (1day 10hours 4mins 57secs)
    -> provider.net
        nameserver = NS1.PIPEX.net
        ttl = 122697 (1day 10hours 4mins 57secs)
    -> provider.net
        nameserver = ns.provider.net
        ttl = 122697 (1day 10hours 4mins 57secs)
    -> provider.net
        nameserver = NS1.provider.net
        ttl = 122697 (1day 10hours 4mins 57secs)
    ADDITIONAL RECORDS:
    -> NS0.PIPEX.net
        internet address = 158.43.128.8
        ttl = 143625 (1day 15hours 53mins 45secs)
    -> NS1.PIPEX.net
        internet address = 158.43.192.7
        ttl = 143625 (1day 15hours 53mins 45secs)
    -> ns.provider.net
        internet address = 194.149.105.18
        ttl = 129175 (1day 11hours 52mins 55secs)
    -> NS1.provider.net
        internet address = 194.149.103.201
        ttl = 129175 (1day 11hours 52mins 55secs)
    -----------
    Non-authoritative answer:
    Name: test100.provider.net
    Address: 194.149.100.1
```

The resolver sent two queries to the name server and received two packets as an answer. You should understand why there are two queries. If you do not know, see Section 1.8.1 and look carefully at the domain name, which the resolver is asking about in the query.

5.1.4.3 d2 Debugging Level

The d2 debugging level displays in detail the contents of outgoing packets (queries) and incoming packets (answers). Using the d2 debugging level enables you to acquire detailed information about the communication of a resolver with a name server, which is almost as thorough as the MS Network Monitor output.

To demonstrate its use, we will use the same example that was used for the debug debugging level. This will allow you to compare the answers.

Query:

```
>set d2
>test100.provider.net
Server: ns.company.com
Address: 0.0.0.0
```

Answer:

```
------------
SendRequest0, len 40
    HEADER:
        opcode: QUERY, id = 3, rcode = NOERROR
        header flags: query, want recursion
        questions = 1, answers = 0, authority records = 0, additional = 0

    QUESTIONS:
        test100.provider.net.company.com type = A, class = IN

------------
------------
Got answer (96 bytes):
    HEADER:
    opcode = QUERY, id = 3, rcode = NXDOMAIN
    header flags: response, auth. answer, want recursion, recursion avail.

    questions = 1, answers = 0, authority records = 1, additional = 0

    QUESTIONS:
        test100.provider.net.company.com type = A, class = IN
    AUTHORITY RECORDS:
    ->company.com
    type = SOA, class = IN, dlen = 38
    nl = 129600 (1day 12hours)
    origin = mh.company.com
    mail addr = hostmaster.company.com
    serial = 1996020802
    refresh = 10800 (3 hours)
    retry = 3600 (1hour)
    expire = 360000 (4days 4hours)
    minimum ttl = 129600 (1day 12hours)

--------------
--------------
SendRequest0, len 33
    HEADER:
        opcode = QUERY, id = 4, rcode = NOERROR
        header  flags: query, want recursion
        questions = 1, answers =0, authority records = 0, additional = 0

    QUESTIONS:
        test100.provider.net type = A, class = IN
--------------
--------------
```

```
Got answer (208 bytes):
    HEADER:
        opcode = QUERY, id = 4, rcode = NOERROR
        header flags: response, want recursion, recursion avail.
        questions = 1, answers = 1, authority records = 4, additional = 4
    QUESTIONS:
        test100.provider.net type = A, class = IN
    ANSWERS:
    ->test100.provider.net
        type = A, class = IN, dlen = 4
        internet address = 194.149.100.1
        ttl = 129025 (1day 11hours 50mins 25secs)
    AUTHORITY RECORDS:
    ->provider.net
        type = NS, class = IN, dlen = 6
        nameserver = NS1.PIPEX.net
        ttl = 122547 (1day 10hours 2mins 27secs)
    ->provider.net
        type = NS, class = IN, dlen = 6
        nameserver = NS1.PIPEX.net
        ttl = 122547 (1day 10hours 2mins 27secs)
    ->provider.net
        type = NS, class = IN, dlen = 9
        nameserver = ns.provider.net
        ttl = 122547 (1day 10hours 2mins 27secs)
    ->provider.net
        type = NS, class = IN, dlen = 10
        nameserver = NS1.provider.net
        ttl = 122547 (1day 10hours 2mins 27secs)
    ADDITIONAL RECORDS:
    ->NS0.PIPEX.net
        type = A, class = IN. dlen = 4
        internet address = 158.43.128.8
        ttl = 143475 (1day 15hours 51mins 15secs)
    -> NS1.PIPEX.net
        type = A, class = IN, dlen = 4
        internet address = 158.43.192.7
        ttl = 143475 (1day 15hours 51mins 15secs)
    ->ns.provider.net
        type = A, class = IN, dlen = 4
        internet address = 194.149.105.18
        ttl = 129025 (1day 11hours 50mins 25secs)
    ->NS1.provider.net
        type = A, class = IN, dlen = 4
        internet address = 194.149.103.201
        ttl = 129025 (1day 11hours 50mins 25secs)

--------------
Non-authoritative answer:
Name: test100.provider.net
Address: 194.149.100.1
>
```

Change of the Default Name Server

The nslookup program can also be used for sending a DNS packet with a query to any name server. The name of the server to be tested is chosen using the server command:

>server ns.internic.net

When you use this command, all following DNS queries will be resolved by the newly chosen server, in this case, the ns.internic.net server.

This setting is very practical because your name server usually appears to be correctly working from your LAN. To make sure that this is the case, you can check your name server from a different name server.

Zone Extract

If you want the name server to send you complete information about a certain zone, you need to use the `ls -d` command. In this case, the query must be directed to an authoritative server for the particular domain. Therefore, you usually need to include the `server` command before the `ls -d` command:

```
>server ns.provider.net
>ls -d company.com
```

The `ls -d` command simulates zone transfer (AXFR) from a name server and that is why it is often used for the configuration of secondary name servers. Using the `ls -d` command allows you to check very easily whether the primary server provides the data of the particular zone and consequently whether it will provide it to the secondary name server for the zone. If you cannot get an answer from the primary server using this command, you can be almost sure that the secondary name server will not be able to do it either.

Unfortunately most important name server denied `ls -d` command from security reasons today. No positive answer may mean that answer is forbidden by server.

Simulation of Queries from a Name Server

If you want to simulate communication between name servers, you have to override two default settings of the `nslookup` program. The `nslookup` program by default uses search a list that is similar to a resolver adds the default domain after any domain name that does not have a dot at the end. This can be blocked by the following command:

```
>set nosearch
```

The `nslookup` program by default requires a recursion, i.e., final answer from a name server. As we know, servers send each other nonrecursive answers and therefore, this behavior needs to be blocked by the following command:

```
>set norecurse
```

Error Messages of the nslookup Program

The following are the most common error messages of the `nslookup` program:

No records available: No record of the required type exists.

No response from the server: The server is not running.

No information: The server is running, but has no information about the particular domain.

Non-existent domain: The reverse record for the name of the name server does not exist.

Can't list domain…Query refused: The server is running, but has no data for the domain. (The data has expired.)

Unspecified error: Unspecified error.

5.1.5 Other Programs Used for Debugging DNS

RFC 1713 informs us about some more tools for DNS debugging. This includes programs such as ddt2, dnsparse, doc, host, inetrover, and lamer, which are available at ftp://ftp.uu.net/networking/ip/dns.

5.1.5.1 The dnswalk Program

The dnswalk program is the best known program for DNS debugging. It is a script written in the Perl language. The dnswalk program knows the rules for DNS configuration and checks the configuration of the selected domain according to these rules. The dnswalk program carries out a zone transfer from the authoritative name server and checks the correctness of the domain configuration from many perspectives. This program can check forward as well as reverse domains. The name of the domain to be checked is entered into the program as a parameter and *must* have a dot at the end.

Again, it is better to start dnswalk from a different computer (not locally on name server which are tested). That is why certain web servers in the Internet offer forms for testing foreign domains. These web servers start dnswalk as a CGI (Common Gateway Interface) script.

The following example shows the use of the dnswalk program for checking the provider.net. zone. (the dot at the end is compulsory):

```
$perl dnswalk provider.net.
Getting zone transfer of provider.net from ns.provider.net. ...done
Checking provider.net.
SOA=ns.provider.net. contact=dostalek.company.com
  dhcp.provider.net.           A       194.149.104.3: no PTR record
  dhcp.provider.net.           A       194.149.104.11: no PTR record
  cbu.provider.net.  129600    CNAME   dhcp.provider.net.provider.net.: domain
occurred twice, forget trailing'.'?
  cbun01.provider.net.         CNAME   gw.provider.net.provider.net : unknown
host
```

dnswalk detected three mistakes during the check. The provider.net domain includes two A records that do not have a relevant PTR record. The name pipex-gw.provider.net does not have a dot at the end and CNAME points to a nonexistent host gw.provider.net.provider.net.

dnswalk can be started with various parameters. Let's at least look at the parameters that are used most often for checks:

The most common use of dnswalk is for checking a domain. It is usually called with the following parameters:

```
dnswalk -Fralf  domain.cz.
```

dnswalk is available at http://www.tucows.com/preview/8173.

5.1.5.2 The dig Program

The dig program is also one of the well-known programs used for checking DNS. The dig program sends DNS query packets to the selected name server and gives the user information about DNS. The user can specify which server should answer the particular query, what information he or she wants to know, and can also specify additional conditions for the query.

The standardized format of answers is an advantage of this program because this allows you to continue processing the answers using your program. While nslookup is most often used interactively, dig is often started from scripts.

The syntax used most often is as follows:

```
dig @server domain query-type
```

The name of a server we would like to query should be stated after the @ symbol. The second parameter is the name of a domain to be checked, query-type is the requested type of a record. Any type of RR record or the AXFR sequence, which requires a zone transfer, or the any string, which requires any type of a record, can be typed in the place of the query-type sequence.

Here is an example of the dig program. In this example, we are requesting a check of MX records for the provider.net domain. We want the ns.provider.net server to provide us with the information:

```
dig @ns.provider.net provider.net mx
: <<>>DiG 2.1<<>>@ns.provider.net provider.net mx
;(1 server found)
;;res options: init recurs defnam dnsrch
;;got answer;
;;->>HEADER<<-opcode: QUERY, status: NOERROR, id: 10
;;flags: qr aard ra; Ques: 1, Ans: 2, Auth: 5, Addit: 15
;;QUESTIONS:
;;    provider.net. type=MX, class = IN

;;ANSWERS:
provider.net.    86400    MX    20 mail.uu.net
provider.net.    86400    MX    10 cbu.provider.net

;;AUTHORITY RECORDS:
provider.net.    86400    NS    ns.provider.net
provider.net.    86400    NS    ns1.provider.net
provider.net.    86400    NS    snmp0.provider.net
provider.net.    86400    NS    ns0.pipex.net
provider.net.    86400    NS    ns1.pipex.net

;;ADDITIONAL RECORDS:
mail.uu.net.    74570    A    192.48.96.15
mail.uu.net.    74570    A    192.48.96.16
mail.uu.net.    74570    A    192.48.96.17
mail.uu.net.    74570    A    192.48.96.5
mail.uu.net.    74570    A    192.48.96.7
mail.uu.net.    74570    A    192.48.96.8
mail.uu.net.    74570    A    192.48.96.14
cbu.pvtnet.cz. 86400    A    194.149.105.18
ns.provider.net.    86400    A    194.149.105.18
ns1.provider.net.    86400    A    194.149.103.201
snmp0.provider.net.    86400    A    194.149.103.34
ns0.pipex.net. 16958    A    158.43.128.103
ns0.pipex.net. 16958    A    158.43.128.8
ns1.pipex.net. 16970    A    158.43.192.7
ns1.pipex.net. 16970    A    158.43.192.40

;;Total query time: 7msec
;;FROM: info.provider.net to SERVER: ns.provider.net 194.149.105.18
;;WHEN: Tue Aug 18 11:15:20 1998
;;MSG SIZE sent: 25 rcvd: 418
```

When calling the dig program, you can state the IP address of the server you are inquiring about instead of the name of the server.

5.2 The rndc Program

The rndc (remote name server control) program is a program that allows you to control a name server both remotely and safely. A name server administrator can use this program to carry out the actions stated in the later table. The program can find out the name server's PID and send the server the appropriate signal.

The rndc program has gradually developed over the years. Version 4 defined signals (see Section 5.2.1) for this purpose. A DNS administrator would send these signals to a name server using operating system commands. Version 8 introduced the rndc utility that offered a similar group of functions, but did not ensure security. BIND 9 added the authentication of the connection used.

BIND 9 and its client use a prepared symmetric key to mutually identify each other. The server has the key stored in the key clause in the named.conf file. The client has the same key and it is stored in the rndc.key file or in the rndc.conf configuration file. The rndc-confgen -a utility can be used to generate this shared key. This utility creates the rndc.key file. Remember that you have to save the key from the rndc.key file into the named.conf file. It is important that not only is the key itself identical, but also its identification.

Syntax for calling the rndc program:

```
rndc [-c config][-s server][-p port][-key] command
```

You can see the simple use of the rndc program in the following example. Here are the contents of the rndc.key file:

```
key "rndc-key" {
algorithm hmac-md5;
secret "WjaYvvX40PPmL0dzv8TsnA==";
};
```

The part of the named.conf file relating to the rndc utility:

```
key "rndc-key" {
algorithm hmac-md5;
secret "WjaYvvX40PPmL0dzv8TsnA==";
};
controls {
    inet 194.17.165.23 port 953 allow { 194.17.165.23; 194.17.14.148; } keys {
"rndc-key";};
};
```

Use of the rndc stop command:

```
$rndc-y etc\rndc.key -s 194.17.165.23 stop
Name server writes the following lines into the protocol and stops its
activity.
Mar 25 10:48:46.902 stopping command channel on 194.17.14.148#953
Mar 25 10:48:46.902 no longer listening on 127.0.0.1#53
Mar 25 10:48:46.902 no longer listening on 194.17.165.23#53
Mar 25 10:48:46.972 exiting
```

Use of the rndc status command:

```
$rndc-y etc\rndc.key -s 194.17.165.23 status
```

Extract:

```
number of zones: 5
debug level: 0
xfers running: 0
xfers deferred: 0
soa queries in progress: 0
query logging is OFF
server is up and running
```

Further details about the program and its configuration can be found in the documentation, which is a part of every BIND distribution.

Overview of `rndc` commands:

Command	Description
reload	Reloads the configuration file and zone files
reconfig	Reloads the configuration file and new or changed zone files; unchanged zone files are not loaded
stats	Records the statistics into a file
querylog	Switches on logging queries about the name server
dumpdb	Records the server's cache memory in the dump file
stop	Stops the server and records changes acquired by IXFR or by a dynamic update into files
halt	Stops the server immediately
trace	Increases the debugging level of the server by 1
notrace	Sets the debugging level of the server at 0
flush	Cleans the server's cache memory
status	Displays the status of the server

5.2.1 Signals

The `kill` command can be used to send a signal to the `named` program in UNIX. A similar group of actions can be carried out using signals to those available using the `rndc` program. The following signals are usually processed: HUP, INT, IOT, TERM, KILL, USR1, and USR2. In the actual implementation of a name server, the parameters that were used during compiling the `named` program are also important.

The `kill` command has, as the second parameter, a process number (PID). You can find out the process number the named program is running under by, for example, using the `ps` command. However, the `named` program writes the process number into the `/path/named.pid` file during its startup. The location and the name of the file can be influenced during the compilation of the `named` program.

The syntax of the `kill` command, for example, with the HUP signal is the following:

```
kill -HUP 'cat /path/named.pid'
```

If you wish to start the diagnostics of the named program during its startup, you need to state the relevant parameter in the command line that is used to start the named program. For more details, see the man named command.

5.2.1.1 HUP Signal

The HUP signal forces the name server to read the data from the disk again. However, the cache is not usually cleaned by the HUP signal.

5.2.1.2 INT Signal

The INT signal extracts all data (authoritative and nonauthoritative) from the memory into a file usually called /tmp/named_dump.bd. An example of a part of the file is as follows:

```
; Dumped at Fri Feb 16 18:12:49 1996
; Note: Cr=(auth, answer, addtnl, cache) tag only shown for non-authorised
RR's
; Note: NT=milliseconds for any A RR which we've used as a nameserver
; ----Cache & Data----
$ORIGIN .
.    518339      IN  NS  A.ROOT-SERVERS.NET.
     5188339     IN  NS  H.ROOT-SERVERS.NET.
     5188339     IN  NS  B.ROOT-SERVERS.NET.
     5188339     IN  NS  C.ROOT-SERVERS.NET.
     5188339     IN  NS  D.ROOT-SERVERS.NET.
     5188339     IN  NS  E.ROOT-SERVERS.NET.
     5188339     IN  NS  I.ROOT-SERVERS.NET.
     5188339     IN  NS  F.ROOT-SERVERS.NET.
     5188339     IN  NS  G.ROOT-SERVERS.NET.
     86348       IN  SOA A.ROOT-SERVERS.NET. HOSTMASTER.INTERNIC.NET. (
          1996021400 10800 900 604800 86400)    ;Cr=addtnl
;workgroup 548 IN  A    NXDOMAIN       ;-$
cz  172768       IN  NS  NS.EUNET.CZ.        ;Cr=addtnl
    172768       IN  NS  NS.CESNET.CZ.       ;Cr=addtnl
    172768       IN  NS  NS.EU.NET.      ;Cr=addtnl
    172768       IN  NS  SUNIC.SUNSET.SE.    ;Cr=addtnl
    172768       IN  NS  NS.UU.NET.      ;Cr=addtnl
    172768       IN  NS  SPARKY.ARL.MIL.     ;Cr=addtnl
$ORIGIN 48.192.IN-ADDR.ARPA.
96  518384       IN  NS  NS.UU.NET.      ;Cr=addtnl
    518384       IN  NS  UUCP-GW-1.PA.DEC.COM.  ;Cr=addtnl
    518384       IN  NS  UUCP-GW-2.PA.DEC.COM.  ;Cr=addtnl
    518384       IN  NS  NS.EU.NET      ;Cr=addtnl
$ORIGIN 96.48.192.IN-ADDR.ARPA.
16  86385        IN  PTR relay6.UU.NET.
$ORIGIN 147.IN-ADDR.ARPA.
230 518391       IN  NS  BUBO.VSLIB.CZ.  ;Cr=addtnl
    518391       IN  NS  NS.CESNET.CZ.       ;Cr=addtnl
$ORIGIN 16.230.147.IN-ADDR.ARPA.
1   3591         IN  PTR bubo.vslib.cz.
$ORIGIN 0.127.IN-ADDR.ARPA.
0                IN  SOA mh.company.com. hostmaster.company.com. (
                 94082701 10800 3600 360000 1 29600 )
                 IN  NS  mh.company.com.
$ORIGIN 0.0.127.IN-ADDR.ARPA.
1                IN  PTR localhost.
$ORIGIN 85.193.IN-ADDR.ARPA.
240              IN  SOA mh.company.com. hostmaster.company.com. (
                 1996020801 28800 3600 604800 864000 )
                 IN  NS  mh.company.com.
                 IN  NS  ns.company.com.
                 IN  NS  ns.eunet.cz.
```

```
$ORIGIN 240.85.193.IN-ADDR.ARPA.
1              IN   PTR Ceske-Budejovice.company.com.
$ORIGIN MIL.
ARL 518368     IN   NS  ADMII.ARL.mil. ;Cr=addtnl
    518368     IN   NS  VGR.ARL.ARMY.mil. ;Cr=addtnl
    518368     IN   NS  SLADW.ARL.mil. ;Cr=addtnl
    518368     IN   NS  DNS1.ARL.mil. ;Cr=addtnl
$ORIGIN ARL.MIL.
DNS1   518368 IN   A   131.218.24.3   ;Cr=addtnl
SLADW  518368 IN   A   155.148.8.2;Cr=addtnl
       518368 IN   A   155.148.6.90   ;Cr=addtnl
ADMII  518368 IN   A   128.63.31.4;Cr=addtnl
       518368 IN   A   128.63.5.4 ;Cr=addtnl
       518368 IN   A   192.5.25.5 ;Cr=addtnl
SPARKY 81548  IN   A   128.63.48.85   ;NT=481 Cr=answer
       81548  IN   A   192.5.23.200   ;NT=745 Cr=answer
$ORIGIN ARL.ARMY.MIL.
VGR    518368 IN   A   128.63.16.6;Cr=addtnl
       518368 IN   A   128.63.4.4 ;Cr=addtnl
       518368 IN   A   128.63.2.6 ;Cr=addtnl
$ORIGIN SUNSET.SE.
SUNIC  172768 IN   A   192.36.125.2   ;NT=459 Cr=addtnl
       172768 IN   A   192.36.148.18  ;NT=459 Cr=addtnl
$ORIGIN COM.
GreatCircle172787 IN  NS  MILES.GreatCircle.COM. ;Cr=addtnl
       172787 IN   NS  NS.UU.NET. ;Cr=addtnl
       3591   IN   A   198.102.244.34
pvt           IN   SOA mh.company.com. hostmaster.company.com (
              1996020802 10800 3600 360000 129600 )
              IN   NS  mh.company.com.
              IN   NS  ns.company.com.
              IN   NS  ns.eunet.cz.
              IN   MX  10 mh.company.com.
              IN   MX  20 bb-prg.eunet.cz.
              IN   MX  150 mcsun.eu.net.
              IN   MX  200 relay1.uu.net.
              IN   MX  200 relay2.uu.net.
$ORIGIN company.com.
Ceske-Budejovice  IN  A   193.85.240.1
              IN   HINFO  "Cisco" ""
$ORIGIN unl.company.com.
p56x01        IN   MX  10 mh.company.com.
              IN   MX  20 bb-prg.eunet.cz.
$ORIGIN NET.
pvt 172781    IN   NS  ns.provider.net.   ;Cr=addtnl
    172781    IN   NS  NS1.PROVIDER.NET.  ;Cr=addtnl
    172781    IN   NS  NS0.PIPEX.NET. ;Cr=addtnl
    172781    IN   NS  NS1.PIPEX.NET. ;Cr=addtnl
$ORIGIN ROOT-SERVERS.NET.
A   518339    IN   A   198.41.0.4 ;NT=475 Cr=addtnl
B   518339    IN   A   128.9.0.107;NT=16833 Cr=addtnl
C   518339    IN   A   192.33.4.12;NT=19544 Cr=addtnl
D   518339    IN   A   128.8.10.90;NT=1040 Cr=addtnl
E   518339    IN   A   192.203.230.10 ;NT=1279 Cr=addtnl
F   518339    IN   A   192.5.5.241;NT=1076 Cr=addtnl
G   518339    IN   A   192.112.36.4   ;NT=411 Cr=addtnl
H   518339    IN   A   128.63.2.53;NT=19544 Cr=addtnl
I   518339    IN   A   192.36.148.17  ;NT=940 Cr=addtnl
$ORIGIN UU.NET.
NS  172787    IN   A   137.39.1.3 ;NT=940 Cr=addtnl
$ORIGIN EU.NET.
NS  172784    IN   A   192.16.202.11  ;NT=280 Cr=addtnl
$ORIGIN pipex.NET.
ns0 172781    IN   A   158.43.128.8   ; Cr=addtnl
NS1 172781    IN   A   158.43.92.7; Cr=addtnl
$ORIGIN provider.net.
```

```
ns1 172781     IN  A   194.149.103.201   ; Cr=addtnl
ns  172781     IN  A   194.149.105.18 ; Cr=answer
;----Hints----
$ORIGIN .
.   3600       IN  NS  NS.INTERNIC.NET.
    3600       IN  NS  NS1.ISI.EDU.
    3600       IN  NS  C.NYSER.NET.
    3600       IN  NS  TERP.UMD.EDU.
    3600       IN  NS  NS.NASA.GOV.
    3600       IN  NS  NS.NIC.DDN.MIL.
    3600       IN  NS  AOS.ARL.ARMY.MIL.
    3600       IN  NS  NIC.NORDU.NET.
$ORIGIN NIC.DDN.MIL.
NS  3600       IN  A   192.112.36.4
$ORIGIN ARL.ARMY.MIL.
AOS 3600       IN  A   128.63.4.82
    3600       IN  A   192.5.25.82
$ORIGIN NASA.GOV.
NS  3600       IN  A   128.102.16.10
    3600       IN  A   192.52.195.10
$ORIGIN UMD.EDU.
TERP    3600   IN  A   128.8.10.90
$ORIGIN ISI.EDU.
NS1 3600       IN  A   128.9.0.107
$ORIGIN NYSER.NET.
C   3600       IN  A   192.33.4.12
$ORIGIN NORDU.NET.
NIC 3600       IN  A   192.36.148.17
$ORIGIN INTERNIC.NET.
NS  3600       IN  A   198.41.0.4 ;NT=683
```

5.2.1.3 IOT Signal

The IOT signal ensures the extraction of the statistics, usually into the /tmp/named.stats file. Here is an example:

```
###(82490113) Fri Feb 16 18:01:53 1996
551359 time since boot (secs)    number of seconds from the start
551359 time since reset (secs)
631708 input packets     number of input packets
637573 output packets number of output packets
621627 queries     number of queries
0      iqueries        number of inversion queries
552    duplicate queries  number of queries repeated after reaching the
interval
13053  responses   number of responses from distant name servers
282    duplicate responses    number of repeated responses from name servers
426098 OK answers number of answers without an error indication
178    FAIL answers   number of answers with an error indication
2      FORMERR answers    number of refused answers
3525      system queries number of queries of a local server
3      prime cache calls  how many times the data about the root servers were
read
2      check_ns calls how many times the TTL field expired for records
describing access to the root name servers; after such expiration the file is
read again
345    bad responses drooped number of faulty responses from distant servers
2      martian responses      number of responses sent by "Martians"
(responses from unknown distant servers)
194894 negative responses cached number of cached negative responses
0      unknown query types    number of queries about unknown record types
520940 A queries       number of queries about A type of records
14     NS queries   number of queries about NS type of records
316    CNAME queries      number of queries about CNAME type of records
```

```
819      SOA queries    number of queries about SOA type of records
2        MR queries     number of queries about MR type of records
13045    PTR queries    number of queries about PTR type of records
86064    MX queries     number of queries about MX type of records
2        AXFR queries      number of queries about AXFR type of records (zone
transfer)
425      ANY queries    number of queries about ANY type of records (*)
```

5.2.1.4 TERM Signal

The TERM signal properly stops the named program. Information obtained by the IXFR or by Dynamic Update is saved into files.

5.2.1.5 KILL Signal

The KILL signal immediately stops the named program; this termination is abnormal. It is recommended to use this signal only in a situation when the TERM signal doesn't work.

5.2.1.6 USR1 and USR2 Signals

The USR1 signal is used for turning on the debugging output into the /tmp/named.run file. Another USR1 signal increases the debugging level, i.e., the quantity of recorded information. There are up to 11 levels. The USR2 signal is used for turning the debugging output off completely (and not to gradually decrease the debugging level). The debugging output records individual steps of a name server.

The following example is an example of debugging level 1. It is a translation of the test97.provider.net name to an IP address. As the name was submitted without a dot, the default company.com domain was first added after the name. The translation of test97.provider.net .company.com was not successful; the following attempt is to translate test97.provider.net. The query was sent to an authoritative name server for the provider.net domain, which has an IP address 158.43.128.8.

```
Debug turned ON, Level 1   (Kill  -USR1 ...)

datagram from [193.85.240.30].1824, fd 5, len 39; now Fri Feb16 18:18:56 1996
req: nlookup(test97.provider.net.company.com) id 512 type=1
req: found 'test97.provider.net.company.com' as 'company.com' (cname=0)
ns_req: answer - [193.85.240.30].1824 fd=5 id=2 Local

datagram from [193.85.240.30].1825, fd 5, len 32; now Fri Feb16 18:18:56 1996
req: nlookup(test97.provider.net) id 718 type=1
req: found 'test97.provider.net' as 'provider.net' (cname=0)
forw: forw - [158.43.128.8].53 ds=7 nsid=3 0ms retry 4sec

datagram from [158.43.128.8].53, fd 5, len 196; now Fri Feb 16 18:18:57 1996
update_msg: msglen:196, c:9
update failed (-10)
send_msg - [193.85.240.30] (UDP 5 1825) id=3
Debug turned OFF       (kill  -USR2 ...)
```

5.3 Errors in DNS Configuration

The 10 most common errors in DNS configuration are as follows:

1. Every host in the Internet should have a domain name correctly established in the DNS. Some services check the existence of the name in the DNS and do not communicate with the host if this DNS name does not exist.

2. The domain name must not contain any other symbols than ASCII letters, digits, and a dash (not underscore!). A name should not consist of digits only. A name must not start or end with a dash. RFC 1033 permits the use of an underscore in a domain name; however, it is not defined as a standard and some implementations have problems with it, and it is therefore better to avoid its use.

3. Full domain names must end with a dot. A dot is not used at the end of an IP address.

4. The symbol @ in a mail address for an SOA record must be replaced by a dot.

5. The right side of an NS record must include a canonical name; it must not include an IP address.

6. An A record and matching PTR record must include identical information.

7. An alias must *not* be used on the right side of PTR, MX, NS, and CNAME records. If you want the host to have the same name as the domain, use the following construction:

    ```
    company.com    IN    NS    ns1.company.com
                   IN    NS    ns2.company.com
                   IN    A     1.2.3.4
    ```

8. Corresponding PTR record must exist for every A record. A host with more addresses must have more PTR records.

9. Lame delegation: an authoritative name server does not contain the data for a domain. This situation usually happens after crashing a secondary name server.

    A typical example of lame delegation is a situation where the primary name server works correctly and a secondary name server is incorrectly configured (a record in named.boot or named.conf file is missing, a zone transfer has not been carried out, and so on). This name server that has not been configured may be then set in a superordinate domain as an authoritative name server for a domain.

    A query about the name of this domain is requested from somewhere. The superior name server answers that the query should be sent to the incorrectly configured name server as it is the authority. The query is then sent to the server, which has not been configured, but should be the authority. This server does not know the answer.

10. A glue record is not added in reverse domains.

11. If the name server has several IP addresses in subordinate zone, the superior domain must contain glue records for all IP addresses.

6

Domain Delegation and Registration

The process of delegating a domain is carried out in several steps:

1. Setting up a primary **Domain Name Server**
2. Configuring a secondary name server for the domain, or requesting the configuration of the name server from your Internet service provider
3. Requesting that the domain be delegated to a higher-level domain
4. If the domain is a second-level domain, registering the domain in an Internet registry domain database

Let us say that, somewhere in the world, there is a magical land that uses the top-level domain `tld` as its country code. This top-level domain is similar to `com`, `info`, `cz`, `fj`, `ru`, `de`, or other domains used in neighboring fairytale lands. The wise old TLD manager of this land controls the primary name server for the `tld` domain in this country called `ns.manager-tld.tld`. The secondary name servers for the `tld` domain are held by his good friends, the hostmasters of other TLDs that are equally accessible from any place on the globe.

The hostmaster of a company called Company Ltd. also works in this far-away country. This company decides to establish and use the `company.tld` domain. Company Ltd. has a leased line connection to the Internet. If the company only had a dial-up connection to the Internet, it would not be allowed to administer its name server itself. In that case, the company would have to assign the administration of its domain to its Internet Service Provider.

6.1 Example 1

The hostmaster of the company decides to administer the primary name server on one of the company's computers. The server is called `ns.company.tld` and has the IP address 194.149.10.11. The `ns.company.tld` server runs on UNIX and BIND version 4.9. (Windows 2000/2003 has a similar configuration.) The administrator wants to administer the secondary name server on an ISP name server called `ns.provider.net`.

The following diagram shows the hierarchy of name servers, and the sections below describe the individual configuration files or their sections that specify the required delegation:

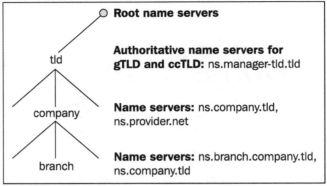

Figure 6.1: Domain delegation

6.1.1 Server ns.company.tld

This server acts as a primary server for the company.tld zone.

File named.boot

```
...
primary     company.tld          company.tld.zone
...
```

File company.tld.zone

```
@        IN  SOA ns.company.tld hostmaster.company.tld (
                            1998082402     ; Serial
                               28800       ; Refresh 8 hours
                                7200       ; Retry   2 hour
                              604800       ; Expire  7 days
                               86400 )     ; Minimum TTL 1 day
; ns records specifying the authoritative nameservers
              IN         NS          ns.company.tld.
              IN         NS          ns.provider.net.
; valid record A for the ns.company.tld server
ns       IN         A           194.149.10.11
...
```

6.1.2 Server ns.provider.net

This server acts as secondary name server for the company.tld zone.

File named.boot

```
...
secondary        company.tld    194.149.10.11  company.tld.zone
...
```

Now let us verify that the primary and secondary name servers are configured and functioning properly. Do not test the servers from the computers on which the primary or secondary name server of the `tld` domain is running. The simplest test can be done using the `nslookup` command. Run `nslookup` and type `server ns.company.tld` to direct the resolver to this name server. The `ls -d` command lists the content of the configured zone. Then direct the resolver to the secondary name server(s). You should see the same zone data. If the command does not list the zone content, you have to look for and correct any misconfigurations on the servers.

You can also use more user-friendly tools such as the `dig` program (for more information visit `http://www.kloth.net/services/dig.php`) or other more sophisticated tools such as dnswalk (for more information visit `http://www.visi.com/~barr/dnswalk/`). If you do not want to allow zone content to be listed from outside computers, you should follow these three steps:

1. Allow the whole zone to be read without limitations, but only put one or two RR records into the zone.
2. Let the administrator of the superior zone make a delegation (see the following section).
3. Set up restrictions to only allow zone transfer between the authoritative name servers of this zone and fill the zone database with the real data.

6.1.3 Server ns.manager-tld.tld

This name server is a primary name server for the `tld` domain.

You can now specify the information that needs to be added into the `tld` zone configuration file (on the `ns.manager-tld.tld` name server). The administrator of the `tld` domain will add this information after the appropriate administrative procedures have been carried out.

File tld.zone

```
...
; ns records ensuring the delegation of a domain
company         IN    NS          ns.company.tld.
                IN    NS          ns.provider.net.
; glue record for the ns.company.tld  server:
ns.company      IN    A           194.149.10.11
```

This registration enables your zone to be translated from any computer on the Internet, and not just from those computers whose resolvers are directed to your name server when testing the zone, as was recommended in the last section.

6.2 Example 2

For its branch office, Company Ltd. plans to create a subdomain within the `company.tld` domain called `branch.company.tld`. The branch will administer its own name server called `ns.branch.company.tld` with the IP address 194.149.10.129. The secondary name server for the `branch.company.tld` domain will be configured on the `ns.company.tld` name server.

The following list shows the individual configuration files or their sections that specify the required delegation. The bold lines are the lines that relate to the delegation of the `branch.company.tld` domain. These lines have been added to the configuration files from the previous example.

6.2.1 Server ns.company.com

File named.boot

```
...
primary    company.tld    company.tld.zone
secondary  branch.company.tld   194.149.10.129
branch.company.tld.zone
...
```

File company.tld.zone

```
@       IN  SOA ns.company.tld hostmaster.company.tld (
                        1998082402      ; Serial
                        28800           ; Refresh 8 hours
                        7200            ; Retry   2 hour
                        604800          ; Expire  7 days
                        86400 )         ; Minimum TTL 1 day

; ns records specifying authoritative nameservers
                IN      NS      ns.company.tld.
                IN      NS      ns.provider.net.
; glue A record for the ns.company.tld server:
ns      IN      A       194.149.10.11
;
; delegation of the branch.company.tld  subdomain to the
ns.branch.company.tld name ,server
; following ns records specifying the delegation:

branch      IN      NS      ns.branch.company.tld.
            IN      NS      ns.company.tld.

; glue record for the nsbranch.company.tldz server

ns.branch   IN      A       194.149.10.129
```

6.2.2 Server ns.branch.company.tld

File named.boot

```
...
primary branch.company.tld branch.company.tld.zone
...
```

File branch.company.tld.zone

```
@       IN  SOA ns.branch.company.tld  hostmaster.branch.company.tld (
                        1998082502      ; Serial
                        28800           ; Refresh 8 hours
                        7200            ; Retry   2 hour
                        604800          ; Expire  7 days
                        86400 )         ; Minimum TTL 1 day
; ns clauses determining the authoritative nameservers
                IN      NS      ns.branch.company.tld.
                IN      NS      ns.company.tld.
; valid A record for the ns.branch.company.tld  server
ns              IN      A       194.149.10.129
```

The significance of the **A-type glue record** should be noted here as well. The A-type glue record must be included in the higher-level domain provided the domain is delegated to a server using a name in the delegated domain. In the above example, the name server of the `tld` domain delegates the authority for the `company.tld` domain to the `ns.company.tld` server. Therefore, the name of the `ns.company.tld` primary name server comes from the `company.tld` domain.

The glue record from the first example is used to delegate the `ns.company.tld` name at the TLD zone.

It is important to point out that the glue record is stored in memory along with the NS records of each name server that may deal with the translation of a name from the `company.tld` domain. The glue record is maintained in line with the TTL included in the higher-level zone.

Once we have successfully configured and launched the primary and secondary name servers for the `company.tld` domain, all nodes whose resolvers are directed to this server will be able to translate names from the `company.tld` domain. Our aim is to ensure that all resolvers within the Internet network are able to translate names from the `company.tld` domain. This is possible provided the administrator of the higher-level domain delegates the authority to your name servers. You must therefore request the delegation of the `company.tld` domain at the `ns.company.tld` and the `ns.provider.net` name servers.

6.3 Domain Registration

Note that there is a charge for registering and holding a domain. You can pay the charge yourself or through your Internet Service Provider. You should decide how you are going to pay before you register the domain. We have not dealt with registration and payment in our examples.

The domain registration (including eventual payment) must be done before the TLD hostmaster makes a particular delegation. There are more than 250 TLDs and each of them probably has slightly different registration rules.

In Chapter 8, you will learn that the TLD register is held by IANA. If you want to know who the administrator of a particular domain is and find contact information, visit `http://whois.iana.org`. This website contains the following form with which you can search for a TLD by name.

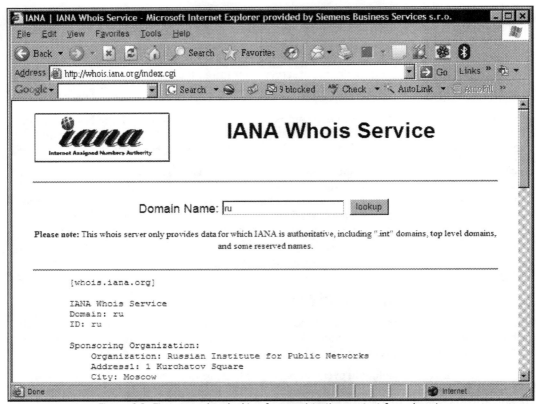

Figure 6.2: First step when looking for a registration contact for a domain

For example, for the ru domain you will see:

```
[whois.iana.org]

IANA Whois Service
Domain: ru
ID: ru

Sponsoring Organization:
    Organization: Russian Institute for Public Networks
    Address1: 1 Kurchatov Square
    City: Moscow
    Country: Russian Federation
    Postal Code: 123182
    Registration Date: 01-January-1985
    Last Updated Date: 01-January-1985

Administrative Contact:
    Name: .RU domain Administrative group
    Organization: Russian Institute for Public Networks
    Address1: 1 Kurchatov Square
    City: Moscow
    Country: Russian Federation
    Postal Code: 123182
```

```
            Phone: +7 095 196 7278, +7 095 737 6976
            Fax: +7 095 196 4984
            Email: ru--adm@ripn.net
            Registration Date: 15-June-2005
            Last Updated Date: 15-June-2005

        Technical Contact:
            Name: .RU domain Technical Center
            Organization: Russian Institute for Public Networks
            Address1: 1 Kurchatov Square
            City: Moscow
            Country: Russian Federation
            Postal Code: 123182
            Phone: +7 095 196 7278, +7 095 737 6976
            Fax: +7 095 196 4984
            Email: ru--tech@ripn.net
            Registration Date: 15-June-2005
            Last Updated Date: 15-June-2005
        URL for registration services: http://www.ripn.net/nic/dns/en/index.html
        whois Server (port 43): whois.ripn.net

        Nameserver Information:
            Nameserver: auth60.ns.uu.net.
            IP Address: 198.6.1.181
            Nameserver: ns.ripn.net.
            IP Address: 194.85.119.1
            Nameserver: ns1.relcom.ru.
            IP Address: 193.125.152.3
            Nameserver: ns2.nic.fr.
            IP Address: 192.93.0.4
            Nameserver: ns2.ripn.net.
            IP Address: 194.226.96.30
            Nameserver: ns5.msk-ix.net.
            IP Address: 193.232.128.6
            Nameserver: ns9.ripn.net.
            IP Address: 194.85.252.62
            Nameserver: sunic.sunet.se.
            IP Address: 192.36.125.2

        Registration Date: 07-April-1994
        Last Updated Date: 16-June-2005
```

We are especially interested in the row containing URL for registration services: This website contains basic information in English about registration, payment, and the delegation of subdomains bound to the .ru TLD domain.

For the .com domain, you see the following:

```
        URL for registration services: http://www.verisign-grs.com
```

Information and contact information for domains are generally kept in Internet registry databases as mentioned in Section 8.4.

7

Reverse Domain Delegation

A reverse translation is the mapping of an IP address to a domain name. We already know that a record defining the mapping of an IP address to a domain name is a **pointer record (PTR)**. Some programs such as ftp, traceroute, etc., use reverse translation. If a reverse record for a domain name is missing in DNS, some services such as FTP might refuse to work properly. Therefore, it is very important not to forget about PTR records and thus about reverse domains.

A reverse domain is always created and delegated for an entire IP address network. For example for a network 194.149.177, a reverse domain 177.149.194 in-addr.arpa must be created and delegated in DNS. A reverse domain has no connection to a forward domain. Domain names of various domains can coexist, and often do so, within one reverse domain.

The types of reverse domains are derived from the extent of the used network. The user makes use of 256 IP addresses of a C class or a subnetwork of a C class for his or her network. Providers then can have 256 IP addresses of a C class assigned, thus a B class network. There are three variants of the IP address range and therefore three variations of reverse domains:

- 255 C class addresses are assigned (i.e., as a B class address, i.e., prefix/16). This situation is not so common for regular users, but more for Internet providers.
- One or more C class addresses are affiliated (less than 255 or more than 255, but not creating a prefix/16).
- An interval of IP addresses smaller than one C class address is affiliated.

The delegation of reverse domains for B and C class networks is not looked after by the managers ccTLD or gTLD, but by regional Internet registries (RIPE, APNIC, ARIN, AfriNIC, or LACNIC). Reverse domains for IP address networks that RIPE gives to providers are delegated to the RIPE name server ns.ripe.net, for example, 193.in-addr.arpa, 194.in-addr.arpa, 195.in-addr.arpa, and so on. RIPE later delegates reverse domains for smaller intervals of IP addresses than a C class network to the name servers of providers or end users.

A reverse domain, like a forward domain, must be delegated to a minimum of two name servers. Internet providers usually provide a secondary name server for a reverse domain on their name servers.

The delegation of a reverse domain like the delegation of a forward domain consists of several steps:

1. Configuration of the primary name server
2. Configuration of the secondary name server
3. Delegation of the reverse domain
4. Registration of the reverse domain

We will demonstrate the process of delegation of a reverse domain with an example.

In the example, we will use our already-known company, Company Ltd. The Company Ltd. uses network 194.149.10.0 (a C class network) for its connection to the Internet. Company Ltd. has its own name server on a computer with the name ns.company.com and an IP address of 194.149.10.11. UNIX and BIND version 4.9 are installed on the name server ns.company.com.

The network administrator of Company Ltd. must delegate the reverse domain 10.149.194.id-addr.arpa. to the name server ns.company.com. An Internet provider will provide the secondary name server for the reverse domain on its name server ns.provider.net as shown in the following figure:

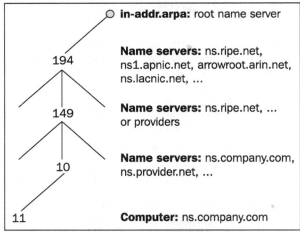

Figure 7.1: Reverse delegation for ns.company.com.

Let us now see the essential parts of the particular configuration files that provide the required delegations.

Server ns.company.com

File named.boot

```
...
primary     10.149.194.in-addr.arpa                    10.149.194.zone
```

File 10.149.194.zone

```
@           IN    SOA       ns.company.com hostmaster.company.com (
                            1998082402    ; Serial
                            28800         ; Refresh 8 hours
                                          ; Retry 2 hours
            604800                        ; Expire 7 days
            86400                         ; Minimum TTL 1 day
            IN    NS        ns.company.com.
            IN    NS        ns.provider.net.
            11    IN    PTR ns.company.com.
            ...
```

Server ns.provider.net

File named.boot

```
    ...
    secondary 10.149.194.in-addr.arpa    10.149.194.zone    194.149.10.11
```

Server ns.ripe.net (authoritative server for a superior domain)

File 149.194.zone

```
    ...
    10                  IN    NS          ns.company.com.
                        IN    NS          ns.provider.net.
```

The delegation of a domain to functional name servers must be performed by regional Internet registries (RIPE, APNIC, ARIN, AfriNIC, or LACNIC). The hostmaster must request this delegation from the RIPE, APNIC, ARIN, or LACNIC hostmaster using a form. An example is listed in Section 7.1.

The company, Company Ltd., has a branch. This branch uses 128 IP addresses, i.e., the subnetwork 194.149.10.128–194.149.10.255. The branch is administering its own name server with the name ns.branch.company.com and an IP address of 194.149.10.129. Therefore it is convenient that the reverse domain for the subnetwork 194.149.10/25 will be delegated to the name server ns.branch.company.com.

This example is quite common in practice, and we will use it for a demonstration of delegating a reverse domain for a subnetwork. But first a little theory.

The delegation of reverse domains for subnetworks was not used from the very beginning of DNS usage. Reverse domains for subnetworks are described in RFC 2317 and are called **Classless IN-ADDR.ARPA delegations**. The method used is compatible with the DNS mechanism and does not require modification of the software used.

Delegating Classless IN-ADDR.ARPA solves an unpleasant situation that used to occur in the past. A customer with an affiliated subnetwork of IP addresses, who had his or her own name server, used to be in a situation where he or she administered the forward domain, but the reverse domain was administered by his or her provider. Each addition of a new A type record brought with itself the necessity of asking the provider to add a PTR record into the reverse domain.

Let us also think about the marking of a reverse domain for a subnetwork.

If a customer has an affiliated network 194.149.10.0/24 (network class C), he or she has a reverse domain of 10.149.194.in-addr.arpa. The computer of ns.company.com with an IP address of 194.149.10.11 then has a record 11.10.149.194.in-addr.arpa in a reverse domain. Let the name ns.company.com has the pointer 11.10.149.194.in-addr.arpa in the DNS.

If a customer has a subnetwork 194.149.10.128/25, he or she has a reverse domain 128.10.149.194.in-addr.arpa. The marking of a reverse domain for a subnetwork is unusual, because it contains four digits separated by a dot, similar to an IP address. Then the computer ns.branch.company.com with an IP address 194.149.10.129 has a reverse domain of 129.128.10.149.194.in-addr.arpa, which is even more unusual. In fact, it is an artificial construction in which a principle of domain name creation is implemented. To make the construction even more bizarre, the superior name server uses a PTR type of record pointing to a CNAME type record, which is defined in a name server of a lower-level as shown in the following figure:

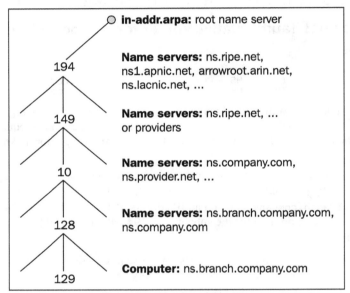

Figure 7.2: Classless delegation

Now, we will continue with the previous example.

Particular configuration files or their parts follow. They provide delegation of a reverse domain for a subnetwork 194.149.10.128/25. We will insert lines that are related to the delegation of a domain 128.10.149.194.in-addr.arpa into the configuration files from the previous example shown.

Server ns.company.com

File named.boot

```
primary 10.149.194.in-addr.arpa                        10.149.194.zone
secondary    128.10.149.194.in-addr.arpa    194.149.10.129  128.10.149.194.zone
```

File 10.149.194.zone

```
@              IN         SOA     ns.company.com hostmaster.company.com (
                                     1998082402        ; Serial
                                          28800        ; Refresh 8 hours
                                           7200        ; Retry   2 hour
                                         604800        ; Expire  7 days
                                          86400 )      ; Minimum TTL 1 day
               IN         NS      ns.company.com.
               IN         NS      ns.provider.net.
11             IN         PTR     ns.company.com.
128            IN         NS      ns.branch.company.com.
               IN         NS      ns.company.com.
129            IN         CNAME   129.128.10.149.194.in-addr.arpa.
130            IN         CNAME   130.128.10.149.194.in-addr.arpa.
131            IN         CNAME   131.128.10.149.194.in-addr.arpa.
132            IN         CNAME   132.128.10.149.194.in-addr.arpa.
133            IN         CNAME   133.128.10.149.194.in-addr.arpa.
134            IN         CNAME   134.128.10.149.194.in-addr.arpa.
... Etc. up to
254            IN         CNAME   254.128.10.149.194.in-addr.arpa.
```

Server ns.branch.company.com

File named.boot

```
primary    128.10.149.194.in-addr-arpa    128.10.149.194.zone
```

File 128.10.149.194.zone

```
@              IN         SOA     ns.branch.company.com
hostmaster.branch.company.com (
                                     1998082502        ; Serial
                                          28800        ; Refresh 8 hours
                                           7200        ; Retry   2 hour
                                         604800        ; Expire  7 days
                                          86400 )      ; Minimum TTL 1 day
               IN         NS      ns.branch.company.com.
               IN         NS      ns.company.com.
129            IN         PTR     ns.branch.company.com.
130            IN         PTR     name1.branch.company.com.
131            IN         PTR     name2.branch.company.com.
... Etc. up to
254            IN         PTR     name.branch.company.com.
```

8

Internet Registry

8.1 International Organizations

A history of organizations that focus on the Internet would be enough for an independent and very interesting publication. The Internet was born in the USA and was financed for many years by American taxpayers. This situation became no longer viable in the '90s resulting in the creation of a new structure of Internet organization. End users participate in financing this structure by paying their Internet providers for connectivity and for registration of their subdomains. Providers then put part of these payments towards the activities of these international organizations.

Two links from the original structure are important for us as ordinary Internet users:

- **RFC-editor**, which publishes the RFC standards (`http://www.rfc-editor.org/`). This link is a source for Internet standards for us. To better understand the process of Internet standards, it is recommended to look at RFC 2026.

- **The Internet Assigned Numbers Authority (IANA)**. Its home page `http://www.iana.org/` states: *Dedicated to preserving the central coordinating functions of the global Internet for the public good.* IANA maintains three very important registers:

    - The **Top-Level Domain (TLD)** register (`http://www.iana.org/domain-names.htm`).
    - A register of allocation of the addresses in Internet space (IP version 4 addresses as well as IP version 6 addresses), i.e., assigning the address space to the individual regions of the world (`http://www.iana.org/ipaddress/ip-addresses.htm`).
    - Assigned numbers (`http://www.iana.org/numbers.html`), i.e., a register of other assigned numbers, contains not only numbers for individual protocols, but also, for example, allocation of AS numbers for individual regions of the world. If you study packets of certain protocols in detail and come across a certain field with a value you do not know, you will appreciate Assigned Numbers. Assigned Numbers were originally published from time to time as RFC (for example, RFC 1700). This mechanism was later replaced (see RFC 3232) by an online database.

The new structure falls under the umbrella of **The Internet Corporation for Assigned Names and Numbers (ICANN)** (http://www.icann.org), whose web pages include the preambles. ICANN is a nonprofit corporation that was formed to assume responsibility for the IP address space allocation, protocol parameter assignment, domain name system management, and root server system management functions previously performed under U.S. government contract by IANA and other entities. ICANN has a contract with IANA, which also specifies activities of IANA. IANA is currently working on those areas specified in the previous paragraphs about it.

From our point of view, three policies issued by ICANN are most important:

- Criteria for Establishment of New Regional Internet Registries: **Regional Internet Registries (RIR)** have parts of the address space allocated by IANA and are responsible for assigning IP addresses and AS numbers in a particular region. Currently, valid policy designates the following regions:
    o Europe and the Middle East
    o Africa
    o North America
    o Latin America including the Caribbean
    o Asia-Pacific
- ccTLD Administration and Delegation: It concerns the **country code TLD (ccTLD)** as well as **generic TLD (gTLD)**. A TLD manager, who is responsible for the operation of a particular TLD and for allocation of domains of the second and following levels (TLD Registries), is determined for each TLD. The process of identifying and determining a TLD manager is quite difficult.
- A Unique Authoritative Root for the DNS: It is the operation of root name servers that is vital for the Internet. Root name servers not only administer TLDs and their subdomains, but also service TLD arpa, which is vital for reverse translations.

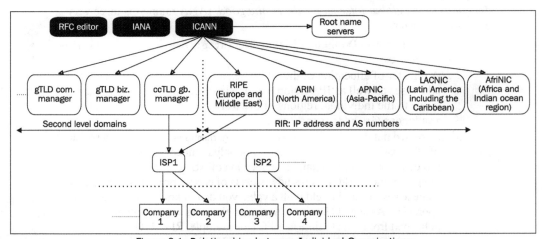

Figure 8.1: Relationships between Individual Organizations

8.2 Regional Internet Registry (RIR)

As we have already mentioned, the world is geographically divided into five regions. Five RIRs are currently established:

- **RIPE NCC (Réseaux IP Européens Network Coordination Centre)**, which administers Europe and the Middle East. For more details see `http://www.ripe.net/`.

- **ARIN (American Registry for Internet Numbers)**, which administers North America and Africa south of the Equator. For more details see `http://www.arin.net/`.

- **APNIC (Asia-Pacific Network Information Centre)**, which administers the Asia-Pacific region. For more details see `http://www.apnic.net/`.

- **LACNIC (Latin America and Caribbean Network Information Centre)**, which administers Latin America and the Caribbean. For more details see `http://www.lacnic.net/`.

- **AfriNIC (Africa Network Information Centre)** for Africa and the Indian Ocean region, see `http://www.afrinic.net/`.

End users do not communicate directly with RIR. They usually communicate through **Local Internet Registries (LIRs)**. LIRs are, in most, cases ISPs. To ensure that an RIR will communicate with the ISP, the ISP has to conclude an agreement with the particular RIR in advance and contribute financially to its activities, i.e., to become an LIR. In some regions, additional bodies are inserted between RIR and LIR. These are then called **National Internet Registers, (NIR)** and they usually operate within one state. In this case, the end user addresses his or her requests to an LIR. The LIR hands the request over to the NIR, which then addresses it to the RIR.

On the basis of a request, the RIR assigns the IP addresses and numbers of autonomous systems. The RIR registers the assigned IP addresses and other information in its database. This information creates objects in the RIR database. Apart from objects such as an IP address number or an AS number, the RIR database also includes objects describing people responsible for administrative and technical contact, i.e., network administrators. It also includes route objects, which describe routing between AS, and mntner objects, which authorize the access to change the objects' properties.

The RIR database is publicly accessible. The whois command is used for reading information from the databases of a regional IR. The web interface, which is available on the web pages of individual RIR, is usually intended for end users. For example, the WWW server RIPE (`http://www.ripe.net/`) is also included in this database.

An RIR creates norms that LIRs (providers) and end users have to observe. RIPE creates norms called RIPE number (e.g., RIPE 159). All RIPE norms are readily available at `ftp://ftp.ripe.net/ripe/docs/`. Similarly, APNIC has norms such as APNIC 86 (Policies for IP version 4 address space management in the Asia-Pacific region), which is also publicly accessible on the APNIC server at `ftp://ftp.apnic.net/apnic/docs/`.

An RIR is also responsible for the delegation of reverse domains. In particular, if, for example, subnet 193.0.0.0/8 has been allocated to an RIR, this RIR is then responsible for the correct operation of the 193.in-arddr.arpa reverse domain.

A list of RIRs and country codes is given in Appendix A.

8.3 IP Addresses and AS Numbers

The allocation of blocks of IP addresses can be found at `http://www.iana.org/ipaddress/ip-addresses.htm`. The allocations of space for IP version 6 global unicast are shown in the following table (for the latest assignments, see `http://www.iana.org/assignments/ipv6-unicast-address-assignments`):

Global Unicast Prefix	Assignment
2001:0000::/23	IANA
2001:0200::/23	APNIC
2001:0400::/23	ARIN
2001:0600::/23	RIPE NCC
2001:0800::/23	RIPE NCC
2001:0A00::/23	RIPE NCC
2001:0C00::/23	APNIC
2001:0E00::/23	APNIC
2001:1200::/23	LACNIC
2001:1400::/23	RIPE NCC
2001:1600::/23	RIPE NCC
2001:1800::/23	ARIN
2001:1A00::/23	RIPE NCC
2001:1C00::/22	RIPE NCC
2001:2000::/20	RIPE NCC
2001:3000::/21	RIPE NCC
2001:3800::/22	RIPE NCC
2001:3C00::/22	RESERVED
2001:4000::/23	RIPE NCC
2001:4200::/23	AfriNIC
2001:4400::/23	APNIC
2001:4600::/23	RIPE NCC
2001:4800::/23	ARIN
2001:4A00::/23	RIPE NCC
2001:4C00::/23	RIPE NCC
2001:5000::/20	RIPE NCC
2001:8000::/19	APNIC
2001:A000::/20	APNIC

Global Unicast Prefix	Assignment
2002:0000::/16	6to4
2003:0000::/18	RIPE NCC
2400:0000::/19	APNIC
2400:2000::/19	APNIC
2400:4000::/21	APNIC
2600:0000::/22	ARIN
2604:0000::/22	ARIN
2608:0000::/22	ARIN
260C:0000::/22	ARIN
2610:0000::/23	ARIN
2800:0000::/23	LACNIC
2A00:0000::/21	RIPE NCC
2A01:0000::/16	RIPE NCC
3FFE:0000::/16	6BONE

Table 8.1: IPv6 global unicast address assignment

The allocation of IP version 4 addresses for RIRs is currently the following:

```
024.0.0.0 - 024.255.255.255   - ARIN
041.0.0.0 - 041.255.255.255   - AfriNIC
058.0.0.0 - 061.255.255.255   - APNIC
062.0.0.0 - 062.255.255.255   - RIPE
063.0.0.0 - 076.255.255.255   - ARIN
080.0.0.0 - 091.255.255.255   - RIPE
124.0.0.0 - 126.255.255.255   - APNIC
189.0.0.0 - 190.255.255.255   - LACNIC
193.0.0.0 - 195.255.255.255   - RIPE
199.0.0.0 - 199.255.255.255   - ARIN
200.0.0.0 - 201.255.255.255   - LACNIC
202.0.0.0 - 203.255.255.255   - APNIC
204.0.0.0 - 209.255.255.255   - ARIN
210.0.0.0 - 211.255.255.255   - APNIC
212.0.0.0 - 213.255.255.255   - RIPE
216.0.0.0 - 216.255.255.255   - ARIN
217.0.0.0 - 217.255.255.255   - RIPE
218.0.0.0 - 222.255.255.255   - APNIC
```

We should also mention intervals of IP addresses for intranets (RFC 1918):

```
10.0.0.0       -   10.255.255.255
172.16.0.0     -   172.31.255.255
192.168.0.0    -   192.168.255.255
```

Allocating intervals of AS numbers to RIRs is similar to allocating intervals of IP addresses to RIRs. The concrete intervals allocated to RIRs can be found in Assigned Numbers (http://www.iana.org/numbers.html). Note that AS numbers in the interval from 64512 to 65534 are reserved, in accordance with RFC 1930, for secure networks (intranets).

8.4 Internet Registry

To become an Internet provider, you need to be able to communicate with an RIR. However, RIRs only accepts requests from LIRs. Therefore, it is first necessary to become an LIR.

8.4.1 Registration of a Local IR

The procedure and rules for LIR registration are described:

- For RIPE in document RIPE 303 (Procedure for Becoming a Member of the RIPE NCC), which can be found at `http://www.ripe.net/ripe/docs/internet-registries.html`
- For APNIC at `http://www.apnic.net/member/membersteps.html`
- For ARIN at `http://www.arin.net/membership/index.html`
- For LACNIC at `http://lacnic.net/en/mem.html`
- For AfriNIC at `http://www.afrinic.net`

Three steps need to be taken to establish a new LIR:

1. Establishing an item about a local IR in the local IR list in RIR database.
2. Familiarizing yourself with registration procedures.
3. Concluding a business agreement to ensure that RIR starts sending you invoices.

8.5 Delegation of Second-Level Domains

From the point of view of IANA and root name server administrators, the particular TLD manager maintains the relevant TLD. From the end user's point of view and especially from the point of view of an ISP, this situation is not as simple. We have to bear in mind that the TLD manager also ensures the registration of **Second Level Domains** (**SLDs**), which are widely used in many countries. The registration of an SLD requires quite a large agenda, which in turn means that a larger office is needed. In many countries, this office is called the **Network Information Center** (**NIC**).

We are most likely to encounter one of the following types of SLD registration:

- There is one authority that registers SLDs. This authority operates name servers for the relevant TLD, registers SLDs, and at the same time tries to settle disputes in those cases where two or more people argue about a certain domain.
- The central authority only operates the central SLD register and name servers and helps to solve disputes about domains. The central authority does not carry out the registration as such, but instead the registration is delegated to different entities such as ISPs. End users register their SLD through an ISP, which has access to the central register. As this solution allows competition in SLD registration, it should help to bring the fees for SLD registration down. This solution needs to be completed by the **LRR** (**Last Resort Registry**), which is usually operated by the central authority. LRR is a backup in case an ISP goes bankrupt. The LRR's task is to take over all SLDs registered by the bankrupt ISP if this bankruptcy occurs. This is a security measure to ensure that the end users of the bankrupt ISP do not lose their SLD registration.

9

DNS in Closed Intranets

A closed intranet is nothing but a network that is not connected to the Internet. One would say that DNS is very simple to configure in relation to closed intranets. What is the problem then?

Your company uses the company.com domain, and you have very little difficulty in configuring your domain's name server; in fact, you configure the primary name server for your company.com domain on one machine and the secondary one on another.

You direct all your clients' resolvers to these name servers. The following figure shows a client asking the name server configured by you for a translation of the name server.company.com to its IP address:

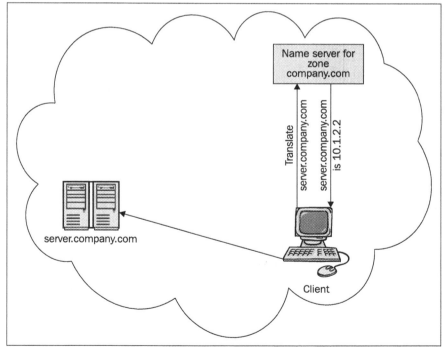

Figure 9.1: Translation of the name server.company.com to its IP address

Everything is working fine until the client sends an incorrect request for `server.ompany.com` instead of the correct `server.company.com` (i.e., there is a one-character error).

Common mistakes like this result in additional time taken to find the server, and in some cases, the application does not respond for several seconds. The following figure explains the reason:

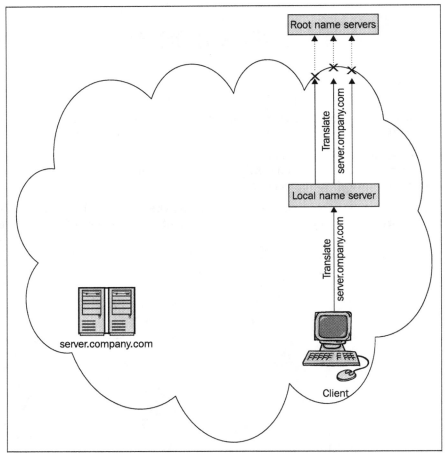

Figure 9.2: The intranet name server is trying to contact (unsuccessfully) root name servers in the Internet

The configured office name server is the `company.com` domain's authority; it does not, however, have any authority over the `ompany.com` domain. As it has no authority over the latter, it has to ask for the translation from the root name servers, which would help it in finding the authoritative name server that is the only one authorized to declare that there is no computer named 'server' in the `ompany.com` domain (or, that it does exist as a completely different machine).

But we are in a closed intranet without an Internet connection. This means that the datagrams containing the requests for the root name servers are thrown away at the network boundaries. The company's name server does not receive a response, and therefore the client is left high and dry.

After an interval without a response, the resolver will realize there must be a problem and send an error message to the user. This error message will only get through if the user has been patient enough not to reboot his or her computer.

The administrator's first reaction is to understand that root name servers cannot be contacted from a closed intranet. He or she remembers that at startup, data about root name servers is loaded into the name server's cache (the file is usually named `cache` and can be loaded by the `cache` command in `/etc/named.boot`). Blaming the file, the administrator deletes it; yet there is no change in the situation. It's simple; if the name server finds no information about the root name servers, the name server's program code implicitly contains IP addresses of some name servers, as they were included by the software developer to handle such situations.

The following figure shows the solution:

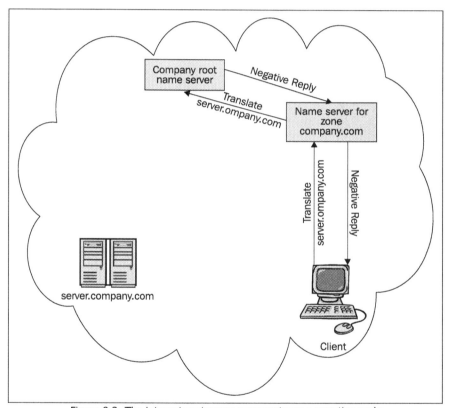

Figure 9.3: The intranet root name server returns a negative reply

You need to create a company root name server (one or more) instead of deleting the file containing information about root name servers. You should make adjustments to it so that everything gets routed to your company's root name server.

> You do not need a separate machine for the root name server as it can be configured on the current name server by creating a primary name server for the root domain.

9.1 Configuring a Root Name Server on the Same Server (BIND Version 4)

Let's say you have two name servers in your closed intranet: ns1.company.com at IP address 10.1.1.1 and ns2.company.com at IP address 10.2.2.2. Configure both name servers as root name servers and, at the same time, as name servers for the company.com domain.

You will need to insert a line in the /etc/named.boot file of the ns1.company.com and ns2.company.com servers. This line will declare that your name server is also the primary name server for the root domain '.':

```
...
primary company.com     file1
primary .               file2
...
```

Note that, there is no line containing the cache command.

It is important to check file2, which specifies the root domain:

```
@                       IN  SOA     ...
                        IN  NS      ns1.company.com.
                        IN  NS      ns2.company.com.
company.com             IN  NS      ns1.company.com.
                        IN  NS      ns2.company.com.

ns1.company.com.        IN  A   10.1.1.1
ns2.company.com.        IN  A   10.1.1.1
```

In this file, we have not inserted any NS resource record for other domains than company.com. That is why there are no other domains within our closed intranet; but additional domains can be easily specified. One way or another, there is no such domain as ompany.com. At the same time, an authority will have to be delegated over the company.com domain to the ns1.company.com and ns2.company.com name servers (that they are identical is a mere coincidence).

Now, the zone file for the company.com domain (file1) looks exactly as you would expect:

```
@                       IN  SOA     ...
                        IN  NS      ns1.company.com.
                        IN  NS      ns2.company.com.
ns1                     IN  A   10.1.1.1
ns2                     IN  A   10.2.2.2
...
```

9.2 Configuring a Root Name Server on a Separate Server (BIND Version 4)

Let's say you have two name servers for the `company.com` domain in our closed Intranet: `ns1.company.com` at IP address 10.1.1.1 and `ns2.company.com` at IP address 10.2.2.2. And an additional third name server for the root domain (.): `ns-root.company.com.` at IP address 10.3.3.3.

9.2.1 Configuring a Name Server for the Root Domain

In the `/etc/named.boot` file of the `ns-root.company.com` server, insert a line declaring that your name server is the primary name server for the root domain "." (dot):

```
...
primary .      file2
...
```

Note that, there is no line with a `cache` command.

`file2` specifying the root domain will delegate authority over the `company.com` domain to the `ns1.company.com` and `ns2.company.com` name servers:

```
@                     IN  SOA   ...
                      IN  NS    ns1.company.com.
                      IN  NS    ns2.company.com.
ns1.company.com.      IN  A     10.1.1.1
ns2.company.com.      IN  A     10.2.2.2
company.com           IN  NS    ns1.company.com.
                      IN  NS    ns2.company.com.
```

As mentioned earlier, since you have not inserted any NS record for any other domain than `company.com` in this file, there are no other domains within the company network. More domains can, however, be easily specified. In this case, there is definitely no other domain than `company.com`. Authority over this domain also needs to be delegated to the `ns1.company.com` and `ns2.company.com` name servers.

9.2.2 Configuring Name Servers for company.com

In the `/etc/named.boot` file of the `ns1.company.com` and `ns2.company.com` servers, you need to add a line with the `cache` command, specifying from which file the information about the root name servers is to be loaded:

```
...
primary company.com    file1
cache .      file3
...
```

`file3` will contain nonauthoritative information about the root name servers (only one is used here, but there can be more):

```
.                        99999   IN  NS  ns-root.company.com.
ns-root.company.com.     99999   IN  A   10 3 3 3
```

This file can never contain a **Start Of Authority** (**SOA**) resource record, as it introduces strictly authoritative data. Also interesting is the second column containing 99999; you don't usually see this column in other files. Its function is to specify the record's lifetime in memory (TTL). Why does it have to be included here? The reason is simply that other databases do not contain this value, and it is taken from the Minimum TTL value within the SOA resource record. Here, you cannot use an SOA resource record so the value needs to be specified explicitly. If it was not specified, the data would expire immediately upon startup (TTL=0). In other words, the data would be declared invalid. The name server would have no information about the root name servers, which would call up IP addresses explicitly stated in the program. The effect is illustrated in Figure 9.2.

The zone file (`file1`) for the `company.com` domain looks then exactly as you would expect:

```
@        IN  SOA   ...
         IN  NS    ns1.company.com.
         IN  NS    ns2.company.com.
ns1      IN  A     10.1.1.1
ns2      IN  A     10.2.2.2
ns3      IN  A     10.3.3.3
...
```

9.3 Root DNS Server in Windows 2000/2003

Windows 2000 behaves in a slightly different way if the DNS server is not configured as root and if the `%SystemRoot%\system32\dns\cache.dns` file is removed, Windows 2000/2003 does not attempt to contact any root name servers. It does not have, for these purposes, the root name server's IP addresses hidden somewhere in the DNS server program code.

The documentation for Windows 2000/2003 actually states at least once that if you have a separate DNS in a closed intranet, you just need to delete the `%SystemRoot%\system32\dns\cache.dns` file. On the other hand, the same documentation recommends in many other places to follow the same instructions as presented here in Section 9.1 and 9.2. In fact, if you are doing the primary configuration of the DNS server, you are asked whether a root name server should be created. In such a case, Windows 2000/2003 will itself create a `%SystemRoot%\system32\dns\root.dns` zone file and it will edit the other files itself. Later, if you want to configure your DNS server as the root server, you simply create a new *forwarding zone* and name it '.'.

The trick with deleting the `%SystemRoot%\system32\dns\cache.dns` file is not really worth trying even in Windows 2000/2003. Not only is it ineffective if the files are read from the Active Directory, but it also becomes questionable if several name servers on varying platforms are used in one company network.

10

DNS and Firewall

A firewall separates the company internal network (intranet) from the Internet. This enables intranet clients to gain information from the Internet, while preventing any aggressors on the Internet from attacking the computers of the internal network.

Let us say that a company has been assigned the company.com domain. It will want to use this domain for both the Internet and its intranet. The company.com domain in the Internet will most likely contain only a few records such as www.company.com, mail.company.com and a few other records (MX records for company.com pointing at mail.company.com, etc.). The company.com domain on the intranet can contain, on the other hand, tens, hundreds, or even thousands of computers.

To put this differently, there will be two company.com domains, with each of them containing different records, but the problem is that they both will have the same company.com name. There cannot be two domains of the same name on the Internet. But both of them are not actually on the Internet, one of the two names is used just for the intranet.

Problems can arise with the firewall as such. The applications (for example, proxy) that need to work with the company.com domain on the intranet as well as other Internet domains are run on the firewall. Additionally, the firewall is the only server that has to act in respect to Internet clients as if it worked with the Internet company.com domain.

The applications that are run on the firewall (such as proxy) use the resolver, while the firewall itself will provide information as a server. As a tool, we can use the fact that the resolver does not need to be directed towards the name server that is run on the local computer (i.e., on 127.0.0.1).

One problem is firewall hook up and assigning an IP address. Another problem is the firewall configuration in respect to DNS. Both problems are independent in their nature.

If a name server, such as BIND version 9.2 and higher, is used on the firewall, then the whole problem can be solved quite nicely by using views. This solution is described in Chapter 4 under Section *view Statement*. On the other hand the view technique is not often used. This chapter deals with a situation where we do not want to use the view technique or we do not have the desired BIND version at our disposal. Then, in respect to the DNS configuration on the firewall, various events might occur as shown in the following sections. We will go through a few model situations that are based on realistic scenarios.

10.1 Shared DNS for Internet and Intranet

The easiest solution is sharing a DNS database between the Internet and intranet. This might be unsuitable for two reasons:

- Translations of computers with nonroutable addresses (net 10/8, 172.16/12, or 192.168/16) are published on the Internet.

- Information concerning the company structure is published (IP addresses of intranet computers). This information is usually confidential.

The most significant question when configuring DNS on the firewall is whether or not all Internet names should be translated on the intranet, and whether the intranet clients should be enabled to translate the names of the company.com domain that are located on the intranet only.

10.1.1 The Whole Internet is Translated on the Intranet

If the whole Internet is translated on the intranet, then the intranet must also route IP addresses of the whole Internet. This has some negative effects as well:

1. The routing of the intranet must be ready for this, i.e., all IP addresses that are not from the intranet must be routed towards the firewall. This is usually done by using the *default* route in the routing tables. Keeping this routing item in the routing table in all routers on the intranet is not, especially in jumbo intranets, an easy task.

2. Security managers monitor the intranet traffic for attacks from other networks. If only the IP datagrams with the 10/8, 172.16/12, or 192.168/16 address range are transmitted in the network, then a security incident can easily be detected upon the occurrence of an address from a different address range. If any other addresses are allowed to be present on the intranet, then we have to take this tool away from the security managers.

The translation of the whole Internet on the intranet is used, especially, in the following two cases:

- If transparent proxies are run on the firewall. A transparent proxy is particularly friendly to those using POP3, Telnet, FTP, etc. If the user wants to use Telnet to log onto, for example, www.packtpub.com, then he/she is not obliged to log onto the proxy (firewall) and then onto the destination server. The user simply writes telnet www.packtpub.com on the intranet. The transparent proxy accepts the connection as if it was the destination server itself and hands the query over, on the user's behalf, to the destination server on the Internet. But Telnet is not used by the majority of users to log onto www.packtpub.com since most of them would just use the regular internet browser, which does not require any transparent proxies.

  The conclusion is that regular users do not use Telnet or FTP (excerpt FTP implementation in browsers) and administrators and developers do not mind them using their regular proxy for the Telnet and FTP applications. Also an employee on the intranet can use the local POP3 server and does not need to use an external one. But from an employee's point of view, it is of course convenient to read personal mails from public mail servers while at work. (It is impossible for the employee to read personal mails via POP3, but they can use webmail instead.)

- If only protection by filtering on the intranet is used and not the traditional firewall with proxy.

The firewall usually works as a primary name server for the company.com domain, which is shared by both the intranet and the Internet:

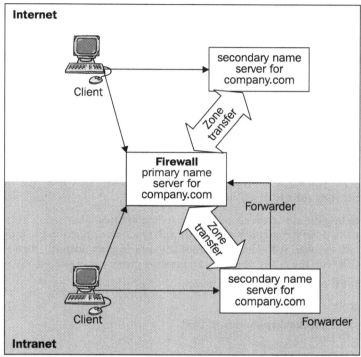

Figure 10.1: Company domain is shared by both the intranet and the Internet

It is wise to have at least two name servers for a domain (primary and secondary). Having two name servers available for both the intranet and Internet is necessary since the firewall is accessible from both networks. Now all that has to be done is to configure one secondary name server for the intranet and the other one for the Internet.

The secondary Internet server for our domain will most likely be set up by our Internet provider.

However on the intranet, the secondary name server can be set up on any other computer. If an intranet client requests the translation of the name from another domain directly on the firewall, then there is not a problem. The firewall can ask Internet root name servers for help and will then fulfill the client's wish. If the client asks an intranet secondary name server for the translation of a name from another domain, the problem is that this secondary name server is not connected to the Internet and, therefore, cannot ask root name servers for help. To be able to do such translations, the intranet secondary name server is configured as a slave server of the firewall, which runs as a DNS forwarder. The firewall does the translation and hands it over to the inferior server that passes it on to the client right away.

10.1.2 Only Intranet Addresses are Translated on Intranet

The translation of Internet addresses in the intranet is not usually necessary at all. On the intranet, just the firewall (proxy) name needs to be translated as the client establishes connection with the proxy before the proxy establishes connection with the destination Internet server on the client's behalf. So, the proxy needs to be capable of translating the destination Internet server name into an IP address.

If you want to practice this, try these two examples:

1. Downloading the www.packtpub.com website by the Internet client using Telnet. Use Telnet but always specify port 80 instead of 23:

    ```
    C:> telnet www.packtpub.com 80
    ```

    Now, you can establish the connection by using Telnet on port 80 and entering the following command (sometimes it is worth setting up local echo in telnet):

    ```
    GET   /  HTTP/1.0
    <Enter> <Enter>
    ```

    This will get you to the homepage, i.e., most likely the index.html file. (<Enter> means simply pressing the *Enter* key on the keyboard).

2. Downloading the www.packtpub.com site by the intranet client using Telnet. If you are located on the intranet behind the firewall (and have access to the Internet through the firewall without the need for any other authentication), then establish the connection with the proxy of the port where the proxy is run (frequently port 8080):

    ```
    C:> telnet proxy.company.com 8080
    ```

    and enter the following command:

    ```
    GET http://www.packtpub.com HTTP/1.0
    <Enter><Enter>
    ```

    This will get you to the homepage, i.e., most likely the index.html file. Note that you handed the destination name server of www.packtpub.com to the proxy in the form of a text chain, not an IP address.

The following figure shows how to configure DNS of the intranet so that it would not translate the Internet:

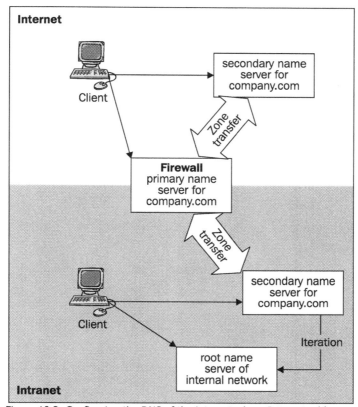

Figure 10.2: Configuring the DNS of the intranet where Internet addresses are not translated

A root name server is set up on the intranet. If a query concerns a domain other than the company.com domain, the root name server replies negatively. Other domains do not exist in this intranet.

Since it is practical to have two name servers on the intranet, two computers are set up. Both computers run secondary name servers for company.com and, at the same time, they run the root name servers.

It is also important to note that if an intranet client routes its resolver directly to the firewall, then the firewall translates any Internet addresses to the client. Therefore, the client's resolver must be routed towards the intranet servers.

10.2 Name Server Installed on Firewall

If we want to have two separated zones for the company.com domain, the primary Internet server is usually located on the firewall and the secondary Internet server on the computer of the Internet provider. A separate pair of primary/secondary servers is set up within the intranet.

And again, we have two possibilities. The first one enables the translation of the whole Internet on the intranet, and the second one enables the translation of only the intranet zone on the intranet.

10.2.1 Translation in Intranet—Whole Internet

We have two separate pairs of name servers as shown in the following figure:

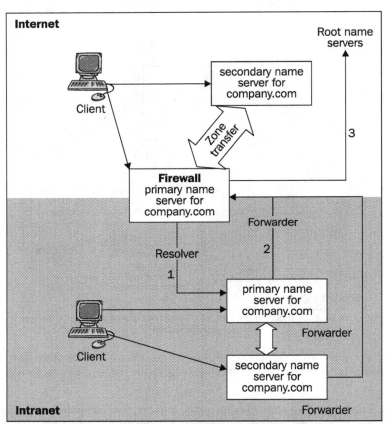

Figure 10.3: Company DNS zone is divided into two independent zones with the same domain name company.com, but with a different content

One of the pairs is on the intranet, while the other is on the Internet.

The first problem is that an application that is run on the firewall (for example, proxy) needs information on the intranet company.com zone, although it also needs the information on all other Internet domains. This is done by setting up the firewall resolver not towards the firewall name server, but towards the intranet name server that has the intranet zone available.

1. The application on the firewall needs to be translated to, for example, www.packtpub.com, so it asks the intranet name server (arrow 1).

2. The intranet name server is a slave server that sends all queries that it is incapable of dealing with to the firewall (arrow 2).

3. The firewall name server has access to the Internet root name servers (arrow 3) and can therefore do the translation.

4. The result is handed back over to the intranet's name server, which then immediately hands it over to the client on the firewall.

5. The intranet client asks the intranet name servers for translations. If the translation is of a local domain, the client receives an answer. If it involves translating an Internet domain, then such a query is handed over to the firewall.

10.2.2 Translation in Intranet without Internet Translation

Not translating the Internet on the intranet means that we need to create an intranet root name server.

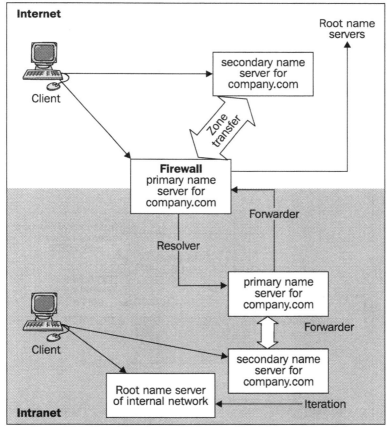

Figure 10.4: Translation in Local Network without Internet Translation

The interesting thing is that there are at least two name servers on the intranet, with each of them having a different function. The first one (labeled as the primary name server) is used by the firewall. If the intranet client routed its resolver towards this name server, the name server would translate anything from the Internet and the intranet company.com zone as well. However, we do not want this to happen, which is why the intranet resolvers of the clients are routed towards other intranet name servers that use the intranet root name server. The intranet root name server then prevents other domains from being translated.

10.3 Dual DNS

If we want to have separate zones for both the Internet and intranet, we have to keep them on two separate computers (since they have the same domain name). The aim of dual DNS is to run the primary name server of the company.com domain of both the Internet and intranet on just one computer if it is a question of money. While in big companies many different servers are run on the intranet, which enables the operation of separate name servers, small companies would often not wish to install another computer just to run the name server.

But how does a dual DNS work? Two name servers are run on the firewall (two processes). Each of them is run on a different port. The following figure shows the Internet name server being run on port 7053, while the intranet name server is run on port 8053:

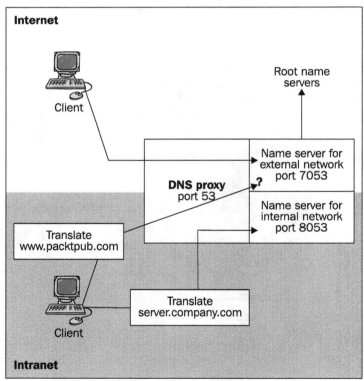

Figure 10.5: Dual DNS

It is improbable that the usual client would use a port other than port 53, since they would not be aware of the existence of ports 7053 and 8053.

A DNS proxy is run on the firewall standard port 53 of the name server. The DNS proxy server identifies the source of queries. Based on their origins, the proxy either refuses them, or hands them over to the name server on port 7053 or the name server on port 8053.

If the queries come from:

- An Internet client, then they are handed over to the Internet name server (port 7053 in the figure)
- An intranet client, then there are two different cases.

  Firstly, any request for a translation from the company.com domain is handed over to the intranet name server (port 8053).

  Secondly, any request for a translation of a different Internet domain is left to the DNS proxy, which decides:

  o If we want to translate the Internet on the intranet, then the request is handed over to the Internet name server (port 7053).
  o If we do not want to translate other Internet domains on the intranet, then it gives a negative response. What is interesting about this is the fact that if we do not have other (for example, secondary) name servers, then we do not even need the intranet root name server. The negative response is issued directly by the DNS proxy.

- An application running on the firewall (such as proxy), then if the request is for the company.com domain it is handed over to the intranet name server (port 8053) or if it concerns a different domain it is handed over to the Internet name server (port 5073).

10.4 End Remarks

In this book, we learned about DNS principles, resolver configuration, and configuration of various name servers. You must have realized that domain registration and delegation is altogether quite easy. However, in spite of its comprehensibility, the DNS is often a source of problems to ordinary computer users.

The correct diagnosis of computer problems is similar to a correct medical diagnosis. In both cases, it is important not only to reach the correct diagnosis, but also to do so in the minimum time. We can suspect mistakes in a DNS configuration if a user complains either that his or her computer does not communicate at all or, more often, the communication seems to be slow from time to time even if the network infrastructure is fast.

In such cases, if a user asks you for help, you should sit down in front of the user's computer, run the command prompt (never mind if it is a UNIX or a Windows machine), and find out the following:

1. Find the IP addresses of an default gateway and a local DNS server (for example, the IP address of the DNS server of your Internet Service Provider). If the TCP/IP protocol stack is installed; the best method to do it is to type a `ipconfig` command (in Windows) or ifconfig (in UNIX).

2. By `ping` with IP address of default gateway command test connection to default gateway. If a default gateway is accessible, simply type the `ping` command along with the IP address of DNS server. If the default gateway or DNS server does not respond, we can see that it is not a DNS problem, but a problem of the network infrastructure.

3. If the DNS server is placed outside your local network, you should also verify the network connection quality with the help of the `ping` command, now with the parameter `-t` (in Windows only). Let the command work for a while, stop it, and look at its statistic. If more than 10% of packets are lost, then the problem is again in the network infrastructure.

4. Now you can focus on the DNS because the problem is probably there. Accomplishing this is very simple. Type the `ping` command, not with an IP address of the DNS server, but with its name. The response must be as fast as if you are using the IP address. If not, check the resolver configuration.

5. Now you can check if a DNS translation of the name of some remote server in Internet to its IP address is functional. Be aware of the fact that known Internet servers are usually configured not to respond to the `ping` command. You must use the `tracert` command (or `traceroute` in UNIX) instead.

If you have passed all the previous steps successfully, verify if the response is faster when using the IP address compared to using a DNS name. If both responses are equally fast, then the problem is neither in the network infrastructure nor in DNS. The problem could not be on the client site, but on the server (application) site (for example, the DNS configuration of the application server is wrong).

You probably think that the previously described problems are too shallow for you, but you should realize that the DNS problems can be found in different levels:

- Ordinary users: Their computers either run or not, and they are usually ignorant about DNS.

- Local administrators: They configure user's computers and should understand the basic DNS principles.

- Local name server administrators (local hostmasters): They must understand the DNS configuration and principles in detail.

- ISP hostmasters: They must know about not only DNS configuration, but also communication with the Internet registries.

- Internet Registry hostmasters: A detailed DNS knowledge is essential, but in this case, it is more of policy than of DNS administration.

Dear reader, we do not know which level you belong to, but we wish you good luck and success at your work and hope that this publication was useful to you.

Country Codes and RIRs

The information included in this appendix comes from `http://www.ripe.net/`. TLDs for individual countries are assigned in accordance with ISO 3166 (`http://www.iso.org/iso/en/prods-services/iso3166ma/02iso-3166-code-lists/index.html`). However, if you look at the following table of assigned ccTLDs and compare it with ISO 3166, you will find that a significantly greater number of ccTLDs are delegated. For example, the United Kingdom has a number of domains assigned for its territories (GB, GI, JE, FK, and so on).

Country	Country code	RIR
AFGHANISTAN	AF	APNIC
ÅLAND ISLANDS	AX	RIPE NCC
ALBANIA	AL	RIPE NCC
ALGERIA	DZ	AfriNIC
AMERICAN SAMOA	AS	APNIC
ANDORRA	AD	RIPE NCC
ANGOLA	AO	AfriNIC
ANGUILLA	AI	ARIN
ANTARCTICA	AQ	ARIN
ANTIGUA AND BARBUDA	AG	ARIN
ARGENTINA	AR	LACNIC
ARMENIA	AM	RIPE NCC
ARUBA	AW	LACNIC
AUSTRALIA	AU	APNIC
AUSTRIA	AT	RIPE NCC
AZERBAIJAN	AZ	RIPE NCC
BAHAMAS	BS	ARIN
BAHRAIN	BH	RIPE NCC
BANGLADESH	BD	APNIC

Country	Country code	RIR
BARBADOS	BB	ARIN
BELARUS	BY	RIPE NCC
BELGIUM	BE	RIPE NCC
BELIZE	BZ	LACNIC
BENIN	BJ	AfriNIC
BERMUDA	BM	ARIN
BHUTAN	BT	APNIC
BOLIVIA	BO	LACNIC
BOSNIA AND HERZEGOVINA	BA	RIPE NCC
BOTSWANA	BW	AfriNIC
BOUVET ISLAND	BV	ARIN
BRAZIL	BR	LACNIC
BRITISH INDIAN OCEAN TERRITORY	IO	APNIC
BRUNEI DARUSSALAM	BN	APNIC
BULGARIA	BG	RIPE NCC
BURKINA FASO	BF	AfriNIC
BURUNDI	BI	AfriNIC
CAMBODIA	KH	APNIC
CAMEROON	CM	AfriNIC
CANADA	CA	ARIN
CAPE VERDE	CV	AfriNIC
CAYMAN ISLANDS	KY	ARIN
CENTRAL AFRICAN REPUBLIC	CF	AfriNIC
CHAD	TD	AfriNIC
CHILE	CL	LACNIC
CHINA	CN	APNIC
CHRISTMAS ISLAND	CX	APNIC
COCOS (KEELING) ISLANDS	CC	APNIC
COLOMBIA	CO	LACNIC
COMOROS	KM	AfriNIC
CONGO	CG	AfriNIC
CONGO, THE DEMOCRATIC REPUBLIC OF THE	CD	AfriNIC
COOK ISLANDS	CK	APNIC

Country	Country code	RIR
COSTA RICA	CR	LACNIC
CÔTE D'IVOIRE	CI	AfriNIC
CROATIA (local name: Hrvatska)	HR	RIPE NCC
CUBA	CU	LACNIC
CYPRUS	CY	RIPE NCC
CZECH REPUBLIC	CZ	RIPE NCC
DENMARK	DK	RIPE NCC
DJIBOUTI	DJ	AfriNIC
DOMINICA	DM	ARIN
DOMINICAN REPUBLIC	DO	LACNIC
EAST TIMOR (TIMOR-LESTE)	TL	APNIC
ECUADOR	EC	LACNIC
EGYPT	EG	AfriNIC
EL SALVADOR	SV	LACNIC
EQUATORIAL GUINEA	GQ	AfriNIC
ERITREA	ER	AfriNIC
ESTONIA	EE	RIPE NCC
ETHIOPIA	ET	AfriNIC
FALKLAND ISLANDS (MALVINAS)	FK	LACNIC
FAROE ISLANDS	FO	RIPE NCC
FIJI	FJ	APNIC
FINLAND	FI	RIPE NCC
FRANCE	FR	RIPE NCC
FRENCH GUIANA	GF	LACNIC
FRENCH POLYNESIA	PF	APNIC
FRENCH SOUTHERN TERRITORIES	TF	APNIC
GABON	GA	AfriNIC
GAMBIA	GM	AfriNIC
GEORGIA	GE	RIPE NCC
GERMANY	DE	RIPE NCC
GHANA	GH	AfriNIC
GIBRALTAR	GI	RIPE NCC
GREECE	GR	RIPE NCC

Country	Country code	RIR
GREENLAND	GL	RIPE NCC
GRENADA	GD	ARIN
GUADELOUPE	GP	ARIN
GUAM	GU	APNIC
GUATEMALA	GT	LACNIC
GUINEA	GN	AfriNIC
GUINEA-BISSAU	GW	AfriNIC
GUYANA	GY	LACNIC
HAITI	HT	LACNIC
HEARD AND MCDONALD ISLANDS	HM	ARIN
HOLY SEE (VATICAN CITY STATE)	VA	RIPE NCC
HONDURAS	HN	LACNIC
HONG KONG	HK	APNIC
HUNGARY	HU	RIPE NCC
ICELAND	IS	RIPE NCC
INDIA	IN	APNIC
INDONESIA	ID	APNIC
IRAN, ISLAMIC REPUBLIC OF	IR	RIPE NCC
IRAQ	IQ	RIPE NCC
IRELAND	IE	RIPE NCC
ISRAEL	IL	RIPE NCC
ITALY	IT	RIPE NCC
JAMAICA	JM	ARIN
JAPAN	JP	APNIC
JORDAN	JO	RIPE NCC
KAZAKHSTAN	KZ	RIPE NCC
KENYA	KE	AfriNIC
KIRIBATI	KI	APNIC
KOREA, DEMOCRATIC PEOPLE'S REPUBLIC OF	KP	APNIC
KOREA, REPUBLIC OF	KR	APNIC
KUWAIT	KW	RIPE NCC
KYRGYZSTAN	KG	RIPE NCC
LAO PEOPLE'S DEMOCRATIC REPUBLIC	LA	APNIC

Country	Country code	RIR
LATVIA	LV	RIPE NCC
LEBANON	LB	RIPE NCC
LESOTHO	LS	AfriNIC
LIBERIA	LR	AfriNIC
LIBYAN ARAB JAMAHIRIYA	LY	AfriNIC
LIECHTENSTEIN	LI	RIPE NCC
LITHUANIA	LT	RIPE NCC
LUXEMBOURG	LU	RIPE NCC
MACAO	MO	APNIC
MACEDONIA, THE FORMER YUGOSLAV REPUBLIC OF	MK	RIPE NCC
MADAGASCAR	MG	AfriNIC
MALAWI	MW	ARIN
MALAYSIA	MY	APNIC
MALDIVES	MV	APNIC
MALI	ML	AfriNIC
MALTA	MT	RIPE NCC
MARSHALL ISLANDS	MH	APNIC
MARTINIQUE	MQ	ARIN
MAURITANIA	MR	AfriNIC
MAURITIUS	MU	AfriNIC
MAYOTTE	YT	APNIC
MEXICO	MX	LACNIC
MICRONESIA, FEDERATED STATES OF	FM	APNIC
MOLDOVA, REPUBLIC OF	MD	RIPE NCC
MONACO	MC	RIPE NCC
MONGOLIA	MN	APNIC
MONTSERRAT	MS	RIPE NCC
MOROCCO	MA	AfriNIC
MOZAMBIQUE	MZ	AfriNIC
MYANMAR	MM	APNIC
NAMIBIA	NA	AfriNIC
NAURU	NR	APNIC
NEPAL	NP	APNIC

Country	Country code	RIR
NETHERLANDS	NL	RIPE NCC
NETHERLANDS ANTILLES	AN	LACNIC
NEW CALEDONIA	NC	APNIC
NEW ZEALAND	NZ	APNIC
NICARAGUA	NI	LACNIC
NIGER	NE	AfriNIC
NIGERIA	NG	AfriNIC
NIUE	NU	APNIC
NORFOLK ISLAND	NF	APNIC
NORTHERN MARIANA ISLANDS	MP	APNIC
NORWAY	NO	RIPE NCC
OMAN	OM	RIPE NCC
PAKISTAN	PK	APNIC
PALAU	PW	APNIC
PALESTINIAN TERRITORY, OCCUPIED	PS	RIPE NCC
PANAMA	PA	LACNIC
PAPUA NEW GUINEA	PG	APNIC
PARAGUAY	PY	LACNIC
PERU	PE	LACNIC
PHILIPPINES	PH	APNIC
PITCAIRN	PN	APNIC
POLAND	PL	RIPE NCC
PORTUGAL	PT	RIPE NCC
PUERTO RICO	PR	ARIN
QATAR	QA	RIPE NCC
RÉUNION	RE	APNIC
ROMANIA	RO	RIPE NCC
RUSSIAN FEDERATION	RU	RIPE NCC
RWANDA	RW	AfriNIC
SAINT KITTS AND NEVIS	KN	ARIN
SAINT LUCIA	LC	ARIN
SAINT VINCENT AND THE GRENADINES	VC	ARIN
SAMOA	WS	APNIC

Country	Country code	RIR
SAN MARINO	SM	RIPE NCC
SAO TOME AND PRINCIPE	ST	AfriNIC
SAUDI ARABIA	SA	RIPE NCC
SENEGAL	SN	AfriNIC
SERBIA AND MONTENEGRO	CS	RIPE NCC
SEYCHELLES	SC	AfriNIC
SIERRA LEONE	SL	AfriNIC
SINGAPORE	SG	APNIC
SLOVAKIA	SK	RIPE NCC
SLOVENIA	SI	RIPE NCC
SOLOMON ISLANDS	SB	APNIC
SOMALIA	SO	AfriNIC
SOUTH AFRICA	ZA	AfriNIC
SOUTH GEORGIA AND THE SOUTH SANDWICH ISLANDS	GS	LACNIC
SPAIN	ES	RIPE NCC
SRI LANKA	LK	APNIC
ST. HELENA	SH	ARIN
ST. PIERRE AND MIQUELON	PM	ARIN
SUDAN	SD	AfriNIC
SURINAME	SR	LACNIC
SVALBARD AND JAN MAYEN ISLANDS	SJ	RIPE NCC
SWAZILAND	SZ	AfriNIC
SWEDEN	SE	RIPE NCC
SWITZERLAND	CH	RIPE NCC
SYRIAN ARAB REPUBLIC	SY	RIPE NCC
TAIWAN, PROVINCE OF CHINA	TW	APNIC
TAJIKISTAN	TJ	RIPE NCC
TANZANIA, UNITED REPUBLIC OF	TZ	AfriNIC
THAILAND	TH	APNIC
TIMOR-LESTE	TL	APNIC
TOGO	TG	AfriNIC
TOKELAU	TK	APNIC
TONGA	TO	APNIC

Country	Country code	RIR
TRINIDAD AND TOBAGO	TT	LACNIC
TUNISIA	TN	AfriNIC
TURKEY	TR	RIPE NCC
TURKMENISTAN	TM	RIPE NCC
TURKS AND CAICOS ISLANDS	TC	ARIN
TUVALU	TV	APNIC
UGANDA	UG	AfriNIC
UKRAINE	UA	RIPE NCC
UNITED ARAB EMIRATES	AE	RIPE NCC
UNITED KINGDOM	GB	RIPE NCC
UNITED STATES	US	ARIN
UNITED STATES MINOR OUTLYING ISLANDS	UM	ARIN
URUGUAY	UY	LACNIC
UZBEKISTAN	UZ	RIPE NCC
VANUATU	VU	APNIC
VENEZUELA	VE	LACNIC
VIET NAM	VN	APNIC
VIRGIN ISLANDS (BRITISH)	VG	ARIN
VIRGIN ISLANDS (U.S.)	VI	ARIN
WALLIS AND FUTUNA ISLANDS	WF	APNIC
WESTERN SAHARA	EH	AfriNIC
YEMEN	YE	RIPE NCC
ZAMBIA	ZM	AfriNIC
ZIMBABWE	ZW	AfriNIC

European TLD managers have created a common body called **Council of European National Top-Level Domain Registries** (**CENTR**). For more detailed information, see http://www.centr.org/.

Index

SOA, 81, 82
SRV records, 87-89
Start Of Authority, file structure, 81, 82
stealth name server, 21
stub resolver, 110
subdomains, 6
subordinate zone, 10
syntax
    DNS record, 80
    SRV record, 87, 88

T

TKEY record, 77
Transaction Signature, 76
translating Internet on intranet, 162, 163
translating in local network
    whole Internet, 166
    without Internet translation, 167
trusted-key statement, 104, 105
TSIG, 76
TTL, 59, 68
TXT records, 83

U

UpdateOptions parameter, 115
User Datagram Protocol, translating hostname
    into IP address, 14, 15

V

view statement, 105-107

Z

zone
    cache, 10
    hint, 10
    journal files, 52
    signature, 73, 74
    statement, 107-109
    stub, 10, 108
    transfer. *See* zone transfer
zone transfer
    incremental. See incremental zone transfer
    parameters, 103, 104

Thank you for buying DNS in Action:
A detailed and practical guide to DNS
implementation, configuration, and administration

About Packt Publishing

Packt, pronounced 'packed', published its first book "*Mastering phpMyAdmin for Effective MySQL Management*" in April 2004 and subsequently continued to specialize in publishing highly focused books on specific technologies and solutions.

Our books and publications share the experiences of your fellow IT professionals in adapting and customizing today's systems, applications, and frameworks. Our solution-based books give you the knowledge and power to customize the software and technologies you're using to get the job done. Packt books are more specific and less general than the IT books you have seen in the past. Our unique business model allows us to bring you more focused information, giving you more of what you need to know, and less of what you don't.

Packt is a modern, yet unique publishing company, which focuses on producing quality, cutting-edge books for communities of developers, administrators, and newbies alike. For more information, please visit our website: www.packtpub.com.

Writing for Packt

We welcome all inquiries from people who are interested in authoring. Book proposals should be sent to authors@packtpub.com. If your book idea is still at an early stage and you would like to discuss it first before writing a formal book proposal, contact us; one of our commissioning editors will get in touch with you.

We're not just looking for published authors; if you have strong technical skills but no writing experience, our experienced editors can help you develop a writing career, or simply get some additional reward for your expertise.